SOULA COASTER

Published in the United States by: SmileyBooks, 250 Park Avenue South, Suite #201, New York, NY 10003 • www.SmileyBooks.com

Photo credits on page 372 are an extension of the copyright page.
Music credits on page 371 are an extension of the copyright page.

Library of Congress Control Number: 2011935631

Hardcover ISBN: 978-1-4019-2835-3
Digital ISBN: 978-1-4019-3177-3

15 14 13 12   4 3 2 1

First Edition, June 2012

Printed in China by Global PSD

DESIGN BY JUAN ROBERTS / CREATIVE LUNACY

SOULA COASTER
The Diary of Me

R. KELLY
with David Ritz

SMILEYBOOKS

New York

I dedicate this book to my mother,

Joann Kelly,

and

my second mom, teacher, and pastor,

Lena McLin.

CONTENTS

ACT I: BACK IN THE DAY

ACT II: GETTIN' BUSY

ACT III: IN THE RING

Author's Note

Soulacoaster is a memoir. I have shared the most challenging times of my life in this diary, but in telling my story, certain episodes could not be included for complicated reasons. Additionally, to protect the privacy of others, specific names and identifying characteristics have been changed. Events and conversations have been recreated from my memory and reconstructed to the best of my recollection. I hope you enjoy the ride.

Look behind myself as I reflect on all the memories

Good times they come and go

Lost everything from friends to family

If I could turn back the hands

There would be some things I'd change about me

I know that my past is not what my future holds

Where I come from who could

believe all the pain and misery

Look in my eyes and you will see . . .

The diary of me

Rewind my life, just go back and correct all the wrong

And ask God to direct my path so then I could make it home

Years ago a child was born and raised without a man

My mom was scorned but still reached out her hand

Just open the book, turn the pages of my life

and you will read

A true story about one man's journey . . .

The diary of me

—R. Kelly

ACT
ONE
{Back in the Day}

Before you go on this Soulacoaster with me, there is one thing I gotta say: No matter what speed it goes, how high it soars, or how low it drops—hold on.

THE MUSIC IS SWARMING

Since the day of my birth, I feel like my soul has been on some kind of roller coaster—with all of the ups and downs, twists and turns, laughing and screaming, smiling and crying. Sometimes I ask myself, *When will this ride stop? Or will it ever stop?*

Before you go on this Soulacoaster with me, though, there is one thing I have to say: No matter what speed it goes, how high it soars, or how low it drops—hold on. Even as I worked on this book, the music was swarming—pushing, inspiring, and challenging me. And I let it; I always accept the challenge. From my earliest memories to last night's recording session, music has been my life's mission and my greatest passion. I feel like God has placed a lifetime of melodies inside me and that's a wonderful thing, but unfortunately a great gift can come with a great price and a helluva responsibility. I call my gift a beautiful disease.

When I'm working on one song, it seems like I'm always interrupted by another song that's knocking—sometimes banging—at the door of my soul. There are times I feel like a radio station with all the channels blasting at once. I often get smothered by songs and lyrics, smothered by ideas about musical pieces and how they mix and match. They're like jigsaw puzzles. As soon as I put one together, I'm on to the next. My mind is always moving fast and furious; it won't let me rest until all the pieces of the song fit together.

When I was a kid, I found out that I couldn't read or write like other kids. I would worry myself sick that something was wrong with me and that my disability would trap me. When the music started flowing through me, at first I was overwhelmed and worried. *Why was I hearing so many songs?* Musical phrasings, lyrics, and song structures were fully formed in my head long before I could understand what these things really were. Even when somebody said that I had a special gift, as a little kid I was scared that it would drive me crazy.

It took me a lot of time, effort, energy—and a lot of God's grace—to learn to recognize the gift for what it was and harness it, even as I struggled in other ways. I've got a leash on my music now and I can walk it. It's not running wild anymore—I can walk it wherever I want it to go.

This book is like my music: It's not just stray melodies. It comes to me late at night—certain scenes, voices, and memories appear unexpectedly—things that made me proud and things that are still hard for me to even think about.

My life is like a mansion with lots of rooms. Some of those rooms are well lit, with bright, joyfully colored party lights and full of happiness. Other rooms are dark. And some of the doors to those rooms have never even been cracked open. Well now, I'm opening those doors. And I'm inviting you in.

{ I'm inviting you in. }

My mom wasn't perfect. She had her bad habits . . . Above all,
Mom was a praying woman who looked to God for a better
way. She was a loving woman who protected her four children
with the strength of a lioness.

Joann "Mom" Kelly

MOM

When I call out *Mom*, it brings the spirit of Joann Kelly into my heart. I'm calling out *Mom* at the beginning of this book because, as I go through the pages of my life and start to wake up the images and feelings of my past, I need to invoke her here in the present. I need the spirit of my mother by my side. She's still my guide and my strength. She was the first one to believe in me. She told me that I could achieve all things through Christ Jesus.

At 45, I can still hear her words, and they're just as comforting now as ever. It was she who taught me to believe I could fly beyond the sky and soar into pure space. No matter what we were going through, no matter how small our Thanksgiving table, my mother's inspiring strength kept our hearts full, even if our bellies were sometimes empty. She was strong in her faith, too—something I carry with me to this day. She taught us how to be thankful. Didn't matter if this neighbor or that neighbor had more than we did. Whatever we had was reason to thank the Lord. Financially, we had nothing. Spiritually, we had everything.

The reason I loved my mother so much is: she was not perfect and she never claimed to be. But I loved her because she was my mother. She had her bad habits. She loved her Winston cigarettes and her Miller beer. Sometimes she'd drink too much and get sick. My mother wasn't ashamed to talk about her imperfections. She'd discuss her faults, telling me how she wanted to stop drinking and smoking like she did. My mother was a praying woman who looked to God for a better way. Above all, she was a loving woman who protected her four children with the strength of a lioness.

My mother was my daddy, too, so to speak, because she raised me on her own. Her husband, Lucious, became my stepfather, but—no disrespect to him—he was not my *real* father. As a kid, when I first understood that my father left my mother when she was pregnant with me, I wasn't really upset about it. But it hurt. Thankfully, I had someone who was a genius at being a mother and a father, too.

Though I'd never met or seen my father, on special occasions like Christmas and birthdays, my siblings' fathers would come by and take them shopping for toys and clothes. I never got jealous, but I do remember being sad and curious. In fact, one day when I was about 11 or 12, I decided to ask my mom questions about my father, like: "Who is he?" "Where is he?" and "Why doesn't he come to take me out for my birthday or bring me anything for Christmas?" My mother would just roll her eyes, look away from me, and say: "Don't say nothing to me about that no-good son of a bitch because the minute he found out I was pregnant with you, his coward ass left. Disappeared in the wind," she'd say. "Didn't want to have nothing to do with either you or me."

I remember my mother's eyes on one of those days—close to blood red as the anger grew and grew while she talked about my father as if he was the Devil himself. I remember my eyes getting baby-blood red, too, because what my mother loved, I loved, and what she hated, I hated. It was that day, that moment, that I decided to hate my father, not knowing really what hate meant or having a clear understanding about love. She told me on that day to never mention him again.

"I'm your mother and your father," she said. I promised her that I'd never talk about him again. And I never did. I remember taking the word *father* and putting it in a little brick box in the back of my mind—until now.

My mother was a woman of strength, love, and courage. She always felt like what we didn't have God gave to us. "Whatever you ain't got, God gave to you so count it all as joy," she would say.

Now most people won't believe this because I'm talking about my mother, but Mama Joann could sing her butt off. People said she sounded like Gladys Knight and Aretha Franklin mixed together. Every time she'd open her mouth to sing—whether it was in church, in a club, or outside on the porch—I would watch the people to get their reactions.

My mother is the reason why I fell in love with old-school music. To this day, the closer I stay to the real soul of music, the closer I am to the spirit of my mother. To me, she *is* the soul of music.

I was five years old in 1972 and already music was all over me. Music was my mother and my mother was music. When she was out of the house, I was never quite right. When she came home, I felt safe. My mother was my comfort zone. All I wanted was to live in the music with her. The first time Mom let me go with her to hear her sing, my heart started hammering so hard. I thought that I was straight-up on my way to heaven.

It was one of those sweet summer nights in Chicago, when the breeze comes off Lake Michigan and everyone wants to go outside and enjoy it. I was holding my mother's hand, walking down the street to the nightclub where she and her band, the Six Pack, were going to play. My mother had grown up with music in the house—my grandfather was a musician who played blues guitar and used to do gigs playing B. B. King numbers. As we passed the original Regal Theater, Mom ignited my imagination with stories of legendary black artists who had once played on that stage— Duke Ellington, Louis Armstrong, Ella Fitzgerald, The Supremes, the Temptations, B. B. King, James Brown, and even "Little" Stevie Wonder.

"Al Green's at the Regal tonight," Mom said. Chicago's South Side in the early '70s was music in motion, bursting with our Southern blues roots and deep urban rhythms just like us. And among Chicago folk, no one was bigger than Al Green. "Let's

Stay Together," "Love and Happiness," and "I'm Still in Love with You" were everyone's favorite jams.

"I'd love to hear Al," my mother said as she looked up at his picture. "But I got some singing of my own to do. Got my own show to put on."

Outside the little lounge where Mom was going to perform, she turned me over to the drummer in her band—a big man with a big laugh and a wide smile. The club wasn't having a five-year-old walk through its front door, but my mother knew they weren't watching the back. Before I knew it, her drummer had scooped me up, hid me in his drum case, and carried me inside.

As the band started to play, I opened the lid to steal a peep. My eyes went wide; I was amazed: clouds of smoke, swells of laughter, women's sweet perfumes, the strong

She smashed the night! Smashed the crowd! Smashed the song!

smell of cigars, the stink of whiskey—I knew that something big, something exciting, was about to happen.

Everything about the place thrilled my soul. The jukebox was playing Marvin Gaye as I waited on my mother to come out. She was in the back room, getting ready like always, smoking a Winston and drinking a Miller. She was taking her time. The longer the folks waited, the more she knew they'd want her to come out and sing.

Finally Mom appeared. She was wearing her only stage outfit, a silky black dress with gold sparkles up and down the sleeves. She was a heavyset woman; flawless brown skin, brown eyes, thick eyebrows. She looked beautiful. She was beautiful. She made her way to the front of the band. No stage, no curtains, no introduction. Just her stepping up to the mic. Strong as she could be. And when the band kicked in and she let that first note go—I still get goose bumps just thinking about it!

8

She smashed the night!

Smashed the crowd!

Smashed the song!

First song she belted out was an Aretha Franklin number, singing "Don't send me no doctor, filling me up with all those pills . . . got me a man named Dr. Feelgood . . . and Lord, he takes care of all my pains and ills."

Me, I had no pains or ills. I had me a mother who could sing. She didn't dance, didn't wave her arms, or do any tricks. She didn't have to: Miss Joann Kelly was a stand-up, straight-up soul singer.

Peeping out of that drum case, I saw how the people loved her. She took that "Midnight Train to Georgia" leaving the Pips behind. My mother didn't need no Pips. She had enough voice for four singers. She was tearing the roof off that little club, and me, well, I was cherishing every minute. The joy of music was the joy of my mother. As far as I could tell, Mom ruled the world.

"Lulu!" "Lulu!" "Lulu!" "Lulu!" "Lulu!" "Lulu!" "Lulu!" "Lulu!" "Lulu!" "Lulu!" "Lulu!" "Lulu!" "Lulu!" "Lulu!" "Lulu!"

LULU

I love *Love*. There's no one on Earth more romantic than me. I've been in love with *Love* ever since I can remember. I've always loved the idea of having a girlfriend. I love the closeness, the sweetness; holding her hand, kissing her cheek, whispering words of affection and hearing her say that she feels the same about me.

My first girlfriend was named Lulu, and she was so special. Though we were only eight, and it was puppy love, I believe she was my first musical inspiration when it comes to love songs. I can still smell the fragrance of our innocence. Lulu and I had a very special bond that—even at our young age—felt futuristic. Ours was that kind of bond that young people talk about when they say they're gonna grow up and get married and just be together forever. And though it sounds much like a fairy tale, it's what me and Lulu believed in our hearts, and nobody could tell us anything different.

Sometimes, Lulu and I would play house. We built a make-believe house out of a big cardboard box that we put in the backyard. We cut out openings for windows and hung fresh paper towels to look like curtains. We took crayons and drew little decorations on the walls. We got a towel to look like a rug and placed it on the ground. We did everything we could to make it pretty.

Inside the cardboard house, we had a make-believe kitchen where Lulu served me a make-believe lunch. We sat on the towel and drank make-believe coffee, just like our mothers did. We just sat there and looked at each other. Lulu had light brown eyes and a smile that made me smile. In our make-believe dream house, Lulu and I made a vow to be girlfriend and boyfriend forever.

"Let's take a walk, Rob," Lulu said to me one day.

It had rained earlier, but the sun finally came out and walking sounded good. We left my backyard, hand in hand. Little eight-year-old me was floating on love.

Across the street, on Concord Drive, sat Beacon Hill Elementary School. A wire fence had been built to keep kids away from Thorn Creek, which rushed like a river between Beacon Boulevard and the railway line.

"I like the river," said Lulu. "I like looking at the water."

"Me, too."

Although there was a sign on the gate that said "Danger! Keep Out!" there was also a hole in the fence that beckoned us in. The rains had swollen Thorn Creek. The water flowed faster and stronger than normal. We were fascinated just to look down at the water, which had a rhythm of its own.

After a while, a bunch of other kids came along. They were laughing and carrying on. One of the kids, a boy bigger than me, said, "Hey, this is our river; what you doing around here?"

"River belongs to everyone," said Lulu. "You can't own a river."

"Hell I can't," said the boy, as he stepped up to Lulu. "I say it's my river and y'all get out."

I stepped in front of Lulu and said, "We were here first. We're not leaving."

"Out!" the boy screamed.

"It's our river, too," I screamed back.

With that, the big kids started pushing and shoving. And one of them pushed Lulu so hard she fell backwards into the water. Before I knew it, she was struggling to get out. I reached for her, but the fast-moving current, stronger after the rain, was carrying her away. I didn't know how to swim, and neither did she. The other kids were running away, and she was screaming, "Rob! Rob!" And I was screaming "Lulu! Lulu!" Suddenly she was out of sight beyond the river's bend.

I started yelling out for help, but I didn't know what to do. I was scared. I was hysterical. I was jumping up and down. After what felt like forever, some grown-ups arrived. I explained what had happened and followed them downstream until they came upon a big rock. There was Lulu, her head crushed against the rock. She wasn't talking, wasn't moving. But there was a lot of blood coming from her head.

"Lulu can't be dead!" I screamed. But the gash and the blood and the women moaning told me what I didn't want to hear.

I wanted Lulu to come back, wanted this day to start over. This time me and Lulu wouldn't go inside the fence. We wouldn't go near the water. We'd go back to our cardboard dream house and sit on our make-believe rug. We'd go there and live happily ever after.

Death couldn't be this real. Lulu's life couldn't be snuffed out like this because some fool pushed her too hard. It didn't make any sense. Lulu couldn't be dead. She's alive. I knew that I'd be seeing her smiling eyes soon as I woke up from this dream.

But it was no dream. It really happened.

That night I was still in a state of shock. Mom, sensing what I was dealing with, held me close in her arms and said, "Wasn't your fault, baby. You couldn't do anything to save her. Lulu is in heaven now. She's with the Lord, sweetheart, and you with me. It's okay to cry. Cry all you need to, baby, 'cause I got you; I'm with you, I'm right here."

My mother's words helped, but she couldn't change the awful truth that Lulu was gone. I kept seeing her caught up in the current, reaching out for me. I heard her screaming out to me. Watched the river washing Lulu away until she disappeared, gone forever; a beautiful butterfly lost in a raging storm.

THE DREAM

When I was about nine years old, I had a strange dream I'll never forget. I was in this house where everything was white—walls, floors, ceiling, carpet, bricks on the fireplace, curtains at the windows. I saw myself seated at a white piano and playing a song. This was weird because at nine I didn't know how to play any kind of instrument. But in this dream the melodies were flying off the keys and filling the room. It was as if I was in the midst of a musical storm.

Then suddenly I heard the doorbell. I stopped playing and ran to see who was there. I opened the door, but no one was there. Stretching my neck to look in all directions, I couldn't see a thing. In the distance, though, I heard the faint sound of giggling. I didn't know who it was that was laughing or what they were laughing about.

So I went back to the piano, and the beautiful melodies and chords just started back up. Then the doorbell rang again. And again, when I got to the door, no one was there. Except this time the giggling was louder.

The third time it happened, I was at the door practically before the bell rang. I desperately wanted to find out who it was doing all that giggling. I quickly opened the door, and standing there were musical notes, except they were all cartoon characters.

I tried to reach out and touch them, but they took off and ran like the wind. I chased after them, giving it all I had, but they were too fast for me.

I yelled as loud as I could: "Hey! Who are you guys?"

They stopped dead in their tracks, turned around, and came back to me and said: "We're your biggest hit song." Then at the blink of an eye, they ran clean out of sight.

I went back to the house and sat back down at the piano, and I played a melody that was like no other melody I'd ever heard. I began to sing the hook to the song, but for some strange reason, when I woke up, I could not remember what I was saying in the hook, couldn't remember the words.

It would take about 20 years, but the words came back and the dream made perfect sense.

COFFEE WITH THREE CREAMS AND SIX SUGARS

We moved around a lot when I was young. We lived in the housing projects on 63rd Street on the South Side before moving to a small place on 107th and Parnell. Back then the projects didn't seem as bad as people make them out to be today. My family knew everybody in the neighborhood, and everybody in the neighborhood knew my family.

We were always broke or not having the things we wanted. But I remember love taking the place of the material things we wanted or needed. We might not have had the money to pay the rent a lot of times, but when I remember sitting out on the porch until 1 or 2 in the morning, listening to Al Green or Marvin Gaye and playing cards with my Mom and my aunties and cousins—I wish I could have brought that part of my childhood with me into the world of success. Because now that I'm successful, that's what's missing in my life.

The world I was born in, though, was filled with its own beauty.

In the 63rd Street projects, nothing was more important than the game of basketball. I started hooping when I was five with street ball and haven't stopped since. Hooping was everywhere, and me and my brothers would hoop any chance we got.

Hooping isn't just a hobby or a sport. It's a way of life.

Unlike indoor, supervised basketball, in street ball you had to adapt to the rules of the neighborhood where you played. Aggressive hand and leg checking was allowed;

you could play full court or half court, sometimes three pointers were three pointers and other times they were just considered beautiful shots. There were no hardwood floors; when you got knocked down, you landed on concrete or asphalt. Some 'hood courts had only a rim and a backboard. Instead of the familiar "whoosh" of the ball through stringed net, you listened for the clang of chain or the sweet sound of nothingness as the ball dropped through a net-less rim.

I love basketball because it helps me blow off steam. It gives me somewhere I can put some space between all the other things going on in my life—even music. Like music, hoop makes life good. I love it for the fast action and high energy, but I'm gonna be straight: I'm also pretty damn good. Thousands of brothers play better than me, but no one loves the game more.

Joann Kelly knew about me and basketball early on. She had vision. Mom never looked behind; she looked ahead. She saw something in me that I could have never seen myself. She understood that I loved basketball more than most other kids. That's why she encouraged my passion for the sport. She knew that nappy-headed little Rob needed to feel worthy, strong, and proud. She saw how I loved to compete, so she let me play hoop as much as I wanted.

Mom and I always had beautiful times together. It could be something as simple as getting up in the morning and walking to McDonald's. She didn't have enough money to buy us breakfast, only coffee for her and a Danish for us to share. To me, that was enough. I just wanted to be with her. She fixed her coffee with three creams and six sugars and tasted it to see if it was sweet enough. She wore this cheap red lipstick, and when she tasted her coffee, she left a red mark on the cup. She always asked me if I wanted a sip and I always did. And because I loved my mother so much, I always turned the cup to where she had left that red mark. I liked to drink from the same spot where she drank.

"One day you're gonna be famous, baby," she would say with a smile. But I didn't really know what "famous" meant.

"I mean famous like Al Green," she added. "Famous like Sam Cooke and Marvin Gaye. See, you got a beautiful little singing voice that's only gonna get bigger and stronger."

"And then I'm gonna have enough money to buy you breakfast here every day, right, Mom?" I would ask.

"Yes, you will, sweetheart. You sure-enough will."

My mother would take me back home and, after dropping me off, get ready for work. She had a job at the hospital where she was training to be an EKG technician. Before she left, she never failed to kiss me goodbye.

"Be good today, baby," she said, "and listen to your grandma."

We lived in a typical Chicago three-family building—we call them three-flats. Grandma lived with her man, Uncle Cary, on the top floor. Uncle Cary owned a TV repair shop, but some of his customers were never happy. They complained that after Uncle Cary fooled with their TVs, they worked worse than before. Uncle Cary said they just didn't want to pay their bills.

Grandma was heavyset like Mom. I loved her, but the woman had her moods. I could tell when she had her mood swings on because she and Uncle Cary would get to screaming at each other. That usually meant they were already hitting the hard stuff. They liked their Old Grand-Dad whiskey, and by early afternoon, they could be down a bottle already.

"I told you to fix that TV of mine a week ago," Grandma was screaming, "and the damn thing still don't work!"

"It was working till you started messin' with the antenna," Cary screamed back. "You the one who done fucked it up!"

"Me? Here you go again, blaming me for shit you can't do. What good are you 'round here if you can't even fix a goddamn television set?"

"If it's so easy, you fix it."

"I'll fix you, you son of a bitch!"

It was World War III. Grandma and Cary went at it something fierce. I couldn't tell if he was beating on her or it was her beating on him. Next thing I heard was Grandma yelling, "Rob! Rob! You get up here!"

I ran upstairs and Grandma told me, "Go to Mr. Ikenberg's store. Get me a pack of Pall Malls, a hunk of Hogshead cheese, and some of them Moon Pies."

I waited for money.

"What you waiting for, boy?"

"Cash money or food stamps."

"Don't got either. Tell Mr. Ikenberg I'll pay him on the first."

I ran over to the store, wondering if Mr. Ikenberg would go along with Grandma's pay plan and let it slide. He did. Back then, small neighborhood store owners still operated on the basic principle of trust and family ties.

"You come from good people," he said. "Plus, I've never seen you try to steal anything from me, not even a candy bar."

"Never would do nothin' like that," I said. And with that, Mr. Ikenberg gave me an Almond Joy candy bar.

Back at the house, after giving Grandma her stuff, I heard my stuttering Uncle Doug calling me from down in the basement. The basement was his kingdom.

"N-n-need your h-h-help, Rob. G-g-get down here," he yelled.

Uncle Doug was a mess. He had a big pot belly, wild woolly hair, and smelled like someone's sweaty feet. That day, like so many others, drinking Wild Irish Rose straight out the bottle, he started in with stories about how he'd been shot four different times and stabbed another six times. I'd heard them all before.

"You call me down to tell me stories, Uncle Doug?" I asked.

"No, b-b-boy, I called you d-d-down to see if that d-d-distant cousin of yours is here."

22

"Which one?"

"The one with the b-b-big t-t-titties."

"Uncle Doug, why you always wanna be looking at big titties?"

"No h-h-harm in looking. Is she around?"

"No."

"Well, I'll just stay d-d-down here and let you h-h-help me get this j-j-job done."

"What job?"

"This here j-j-job b-b-behind the m-m-milk crates."

Uncle Doug walked to the other end of the basement where he'd dumped nasty old car seats and junky lamps. Bunches of old records were scattered on the floor. Dirt and dust everywhere.

When he moved the milk crates, I saw Tempskins, our German shepherd, lying there.

"Tempskins asleep?" I asked.

"No, T-T-Tempskins d-d-dead."

"Dead?"

"D-d-dead, as in the b-b-bitch ain't b-b-breathing."

"How'd he die?"

"Accident."

"What kinda accident?"

"I set some p-p-poison in the p-p-peanut b-b-butter to k-k-kill the rats. K-k-killed T-T-Tempskins instead."

"Mom's gonna be furious," I said. "She loves that dog."

"She can't n-n-know."

"How she not gonna know?"

"You ain't gonna t-t-tell her."

"When she comes to find out Tempskins ain't here, what we gonna say?"

"You b-b-better not s-s-say nothing. D-d-dogs disappear."

"Not this dog. This dog don't even go outside."

"He g-g-going outside n-n-now 'cause we b-b-burying him in that empty lot d-d-down the street. Now p-p-put him in this b-b-bag and f-f-follow me."

I followed my uncle's instructions. I knew better than to argue with my elders, even when my elders did crazy things. Uncle Doug did the supervising, I did the digging, and, after a long while, we managed to bury Tempskins.

That night when my mother got home, the first thing she asked was, "Where's my dog?"

She looked at me. I looked away. She called up to Grandma and Cary. They were asleep from a long day of drinking and fighting. She called down to Uncle Doug,

who didn't answer. She looked at me again.

"You know something, Rob. I can see it in your eyes," she said. "You ain't good at lying. Now tell the truth and shame the devil."

"Truth is . . ." I hesitated. I wasn't comfortable snitching on Uncle Doug. I wasn't comfortable snitching on anyone.

"Truth is what?" Mom insisted.

"Truth is that Uncle Doug's rat poison killed Tempskins."

"Oh Lord!" she cried. "Now I'm gonna have to go down there and kill Uncle Doug."

Next thing I heard was a big commotion from the basement. My mother was down there chasing Uncle Doug, and Uncle Doug was doing all he could to duck and hide.

"You can run, you bastard," she said, "but you can't hide."

"Your b-b-boy's l-l-lying," Uncle Doug lied. "I d-d-didn't k-k-kill your d-d-dog."

"My boy don't ever lie to me," said Joann Kelly, "and never will. There's only one mothafuckin' liar around here and that's you. Now you gonna get me a new dog or I'll kick your sorry ass from here to Mississippi."

By noon the next day, Uncle Doug was presenting Mom with a new-born mongrel puppy.

WOMEN IN THE HOUSE

Growing up in the 'hood, the number-one rule was don't snitch, don't tell. Like learning $2 + 2 = 4$, it was drilled into you. And if you didn't know $2 + 2 = 4$, you failed. In the 'hood if you snitched, you weren't going to make it.

There were always women in our little house at 40th and King, There were cousins, aunties, friends of my aunties, all older women. When my mother wasn't home, the women ran a littler freer, meaning that when my mom or my grandmother were home, they'd dress a certain way. When my mother and grandmother were out, they felt free to wear less clothing. You could see through their blouses. Sometimes they wore bras, sometimes they didn't. When they walked around in nightgowns or pajamas, you could see their panties and on a few occasions, like on a very hot summer days, they wouldn't even wear panties.

As a very young boy, I didn't think much of it. The women didn't really pay much attention to me or my brothers. I looked at them the way any kid would. Kids are naturally fascinated by body parts, and I was no different. As I crept up in age, though, and made my way through grammar school, I found myself more curious and sometimes aroused; and I was ashamed of being aroused. But there was no one I felt I could talk to about this. I couldn't have a sit-down with my mother because I wouldn't know what to say or how to say it. There was no man that I trusted enough to share such shameful feelings with. Growing up with that shame has haunted me throughout my life.

One winter afternoon, I came back from school early when my mother wasn't home. As I came through the door, I heard a strange noise. It sounded like bedsprings squeaking. The walls in our place were paper-thin, and sound came through like there weren't any walls at all. This squeaking got louder and louder.

Then I heard voices. A woman screamed—but it didn't sound like a scream of pain or panic.

Then I heard a man's voice, shouting, but it wasn't in anger.

"Oh God! Do it! Do it! Get it right there! Right there, baby, right there!" the woman pleaded.

"You like it, don't you, bitch?! How much you want? How much can you take?" the man shouted.

"All you got!" the woman shouted back.

I was just eight-years-old. I didn't understand what was happening. I thought the man was maybe hurting the woman, but that didn't seem right. I was confused, curious, so I went to see for myself.

I crept toward the bedroom where the noises were coming from. They were doing so much hollering, I figured they wouldn't hear the door if I opened it just a little.

I opened it just a little.

Then I looked inside.

I was just eight

A man's backside was high in the air, coming down on the lady with her legs spread wide, her big booty propped up on a pillow. I didn't understand how it was all working, but he was moving down on her and she was coming up on him. First the rhythm was slow, then faster, then crazy fast. They were screaming, moaning, going wild. I couldn't stop looking. I'd never seen nothing like this before. Screaming, cursing, bed sagging, bodies bumping.

Just then, the woman caught sight of me. They stopped abruptly.

"Little Robert, what you doing in here, boy?"

years old.

I got scared and started running. She shouted out, "Come on back, it's okay."

They were still in bed, both of them naked, when she said, "You can watch, but you better not say shit to nobody about this."

I knew the women in my house weren't dressing or acting right. My mother or grandmother wouldn't dream of parading around the house half-dressed. At the same time, I couldn't snitch. In my house and growing up in the 'hood, the number-one rule was don't snitch, don't tell. It was the same as learning $2 + 2 = 4$. It was drilled into you, and if you didn't know $2 + 2 = 4$, you failed. In the 'hood if you snitched, you weren't going to make it.

Still, as I grew older, things began to change when I was around these women. When I was nine, they changed in a major way; I began to regret this code of silence.

If my mother had known what was going on in the house, she probably would have burned the house down. She didn't play that. I wanted to tell her but I had a hard time trying to figure out who would really be in trouble—me or them. At that age I didn't really know how to handle it. I knew it wasn't right but I just didn't know how to say anything about it. Talking about it was strange, so I locked it away as my own little secret.

At the time, Mom was going out with Lucious, the man she later married when I was still a kid. I wasn't happy about it 'cause I wanted her to stay home with me. But Lucious was okay. He was a nice man, nice to me, and most times nice to my mother. He liked to tell stories about his Army days. Since my real daddy was long gone, I liked listening to an older man talking 'bout "back in the day." I saw Lucious more like a big brother than a father.

My mother and Lucious went out together often. Sometimes they left me with Uncle Doug. My brothers didn't like Lucious, but my attitude was different from theirs. Anything that made Mom happy made me happy, too.

One Saturday evening we were watching TV. "Don't watch that television set all night," Mom said before she and Lucious left the house.

Me and my brothers liked horror movies. We were watching *The Creature from the Black Lagoon* when the TV crapped out. Picture went dead. I called up to Uncle

Cary to fix it, but he was snoring loud enough to wake the dead. My brothers went off to bed, but I kept banging on the TV, hoping to get the picture back. When it did pop back on, the monster was rising out of the black lagoon. I was waiting to see what would happen next when — just like that — the damn picture crapped out again.

Disgusted, I fell asleep on the couch. I was far away in some dream when I heard that same noise. Bedsprings squeaking.

The guy yelling, "Tell me how much you like it, bitch!"

The lady screaming back, "Give it to me! Gimme all you got!"

I got up and looked around the house to make sure my mother wasn't home yet. She was still out with Lucious.

This time I knew what all the noise was about and, truth be told, I wanted to have another good look.

I opened the door just enough to see them kicking it hard. I mean, they were deep into it. I stood there for a while, and just as I started to close the door, the woman spotted me. "Don't move, Rob," she said.

I was scared. Didn't know what to expect.

"Come over here and get this camera," she said. "Take a picture of us."

I was dumbfounded. Couldn't say a word.

"You do know how to use this thing, don't you?"

I was too stunned to talk. All I could do was shake my head no.

"It's easy," she said. "Just aim this camera and snap a goddamn picture!"

She gave me a Polaroid camera. The guy liked the idea as much as she did. They got into positions where I could see their private parts.

I snapped the picture. When she showed me how it took only a minute to develop, I was amazed. The photographic technology impressed me more than the sex.

She grabbed the photo and kept it for herself. I took the memory of them doing the dirty and stashed it inside my mind's brick box.

A couple of Saturday nights later, Mom was out again and I was sitting on the couch with Uncle Doug. We were watching TV. My favorite show was *The Jeffersons*. But on this particular night, we were looking at *Three's Company*.

Uncle Doug turned to me and asked, "N-n-now this h-h-here is every m-m-man's d-d-dream. Every m-m-man d-d-dreams of living with t-t-two women. Which one d-d-do you l-l-like?"

"The blonde," I said. "Chrissy."

"I l-l-like b-b-both them b-b-bitches," Uncle Doug said. "Ain't 'b-b-bout to k-k-kick either one outta m-m-my b-b-bed."

Halfway through the show, the TV went dead. Again.

"C-C-Cary!" Uncle Doug shouted. "Where's that m-m-mothafuckin' lame-ass repairman when we n-n-need him?"

"Gone out with Grandma," I said.

Uncle Doug let out a big sigh. "Oh well, we p-p-probably b-b-better off. If he start f-f-fooling with the T-T-TV, the fuckin' thing will b-b-blow up and b-b-burn the house d-d-down. B-b-boy, I've had enough for one d-d-day. I'm g-g-going to b-b-bed."

"Goodnight, Uncle Doug."

"G-g-goodnight, Rob."

I stayed on the couch, staring at the dark TV, thinking what it might be like to have a dad like George Jefferson, someone with enough money to move us all into a fancy high-rise in the sky. I started thinking of Jack Tripper, the guy in *Three's Company*, and the cool but confusing situation that he was in.

I drifted off to sleep and fell into a crazy dream about *Three's Company* when a strange feeling in my body woke me up. The "feeling" was down below my belt. I opened my eyes and saw that a female was playing with me. She was at least ten years older than me. I was eight.

"What're you doing?" I asked.

"You'll like it," she said. "It'll feel good. Look what happens when I rub it."

She kept rubbing until I got hard. I didn't say anything. Then she put it in her mouth and started sucking.

At first I was scared she was going to do something crazy like bite me. I tried to push her away, but she wouldn't stop until she was finished. When she was, she said, "You better not say shit to no one or else you gonna get a terrible whupping," she threatened.

I knew she meant business. I knew to keep quiet. Every time she did it—and she did it repeatedly for years—she warned me about what would happen to me if I snitched. No matter how many times it happened, I knew I could never tell anyone. I was too afraid and too ashamed. All I could do was stash the secret—and hide it in my imaginary brick box.

SUNDAY MORNING

My belief in God has been with me since I was a little boy, and I still believe in God now. I believe in the grace and mercy of Jesus. That belief got seeded in me when I was just a kid. No matter how many other crazy things jumped off in my life, God was always there; my mother made sure of that.

On Sundays, I would put on my freshly ironed best—black trousers, clean white shirt, little clip-on bow tie—and follow Mom to the little storefront church where we went to sing and pray. I had to get myself ready for a long day: Church went on for three, sometimes four hours.

The church didn't hold more than 25 people. It was no bigger than a liquor store or pizza joint. Our pastor was Mother Nance. She had these big, frightening eyes but was a sweet lady who was all about the Lord. She preached her sermons like songs, singing the lessons she hoped to impart to us.

A small band backed Mother Nance. The beats came from a drummer banging on nothing but a snare. He worked it hard, and the groove he laid down made me happy. The broken-down organ had a bunch of missing keys. From where I sat, I could see the woman at the old instrument and—don't ask me how—when she hit a key that didn't work, I could fill in the missing note in my mind. It was a game I liked to play. I could hear the whole composition. Everyone else in the room had the music in 2-D; I could hear it in 3-D.

When my mother got up, faced the congregation, and started in on "Amazing Grace," she became a star. She sang so hard until everyone was standing and waving, shouting God's name. They loved my mother's singing. When the saints heard I could sing, they wanted me to do a solo, but I was too shy. Besides, I figured Mom sang good enough for the two of us.

Later in the service, when I got a little bored with the songs, I'd change the words around. When everyone was singing, "Jesus is on the main line, tell him what you want," I sang, "That girl in the choir is so fine, gonna tell her what I want"—and my lyrics went right along with the song. Once, Aunt Rose, sitting right behind me, heard me and slapped me upside the head. "Boy," she said, "you better sing the right lyrics or I'm telling your mama."

Service went on so long I usually couldn't help but nod off. One time, I don't know how long I'd been snoozing when a scream woke me up. It was my mother: Joann Kelly had caught the Holy Ghost and was shaking and shivering like she had some terrible fever. She was yelling out, "Ain't gonna smoke no more! Jesus God, ain't gonna have another cigarette long as I live!" Tears were streaming down her face. She was crying and talking in tongues, reaching into her purse, grabbing her pack of cigarettes, and throwing them in the aisle. "No more!" she was yelling, "Ain't gonna touch 'nother one of these cancer sticks for the rest of my life! Thank you, Jesus! Thank you, Lord!"

After church we went home for a big Sunday dinner, which was always delicious. We were all filled up and satisfied. My mother was drinking her coffee when she leaned over and whispered to me, "Run over to Mr. Ikenberg's and get me a pack of Winstons."

"But Mom . . ." I started to say.

"You heard me, boy. Now go."

When I got back, my mother was waiting for me at the door. She took her Winstons, went to the bathroom, locked the door behind her, and lit up. When she was through, she sprayed the smell away with a can of aerosol. She didn't want anyone to know.

But I knew. I knew more than I should have about the things that happened in our house.

I was there the Sunday that Grandma came back from church and announced that she got saved.

"That mean you ain't drinking no more of that Old Grand-Dad whiskey?" Mom asked.

"Not a drop," said Grandma.

"And what about your Pall Malls?" Mom wanted to know.

"Quit smoking, quit cursing. Just living for the Lord."

I was surprised. Grandma and Uncle Cary loved their Old Grand-Dad. And when they fought, they loved cussin' up a storm.

"What about Cary? He get saved along with you?" asked Mom.

"Yes, he did," said Grandma. Cary was standing next to her. The man was all smiles.

"Well, well," my mother muttered. "The Lord works in mysterious ways."

"Yes, He do," said my grandmother. "He sure-enough do."

From that point on, Grandma's moods were more talking down to you than screaming at Uncle Cary. In fact, we referred to Grandma and Uncle Cary, who lived on the upper floor, as the "Uppities." After Grandma got saved and indulged her uppity attitude, she and my mother would get into heavy arguments. For example, Grandma didn't like my mother playing bingo.

"You going against God," Grandma told her.

"Why you say that?"

"I don't. The Bible does."

"Where in the Bible does it tell you not to play bingo? Back then, they didn't have no bingo."

"Proverbs 13:11. 'Dishonest money dwindles away, but he who gathers money little by little makes it grow.'"

"That's what I'm doing," my mother said. "I'm making my little money grow. Besides, nothing dishonest about bingo."

"You play the numbers," said Grandma.

"Everyone plays the numbers."

"Look here," Grandma explained, opening her Bible. "Ecclesiastes 5:10: 'Whoever loves money never has money enough; whoever loves wealth is never satisfied.'"

"I didn't say I love money. I just said I need money. We need money. You need money."

"We need God."

"We got God," her daughter said. "But to keep from getting kicked out of this here house, we got to pay rent. And you telling me that if I hit the number and collect a few thousand, you won't be following me to a nicer house?"

"I'm following Jesus to wherever He leads."

"Well, I believe Jesus is leading me to the numbers man because this week I got a good hunch. But if my number do come in, I won't bother telling you. I don't want my Bible-believing mother covered in my sin."

With that, my mother walked out of the room. Grandma gave me a look as if to say, "Boy, you better not smile."

I didn't.

{ Enjoying the ride? }

I wanted to do my homework and get all A's. I wanted to prove myself and make my mother proud. But every time I made up my mind to conquer the problem and start reading, every time I opened a book, my mind would turn *off*.

SCHOOL DAYS

When I was at church, I learned to sing the words from memory, but at school, when it came time to open the book and read silently or out loud, I couldn't focus on the words. I didn't even see words.

Every time my teacher called on me to read, my heart sank. I choked up. I stammered and stuttered. It was terrible because the other kids would start giggling. I felt like a cripple and an alien. Here were my schoolmates, learning like nobody's business, building up their vocabularies, reading all these stories. I wanted to read so bad I could taste it. I wanted to do what everyone else was doing. But the more I tried, the worse it became.

Trying to learn how to read and spell in school for me was like throwing a brick on top of the Sears Tower. That's how hard it was for me. I really tried hard because, if for no other reason, I didn't want the other kids calling me "a dummy."

I'd look around at every other kid, and they were reading and writing and spelling and doing math. They were going forth with their books and their studies. But when it came to me being able to study, I just couldn't do it, I couldn't make sense of the words on the page. I desperately wanted to learn how to read, so I made a hell of an effort. But the more I tried to study, my mouth would get dry; I'd get sleepy and start yawning the minute I even tried to read a book or study spelling words.

I wanted to do my homework and get all A's. I wanted to prove myself and make my mother proud. But every time I made up my mind to conquer the problem and start reading, every time I opened a book, my mind would turn off. Time and again, I'd make a mess out of this whole reading business and I'd wish that the ground would open and swallow me whole.

I didn't know what to think about myself. *Was I sick? Was I really a dummy? What was wrong with me?* Those thoughts scared me to death, but I was too afraid to say anything to anybody.

"You got genius," my mother told me after a day at school where kids were laughing at me 'cause I couldn't read. I wanted to believe my mother, but it was hard. To me as a kid, if you were a good reader, it meant you had a good brain. If you were a bad reader, it meant you had no brain. Bad reading meant you were obviously a dummy.

It wasn't until I was an adult that an educator told me about dyslexia. She said dyslexia is where kids have trouble learning to read or interpret words. She also said it's got nothing to do with your intelligence. Steve Jobs, Walt Disney, and even Leonardo da Vinci all had some form of dyslexia. But my disability is something more than dyslexia. They still don't know what caused my problem. I'll never know if it was possibly "brain damage," as one specialist diagnosed, or an accident of Spirit—God's way of making sure that I fulfilled my destiny.

Another crazy thing about my reading problem is that I've always loved words. Still do. I love stories about faraway places and different kinds of people. I wanted to be able to read those stories like everyone else. I always loved listening to how different people—my mother, my aunts, Uncle Doug, Lucious—told stories each in their own special way. I instinctively understood the power of language and the magic of storytelling from a very young age.

Words had a spirit that got all over me. Depending on how they were used, words could scare me, comfort me, encourage me, make me happy, or make me sad. It broke my heart that I found it so hard—in fact, downright impossible—to read words on the page.

Outside of school, I spent a good amount of time with my brothers, Bruce and Cary. My mother wanted all her kids to get along. "Y'all are blood," she would remind us. "Y'all need to be there for each other." Sometimes that was easy—especially if it involved kung fu. Me and my brothers were deep into Bruce Lee. We'd go to the Met movie theater on King Drive down the street from where we lived and sit in there, hypnotized by films like *Enter the Dragon* and *Fist of Fury.*

Bruce Lee was our man—from his lightnin'-fast nunchucks to his awesome sword work to the way he downed a dozen opponents without breaking a sweat. He had that cut-up 12-pack body, that attitude, that look in his eyes that said, "I don't know the meaning of fear."

When we left the theater, we were out of our minds with Bruce Lee cockiness. We were worked up and ready to roll against anyone who even looked at us funny. We'd come out of that movie kicking like we actually knew what we were doing. You better not try to challenge us after a Bruce Lee flick.

Big Bro Bruce and li'l Bro Killer—we called Cary "Killer" after a Flip Wilson character Grandma loved—came charging out of a Bruce Lee film high on the action we'd just seen. Man, we were flying on that Bruce Lee energy. We got home, playing like we were actually in the movie, when I landed a roundabout kick on Killer that sent him through our living room window. He got a little cut up and felt some pain, but it was nothing like the pain we'd feel when Mom got home. We knew that if we didn't think of something quick, Mom would give us the worst whipping of our lives.

So we started thinking and plotting, trying to come up with a story that we were sure Mom would buy. We got it all planned out. We thought we were real smart.

Mom came home and right off yelled, "What the hell happened in here?"

Big Bro Bruce led off. Me and Killer were his backup.

"We was just sitting in the living room watching TV," said Bruce, "when someone, maybe they were gang members or something, came by, hollering and screaming, and the next thing we knew, they threw this brick through the window. We ran to see who it was, but by then they were long gone. You see, Mom, the brick is still there, right where it landed. Thank goodness it didn't hit any of us. We were lucky, Mom, real lucky."

My mother stood there, just staring at us. I mean, seriously staring.

"Gonna ask you boys again," she said. "What happened?"

Me and Killer backed up Bruce's story. We said how scared we were when that brick came flying through.

Mom kept staring. Her eyes were like laser beams going through our heads. "Gonna ask you one more time, boys, and then I'm gonna get me the biggest switch I can find and start whipping your behinds until I hear the truth."

The thought of a whipping had us start defending ourselves even harder. We kept saying we were minding our own business, how we were being good boys, how we didn't do nothing wrong, and then here came this brick.

Then came the bullet.

Mom just stood there, shaking her head. We saw that she wasn't buying a word of it, but at the same time, to our little brains, our story seemed bulletproof.

"If what y'all say is true," she said, "then why is all the broken glass out there on the porch? Why ain't there no broken glass here on the inside? If someone throws a brick in the window, how does the glass shatter backwards?"

We hadn't thought of that. Of course, my mother was right. There wasn't a shard of glass in the living room. The only thing in the living room was that brick sitting on the floor—the cleanest brick you ever saw. It wasn't even sitting crooked.

For days after that, we could barely sit at all. Mom whupped our asses good. All we got out of the whole thing was a bad memory from her switch of fury.

Bruce Lee created the kick-butt genre of kung-fu movies that paved the way for everyone who followed him, from Chuck Norris, Steven Seagal, and Jean-Claude Van Damme to Jackie Chan. The death of our indestructible hero—when Lee's brain swelled in his sleep and he died in 1973—was a painful pill that my brothers and I tearfully swallowed.

There were times like these when my brothers and I stuck together. At other times we could barely stand being in the same room, especially Cary and me. I never got along too well with my little brother and we used to fight all the time.

One night I wanted to watch *Good Times* and he didn't. He had another program he thought was better. Nothing was better than *Good Times*. I not only loved the show, but I loved the theme song and I love singing it to this day. The show opened with a shot of a high-rise housing project. Although it was never mentioned in the opening credits, everyone in Chicago knew it was our very own Cabrini-Green. Back then, the hard and "good times" the Evans family—Florida and James, J.J., Thelma, and Michael ("the militant midget")—faced on every episode was absolute "reality TV" to me.

But Cary was watching an old *Three Stooges* movie and wouldn't let me change channels. He took a swing at me and landed a blow to my left eye. My eye got puffy and I got crazy angry. I grabbed a broom from the kitchen and started chasing him. I planned to hit him over the head with this broom and chased him into the bathroom. Our mother yelled for us to cut it out, but we kept fighting.

"If y'all don't stop," she screamed. "I'm coming in there."

I still wasn't stopping. I got Cary backed into the bathtub when Mom showed up. She happened to be carrying a knife she'd been using to slice some vegetables. I didn't know she was directly behind me, so when I stepped back, I stepped into her knife and got cut. Blood was gushing everywhere and I was hollering, "Y'all trying to kill me! Mom wants to kill me!"

My mother dropped the knife and grabbed me, crying, said she was sorry. She immediately started to bandage me up. Turns out the cut wasn't all that deep, but that didn't keep me from hollering like a baby.

My mother always wanted to show us how family should be able to lean on each other and stand by one another. I wanted to please and obey her.

"Take your brother Cary to the park, Rob," she said one day. "Let him play on the swings, but don't push him too high."

When we got to the playground, Cary was happy as could be. He loved those swings. He jumped on and asked me to push him. I gave him a shove.

"Higher!" he screamed. I pushed him higher.

"Higher!" he screamed even louder, so I pushed him even higher.

Li'l Bro was having the time of his life. "Higher!" he kept demanding.

Now I knew not to push any higher because he was already flying super-high. But he was insisting, so I kept pushing while he kept sailing higher until the swing got loose. I saw him get caught on the chain. He came flying off and hit the grass. Cary was a mess. Blood all over. He was crying. I was scared, but somehow I got him home. Mom rushed him to the emergency room.

All I could think was, *God! What have I done to my little brother?*

One secret was about what was happening to me in the house; **next** was my secret about reading and writing; and the **third** secret, strange as it seems, was music.

SECRETS

As a kid, I had a lot of secrets. Some were terrible, some were beautiful, some were both. There were so many secrets to stuff into my imaginary box that I was running out of room.

The first secret was the sex. I couldn't reveal it because of the rule against snitching. I had a feeling my mother wouldn't play no SECRETS shit—no way, no how. Meanwhile, though, odd things were happening in my body. I was confused by it. I was dying to tell my mother, but I was scared to death about what would happen if the real truth ever came out.

One secret was about what was happening to me in the house; next was my secret about reading and writing; and the third secret, strange as it seems, was music.

I would hear music, like I had a radio playing non-stop in my head. Sometimes it would switch stations. Every now and then it would play one song and then sometimes before the songs even finished, another one comes in. I would hear melodies, although I never knew what they meant. In fact, I thought everybody heard the music.

If I was at school and it was time to read, I'd put my head down on the desk and drift off. While I was drifting off, though, music would start up so heavy and loud that it felt like my head would explode. I'd pick my head up to see if everyone had heard it or I'd say to one of the other kids, "Hey did you hear that?" They'd look at me like I was crazy, and that just made things worse.

It was another problem that I put in my brick box because I didn't want everybody to know, and I was afraid about what would happen if they found out. It was one of the scariest times in my life. I couldn't figure out if I was sick, or retarded, or dying, or if there was just something really messed up about me.

My mother always taught me that, too much of anything can kill you, so I used to worry about too much music happening inside me. *Was it an overload, an overdose?*

I couldn't really tell anyone how music wouldn't leave me alone. No one, except maybe my mother, would understand. As a kid, it was even too much for *me* to understand.

I was writing songs before I even knew what songwriting meant. Just as one melody came pouring out, another one interrupted it, and then another, and then another, and then all kinds of harmonies, all kinds of notes coming from everywhere—ideas, thoughts, endless songs. It was beyond crazy. I didn't want to tell anyone what was happening inside my brain because I couldn't explain it. My brain was overcrowded. Music was overwhelming me.

I wanted to be happy. Wanted to please my mother, please my teacher; I wanted to be like other kids. Instead I was stumbling and falling down over words while melodies were pouring in and singing inside my head.

Here's another thing: Even though there were times when the sheer volume of music inside my head had me thinking I was an alien, there were even more times when music comforted me, ministered to me, gave me life. Because I absorbed music like a sponge absorbs water, I couldn't help but soak up every thirst-quenching drop.

Picture the porch in front of our three-flat on a late afternoon in summer. Sky clear, weather warm, Mom out there with Lucious, Uncle Doug, and Uncle Cuz. (I never did know if the man was my uncle or my cousin.) Picture the neighbors dropping by, caught up in the sound of the radio floating on air. Now hear the sounds: the Isley Brothers singing, "Drifting on a memory . . . ain't no place I'd rather be . . ." The groove so free and easy that you had to sway with Smokey, "Soft and warm, a quiet storm," or Frankie Beverly, "When the sun settles down and it takes a lovely form . . . that's the golden time of day." This was music from heaven, music without pressure, pure magical music. Maze singing, "Shine, children, shine," and Mom swaying along, arms outstretched, "If you believe in love, shine . . ."

That unforced, free-flowing, syncopated sweet sound of voice, horn, and bass made everything seem all right. It took the sting out of life; it was nothing but sugar and cream, nothing but clouds floating on a breeze of love. Music said life, for all the strife, could be heaven on earth—if only we listened to the singers and the songs they sang.

Watching them listening to Teddy Pendergrass or Donny Hathaway, David Ruffin or Eddie Levert, Etta James or Curtis Mayfield, I started dreaming this dream: I imagined that one day people would be relaxing on their porches listening to music that I made, songs that I sang. One day, I prayed, I could take the pressure off and bring the calm to folks like Mama and Lucious. Like Frankie Beverly and Maze, one day I'd be able to lay down grooves that would make people happy, loving—I'd create music from the heart that touches hearts.

In the world of music during the 1970s, Chicago Soul was like an ice-cold pitcher of sweet tea. Known for its blend of Southern and Gospel soul, backed by sweet harmonies, and horn and string arrangements, Chicago Soul was as powerful as the music coming out of Detroit or Memphis. Record labels like Okeh, Chess Records, One-derful, and Chi-Sound promoted artists like Jerry Butler and the Impressions, The Dells, Etta James, the Chi-Lites, Curtis Mayfield, and Gene Chandler.

"Sam Cooke—that's the most loving man you'll ever wanna listen to," Mom said. He was her favorite singer, bar none. "Sam Cooke was raised right here in Chicago," she'd boast. "Not only was Sam a soul music pioneer," Mom said, "Sam Cooke was a businessman who owned his own record label and publishing company.

"He came out the church," she explained, "but took the church with him. That's why you hear God in every note he makes. Ain't no one like Sam." Even though I was only 10 years old, she strongly urged me to study this man. "You learn him good.

There were two sides to him, and you best learn them both—when he was with the Soul Stirrers singing gospel and when he started singing pop, no one could touch him, baby; each side of that man's music was as good as the other."

My mother and I listened to Sam Cooke for hours on end, whether it was "Touch the Hem of His Garment" or "You Send Me"; whether "Jesus, Wash Away My Troubles" or "Twistin' the Night Away"; "Nearer to Thee" or "Cupid"; "He'll Make a Way" or "I Love You for Sentimental Reasons"; "Joy, Joy to My Soul" or "Change Gonna Come."

I could hear the church echo in Cooke's silky voice. His soulful confession helped me understand what I saw at home, in church, and on the streets of South Side Chicago. I understood sorrow with "Chain Gang," dreamed of giddy love with "Cupid," and enjoyed finger-popping fun with "Twistin' the Night Away." Listening to Sam Cooke's music wasn't enough for Mom, though. She wanted to make sure I truly understood his ability to manipulate lyrics and command each genre—no matter if it was a bluesy ballad, soul-felt Gospel, raw rock and roll, or funky rhythm and blues.

"Hear him bend that note, baby," she would say. "That's his specialty. Singers are like great chefs. They got their specialties. Some can bake pies. Some can fry chicken. You'll find your specialty, sweetheart, and when you do, the minute you open your mouth to sing, folks will know it's you. Meanwhile, listen to the chefs. Learn their recipes."

My mother considered Stevie Wonder a master chef. The first Stevie song I learned was "Fingertips." When I got older, she took Stevie's "Master Blaster" cut and taught me how to memorize every last lick, every breath, every riff. She'd place a nickel on the record player's needle to slow down the revolutions so the runs could go really slow, so I could learn them and get them down pat.

Joann Kelly and Stevie Wonder's mother, Lula Mae Hardaway, had a lot in common. Lula Mae also recognized her son's musical gifts at an early age and nurtured his genius. Stevie was barely a teen when his mother heard him repeating just a slice of a lyric: "Here I am, baby. . . Here I am, baby." It was Lula Mae who supplied the hook: "Signed, sealed, delivered. I'm yours." Stevie's mother was by his side when he signed with Motown in 1961, and she helped him write hit records such as "I Was Made to

Love Her," "You Met Your Match," and "I Don't Know Why I Love You." Soon I was sounding more like Stevie than Stevie . . .

Same was true with Marvin Gaye. I could sing "What's Goin' On" or "Let's Get It On" with that Marvin-like attitude—mellow but intense. I could fix my voice like Donny Hathaway. Mom made sure I knew the songs of the older cats like Jackie Wilson and Ray Charles. At Christmas time, it was all about Nat King Cole.

I was born into the perfect musical storm. Everything that Mom loved I loved, from Billie Holiday to Dinah Washington to Aretha. I soaked up everything she had soaked up. She loved Frankie Lymon and the Teenagers, but when Michael and his brothers came out with "ABC" and "I Want You Back," Mom was loving that just as much. When it came to music, the woman had no prejudices.

Her musical history became my history. Like everyone else in the 'hood, when we saw a new history in the making, we jumped on board that musical change. When the Sugar Hill Gang started singin' about "a hip-hop the hippie the hippie to the hip-hop, you don't stop" in "Rapper's Delight," we were euphoric. Those early jams—Kurtis Blow's 1980 hit, "The Breaks," which was the first certified gold rap record, and Grandmaster Flash and the Furious Five's 1982 game changer, "The Message," which is regarded as one of the greatest songs in hip-hop history—had us young kids dancing just as wild and free as when Mom and them were dancing to James Brown.

Like Tarzan in the jungle learning how to talk to the animals and swing from vine to vine, I learned to talk to music; I learned to swing from one musical vine to another. I heard every sound there was to hear, and I could make every sound that I heard. I grew up in a place on the planet where music—beautiful music, God's music, the people's music, my mother's music—spoke to me every minute of every day.

"You got that gift, boy," my mother said. "You got that talent."

But how could a talented person have such a terrible time with simple reading? Didn't that prove that something was wrong? Wasn't that something I had to hide from the world?

And what about what was happening at the house behind my mother's back? Were good little boys supposed to be doing the things that had been happening to me? Shouldn't I have tried to stop those things? Shouldn't I have stopped gazing at these women running around half-naked? Shouldn't I have stopped taking Polaroids of people doing the nasty?

On the Soulacoaster, a talented kid with too many secrets did his best just to hold on.

That was when I understood
the love between Lucious and my Mother.

"devotion"

DEVOTION

One afternoon after school I was walking home, glad to be out of the classroom, when I heard a song blasting from our front porch. It was "Kung Fu Fighting."

That song always made me happy, and seeing Mom and Lucious on the front porch drinking their Millers, I could see they were getting happy, too. They were dancing and hugging like newlyweds, carrying on like they didn't have a care in the world. But then Lucious said something to Mom that she didn't like, and suddenly things started to change. Didn't take much for things to change when Mom and Lucious were drinking.

Now Mom was cussing out Lucious.

Now Lucious was cussing her out.

She said, "I ain't gonna take that."

He said, "I ain't gonna take *that*."

My mother ran in the house; he followed her. She screamed at him to get out of her kitchen. He said, "Screw you." My little heart started beating 'cause I was scared that something bad was gonna happen to her. But Joann Kelly was straight-up tough. The woman could take care of herself. She was out of the kitchen and back on the porch, Lucious close behind her.

"Get outta my face!" Mom warned Lucious.

"Kung Fu Fighting" was playing over and over again; the record was stuck.

"I ain't going nowhere, bitch!" yelled Lucious.

She ran back in the house. When she came out again, she was holding a heavy glass mug.

"Put a hand on me and I'll fuck you up," she threatened.

"Who you gonna fuck up, bitch?" Lucious taunted before grabbing and twisting her arm.

With her free arm, Joann Kelly whacked Lucious across the head. The mug split open and cut his forehead, blood gushing out everywhere. Lucious staggered, fell, passed out unconscious. My mother ran to him, screaming for me to call 911. A neighbor called the police.

By the time the cops arrived, Lucious had come to.

"What happened?" they asked.

Lucious hesitated. I was shaking 'cause I thought they'd take my mother to jail.

Lucious looked at the cops and said, "I drank a few too many and fell down the stairs."

"That's all there is to it?" asked the cop.

"That's all there is to it," said Lucious.

That was the day that I fell in love with Lucious.

Two weeks flew by.

It was a Friday night and the rent was due. Mom was short on cash. Lucious was supposed to pay his share, but he wasn't home; he'd gone out with the boys.

My mother convinced the landlord to give us another week. I was glad 'cause I was tired of hopping from house to house every time our money was funny. We called the landlord the Monster. Seemed like the Monster was always on our tail.

Saturday came, and my mother was still looking for Lucious. She was boiling mad. Sunday we went to church, and when we got back, Lucious was still a no-show. Mom was boiling even more.

Monday evening he showed up.

"Where you been?" she asked.

"Out."

"Any fool knows you been out. But out where?"

"Don't matter," said Lucious.

"You right, it don't matter, long as you got your rent money."

"I don't."

"What you mean, 'I don't'?"

"Can't you understand English, woman? I don't means I don't."

"That ain't gonna cut it."

"Gonna have to."

"Gimme your share of the rent."

"Can't give what I don't got. Besides, I'm tired of talking."

Lucious stormed out, but Joann Kelly wasn't letting him off that easy. She wanted her money. She reached for his wallet, he pushed her away; she scratched his face with her fingernail; he kicked her, then ran out to his car; she ran after him. Lucious got into his car and slammed the door, but my mother's dress got caught in the door. Lucious took off, dragging her down the street. Me and my brother Bruce chased the car, jumping into it, beating on Lucious to stop. The car stopped; Mom was banged up and bruised. With all the screaming and carrying on, somebody had called the cops who arrived soon after.

"Who hurt this woman?" they wanted to know, looking at the black-and-blue marks up and down my mother's arms and legs.

"No one," she said. "I just hurt myself."

Cops looked over at Lucious. "Sure you don't want to press charges?" they asked.

"I'm sure," she said.

MR. BLUE

In one of the neighborhoods where we lived when I was a kid, there was a man named Mr. Blue. My mother always liked him 'cause during the summer he'd put us in his car, drive us out to the country, and show us how to pick fruit. Mr. Blue bought us skateboards and bicycles. Mr. Blue was cool.

On this particular morning, Mr. Blue came by, saw that I was by myself, and told me to come over to his place; I followed him over. When we got there, he said, "Help yourself to the watermelon in the fridge." The melon looked good, so I helped myself to some. Meanwhile, Mr. Blue went to the bathroom and took a shower. I didn't think nothing of it. When he came out, he was wearing a robe loosely tied around the waist.

As I finished my melon, he told me to come into his room.

"When I was a little boy 'bout your age," Mr. Blue recalled, "I had me an uncle who paid me a dollar to rub on his dick. Shit, I'd take that money and buy me all kinds of candy."

At this point Mr. Blue pulled out his penis and started rubbing it with grease. It looked like a monster. The last thing I wanted to do was rub it.

"Well, sir," Mr. Blue said, "a dollar ain't what it used to be. But five dollars ain't nothing to sneeze at. If I give you five dollars to rub on . . ."

But before Mr. Blue could say another word, I was running out the door with his voice trailing after me. He was shouting, "If you know what's good for you, boy, you won't say nothing to no one. Say a word and I'll cook your goddamn goose!" Later that night I was talking to my good friend, Sam. The thought of what happened with Mr. Blue was bothering me to a point where I couldn't think of anything else. I was scared to say anything, but I just couldn't hold it back.

"Hey, Sam," I whispered, "if I tell you something, promise you'll never tell anyone?"

"Okay."

"It's about Mr. Blue."

Sam immediately cut me off. "You, too?" he asked. Sam told me that Mr. Blue had tried the same stuff on him. We vowed never to say anything to anyone.

A month later, I was putting together another cardboard house in the backyard. This time I got real curtains. I got it tricked-out so pretty I wanted my girlfriend Lisette to see it.

"Your playhouse is like a real house, Rob," she said.

We sat on the little rug I put over the grass and pretended to be watching a TV that wasn't there. We pretended we were married. Lisette kissed me on the cheek. I kissed her back, and the puppy love started to grow. We were both ten.

That night I dreamed of Lisette. We lived in a house like you see on television, with a white picket fence, a backyard, and a swimming pool; afterwards we were riding in my fancy car to a fancy restaurant where the rich folk eat. I woke up happy. Beautiful dream, beautiful Lisette.

I had an idea for my playhouse. I decided to take some cushions off Mom's bed, put them on the grass, and pretend it was a couch. Me and Lisette would sit on the couch together and act like husband and wife. The pillows were pink, Lisette's favorite color.

I grabbed the pillows and carried them outside. When I got to the yard, I saw that the playhouse door was ajar. Even stranger, I heard Lisette's laughter and playful voice. When I looked inside, I saw my friend Sam on top of Lisette, kissing her and trying to pull her pants down.

"Get outta here!" I screamed at Sam. "Get away from my girl." But Sam wasn't budging, and neither was Lisette. I couldn't control my fury, so I jumped on Sam. He was stronger than me; he pinned me down and gave me a good licking.

To retaliate, all I could do was scream at the top of my lungs: "You told me not to tell anyone, but I'm telling everyone! I'm telling how Mr. Blue messed with you! You said it was a secret, but it ain't a secret no more 'cause I'm yelling it out! Mr. Blue messed with Sam! Mr. Blue messed with Sam!"

My sister heard me screaming and told my mom, who was shocked. She didn't know about Mr. Blue. She called the cops, and they showed up at Mr. Blue's door. We never saw the man again.

... one day
I'm gonna be
a symbol.
I'm gonna
stand
for
Chicago ...

JUMP SHOT

There were times when I had to get out of my house. There was too much noise, screaming, arguing. There were too many people having sex.

A bike ride was a great escape. By the time I was 11 or 12 years old, I rode my Huffy bike all the way from 34th Street to the Sears Tower, at the time the tallest building in the world, on South Wacker Drive.

When I got near, I'd look up at that awesome skyscraper and think, *It's gonna fall on me!* Crazy as it sounds, I'd get scared. But I wouldn't run. Rather than back away from the tower, I'd get closer. I'd get right underneath it. I'd challenge it and say, "Sears Tower, I dare you to fall on me. I dare you to scare me anymore. You ain't nothing but steel and concrete. You might be some kind of symbol of this city, but one day I'm gonna be a symbol. I'm gonna stand for Chicago; one day I'm gonna stand as tall as you."

I remember that day like it just happened: It had rained the night before and, riding my bike down Martin Luther King Boulevard, the morning mist felt fresh on my face. Inside my head, I was hearing music; music was drowning out the rest of the world. Music was my shield and protector. It was a blessing and a burden. It was heavy on my head when I was peddling down to the playground to hoop with my pals. Like a lot of kids, I was dreaming of playing in the NBA like Dr. J.

Folks said that the South Side of Chicago was rough. But I never fooled with the rough guys. They didn't bother me, their business didn't interest me. I wasn't afraid of the streets. Hearing gunshots, for example, was no big thing. Been hearing them my whole life.

But this gunshot was different. This POW! rang in my ear, and suddenly I felt something hit me in the chest. My head went woozy, and I couldn't control the bike. Then everything got crazy and strange. It was like I was leaving my body. In slow motion, I saw myself falling off the bike. My vision went blurry, and I saw people running towards me. Before long, my mother was running up to me, along with my sister and brothers. I heard them in an echo, saw them in a fog.

"Robert's been shot!" my mother shouted.

"My baby's been shot!"

I closed my eyes and lost consciousness.

When I woke up, I was in the hospital. My shoulder was hurting something fierce. Mom was sitting next to me, holding my hand. "Rob, God is good. God spared your life, baby," she moaned.

"What happened?"

"You got shot, son."

"Who shot me?"

"We don't know."

Years later, after I'd had some success, BET was doing a show about where I grew up. As I was showing the director and the film crew around the 'hood, we ran into the guy who shot me. He'd gone to jail for what he'd done and he talked about it on camera. It was all good. Then he handed me a demo tape to check out, to see if I could do anything for him!

But back then I was only worried about one thing.

"Will I be able to shoot the ball?"

"Doctor said you'll be fine. They can't take out the bullet 'cause it's too close to a nerve. If they touch that nerve, it could paralyze the whole half of your body. So they're gonna leave it in there. They say the tissue will grow up around the bullet. The blessing is that the bullet didn't hit your head or your heart. The blessing is that God has beautiful plans for you, baby."

"But will I still be able to make my jump shot?"
I had to know.

Three weeks later, I was back on my bike, pedaling over to the playground to work on my jump shot. Because of the bullet in my shoulder, my shot was off, and I wasn't happy; I was frustrated and I cried about it because it hurt like hell when I tried to lift my arm. But I really got scared when I started shooting funny. I wanted my jumper back. More than anything in the world, I wanted to feel that sweet power of the ball going in the hoop. The pain didn't matter. How could I go through life without a killer jump shot?

"There are more important things in this world than a good jump shot," my mother told me when I got home.

"Like what?"

"Like music. You were born to sing songs, not shoot basketballs."

I didn't dare talk back to her, but in my mind, I was thinking, *I gotta get my jump shot back. My jump shot was all I had. How else could I get out of the 'hood and take care of my mother?*

{ I grew up in Madden Park.
That's where the big boys hooped.
We called it the Uncles Tournament. }

HOPE

Some kids were scared of the streets—and with good reason. Some kids were scared of the playgrounds, where the bullies and gangbangers acted like they ruled the world. But none of that scared me, not even after I was shot.

nstead, I was scared of the classroom, scared of being called on, scared of everyone learning that I couldn't do what they could do—read and write. No one wanted to learn more than me, and no one seemed more troubled. The minute the bell rang, I ran out of school like a bat outta hell. I couldn't wait to get to the playground and find me a game of basketball.

One day when I was 11, on my way to hoop, me and some of my homies got cornered by thugs looking to steal our lunch money. I wasn't about to get messed up over lunch money, so I gave 'em my change. One homie, though, refused. "It's my goddamn money," he said. Without even hesitating, two of the gangbanger slashed his face with a broken whiskey bottle. That's when I knew that I'd made the right decision. I spent the rest of the afternoon at the playground, working on that jump shot that still wasn't right.

Every year when we were growing up, there was an amazing event called the Bud Billiken Parade and Picnic. Coca-Cola had a float. McDonald's had a float. Jesse Jackson had a float. Entertainers waved at the people, singers sang, musicians played, and there was funky music, good food, and good times.

We looked forward to the parade every year; it was our Disneyland—like Walt Disney was coming to us. You got to see all kinds of celebrities if you were lucky.

Everyone—Mom, Grandma, all the aunties, uncles, and cousins—would start out early setting up their little chairs and crates with their cards and beers and wait for the parade to come by. It was an all-day free party right out in the street.

The parade started at 35th and King, and when we lived on 40th and King, me and my brothers would follow the parade all the way to the end. I went to all the barbecues and picnics and looked at all the floats; I saw all the performances. I was inspired by the parade, I got to see a lot of artists who performed on floats—New Edition, Bell Biv Devoe; everybody wanted to be in the Bud Billiken Parade.

Years later, when I was about 15 or 16, I sang for Lionel Richie. He was performing at the parade that year and somebody had told him that I could sing and write songs. He asked them to bring me over to meet him, and he asked me to sing him something I wrote. I can't remember what the name of the song was, but Lionel Richie offered me $500 on the spot to give him the song. Now at that time I was so broke I couldn't even pay attention, and $500 was a lot of money, but even back then I knew that my work was worth more than that, so I turned him down.

I always wanted to be on a float performing like the groups that were famous back then. I would be in the crowd following the floats and waving. In 2011, I felt truly blessed to be the Honorary Grand Marshall of the oldest and largest African American parade in the country. As my float rolled down King Drive, I pictured my mother sitting in her chair with the rest of the family and her friends watching the parade go by, as she had for so many years; I wished she could have been there to see her son wave to her.

I always loved music and I always loved basketball. In those days when I was hooping, you could always find me at Washington Park, Madden Park at 33rd, or King Drive. Madden Park was where the big boys hooped. The older guys were much stronger than us kids and they played harder; they banged! I always wanted to play with them. I never wanted to play with the guys my age. I knew if I played with the older guys, my game would get tighter. So I'd call "next," meaning we got the next game. But once we got on the court, we regretted it, because the older dudes didn't play. They were rough; they didn't care nothing about our age; they were out to win at any cost. They hit hard. I saw many shoulders dislocated, knees shattered, heads smashed on concrete.

I got banged up so hard I couldn't help but be nervous, but I knew the only way to get over that was to keep on playing. I missed a lot of shots. I threw the ball away more times than I could count. Sometimes the bigger guys literally took the ball out of my hands. They frustrated me until I was ready to quit. But I never did.

One day after a rough game, this older guy came up to me and said, "You know what you're doing wrong, young fella?"

"Yeah; I'm missing a lot of shots. I'm throwing the ball away, and they're taking it from me."

"It's more than that," he said. "You're chasing the game. You're not letting the game come to you."

"Don't know what you mean."

"Well, you need to know, Bro. You need to stop forcing your shots. You gotta find your groove."

"Will that get me points?"

"It's not about shooting the ball in the basket," he said. "It's about being positive."

Dude had an interesting way of talking, so I kept listening. Plus, he saw I had something; he believed in me. His name was Robert Reid. The other guys called him

Hope. At that time, Hope was on his way to becoming a neighborhood legend because of his street ball skills. His mother and my mom were very close; she lived right across the street from us.

Hope was slim and smooth-talking; he was about 14 years older than me, about five-foot-eight, with a face like Dr. J. Later, when I watched him on his Robert Reid All-Stars team, I saw he had Dr. J's moves. Hope was a great point guard. He invited me and Bruce, whose hoop skills were sharper than mine, to his place.

Hope schooled us. He had reels of NBA films. As we watched the movies, he pointed out subtle moves we had been missing. He talked about going with the flow.

"Finding the flow," Hope said, "is everything. The game's got a flow, and you got a flow. The art is to let those two flows flow together."

Hope knew I was into music, so he kept making musical comparisons.

"There's a righteous rhythm to every movement," he explained. "It isn't something you create. The rhythm's already there. You tap into it. You ride it. You let it take you where it wants to go."

Hope was a beautiful guy. I could feel that his mind was elevated, even though I couldn't do everything he suggested. For example, he said that rage always hurts. Well, if I was in a close game and someone tripped me on purpose, I went to rage; didn't know any other way.

"Control that rage," advised Hope. "If you don't, rage will control you. When rage is in charge, your game falls apart."

I knew that was right. I'd seen it happen, but I was still no good at controlling my fits of rage. I got less angry, though, when Hope showed me how to finesse my jump shot.

After I got shot, Hope helped me work on getting my jump shot back.

"You fighting that shoulder injury," he said, talking about that bullet lodged in my body. "Don't fight it, work with it."

Hope is one of my best friends to this very day. I still respect his wisdom when it comes to basketball. It was because of Hope that I started developing and strengthening my shoulder. Hope helped me rediscover my game. Bruce and I used to practice the moves that Hope taught us in the backyard. First we nailed a bottomless crate to a pole, then we moved on up to a bike wheel that we took all the spokes out of, and then we moved on up to a rim. We called it Planet-Dunk-A-Lot. After playing for hours, we went over to 42nd and State for the best foot-longs on the planet—Polish sausages smothered with onions, flaming hot barbecue sauce, and a mountain of fries.

It was all good.

LOVIN'
... BUT PLENTY GOOD LOVIN'
... I KNOW AND I'LL TELL YOU SO
... USE TA BE MY GIRL
...ECTED HER WHEN SHE WAS MINE
... USED TO NEGLECT HER
... WANTED MORE THAN I COULD...
... AS LONG AS I LIVE
SHE'LL BE MY GIRL
SHE USE TA BE MY GIRL
SHE USE TA BE MY GIRL
... HAD A CHARMING PER...
... GIRL WAS SO RIGHT
... MY GIRL

UNTIL YOU JUST CAN'T BOOGIE NO MORE

In Chicago, you love the sweetness of summer because you've made it through the meanness of winter.

One summer Saturday the streets were bouncing, and the whole neighborhood was dancing to the sound of my brother Bruce's band. Me and my mother were singing Taste of Honey's "Boogie Oogie Oogie," she looking over at me, me looking over at her, smiling all the while, a singing team that had everyone up and happy. Wasn't always that way, though. There's a story behind how I got to sing that day.

My brother Bruce's band was pretty cool. Bruce played bass, a guy named Pucci was on lead guitar; Pucci's brothers were also in the band—Al on drums and Terry on synths. They did all-instrumental versions of popular songs. I watched them rehearse on the porch, and I knew the songs that they would rehearse, and I sang along with them in my head. Naturally I wanted to sing with them, but Bruce would always tell me they didn't want a lead singer. I really wanted to be in that band, but the more I wanted it, the more Bruce seemed to be against it.

When it came to anything to do with music, I knew my stuff. For example, Bruce and his band would all tune up at the same time. I'd tell them, "If y'all tune up at the same time, by the end of the tuning session, everyone will be pretty much off key. Better to tune up one at a time."

"Get out of here," Bruce said. "What do you know about this stuff, little brother?"

"Bro," I said, "I can sing."

"We good, Rob," he said. "We don't need no singer."

I may have been younger, but I knew he was wrong. They played songs like Kool and the Gang's "Ladies' Night" that needed a singer. It was just a situation, though, where Big Bro didn't wanna mess with Li'l Bro.

But Li'l Bro wasn't going away.

I kept bugging Bruce to give me a chance, let me rehearse, let me sing. He kept saying they wanted to do only instrumentals. Finally I went to the boss: Mom.

When I told her the story, she was really feeling me. After all, she was a singer, too. She told Bruce, "If you don't let Rob sing in your band, there ain't gonna be no band!"

Bruce had no choice. He told me what songs he wanted to sing, and I was ready. Except for one thing—I didn't know all the lyrics.

"I'll have Lisette write the words out for you," said Bruce.

Lisette had good handwriting, and she printed the lyrics to the O'Jays' "Use Ta Be My Girl" and Earth, Wind & Fire's "Serpentine Fire." The words were written on a yellow pad. The letters were big; the words couldn't be plainer. But I had a hard time reading them. I had a hard time reading anything.

As I stumbled over the lyrics, Bruce and the other guys saw that I couldn't even make out simple words. At first I tried to play it off like I couldn't really see them, but they figured it out. I think Bruce saw this as a way to keep me out of the group. I got embarrassed because I thought he might be right—if I can't read, how am I going to be able to do this? So I stopped singing and left.

That night our mother saw how upset I was.

"What's wrong, baby?"

I told her about how I'd made a fool of myself.

"No child of mine is a fool," she said. "It's just that music comes easy to you and reading don't. What you need to do, son, is listen to the records and get the words directly from the singers. Memorize the lyrics from the record. Then you don't have to read. All you gotta do is sing, and your singing is something no one can make fun of."

I did what my mother said. I learned the words from the records and, to make me feel even more secure, she came out there so we could sing side by side. We sounded as good as Taste of Honey. Maybe better.

Once I learned all the songs, it got to the point where we would plug in and sit on the porch and play and the whole block would turn out with people coming from everywhere just to listen to us.

Growing up, Bruce and I were close; we'd get into all kinds of trouble together, in spite of the fact that in the beginning he didn't want me in the band. We'd act up with all sorts of pranks. Sometimes we played with our food. Our mother hated that, but you know how boys are.

One night Mom fixed us her traditional soul food dinner; Ham hocks, pinto beans, cornbread, and greens. I liked it all—except the greens; couldn't stand greens.

When my mother went back into the kitchen, Bruce and I started messing with our food. I stabbed the greens with my fork, flicked them up, and, just like that, they flew across the room and stuck against the wall. Mom didn't notice them that night, but the next night, with Grandma at the table, she did.

"Who the hell threw those greens against the wall?" she asked.

"Bruce," I said, pointing at my brother.

"Rob," said Bruce, pointing back at me.

"One of y'all is lying," she said. "I wanna know which one."

"Bruce is lying," I said.

"I'm telling the truth," Bruce shot back. "Rob's lying."

"Robert would never lie," said Grandma, my staunchest defender.

If she hadn't said that, maybe I would have confessed, but I didn't want to look like a liar in front of Grandma. She had me up on a pedestal.

"Okay," said Mom, "if that's how y'all wanna play it, fine. I'll be right back."

She went into the yard and came back with a switch.

"Don't whip Rob," said Grandma. "He'd never do nothing like that. And if he did, he'd never lie about it."

"Stay out of this," Mom told her mother. "This here is between me and my sons."

Mom next turned to us and said, "Pull down your pants."

"Right here?" I asked. "Right in front of Grandma?"

"You heard me, boy. Right here."

It was embarrassing, but we did it. We stuck out our booties and Mom started whipping us. First Bruce, then me, then back to Bruce, then back to me.

It got to hurting so bad I finally blurted out the truth.

"Okay," I confessed, "I was the one! I threw the greens!"

"Go to your room, Bruce," she said. "Rob, you stay here."

Before she started whipping me again, I looked over at Grandma and saw the sad look on her face; I had let her down. Meanwhile, Mom was more furious than disappointed. She took that switch and let me have it twice as hard. When she was through, I could barely walk.

"Now get out of here," she said, "and get in your room. Think about what you did. Think about what lying got you. And Rob, if I ever catch you lying like that again, I'm giving you an even worse whipping. You hear me, son?"

"Yes, ma'am," I said.

"HE DON'T SING
LIKE NO BOY.

*Robert sings
like a man.*"

—WILLIE PEARL

WILLIE PEARL

In my book, Willie Pearl gets her own chapter. I want to pay her tribute and, though she's long gone, I want to tell the world how her spirit entered my soul and helped give me the confidence I have today. I owe her so much.

Willie Pearl was Mom's best friend when we lived in the Vista Gardens Apartments. Willie Pearl and her two boys, Bam and Wof, stayed right upstairs above us. The woman had her problems, but she always managed to work and feed her sons. She always kept up appearances. When Willie Pearl came downstairs and showed up at our door, we got happy in a hurry. Her hair was always done up right, her clothes were fashionable and bright, and her smile could cut through anyone's sadness.

In our poor neighborhood, she was the first one to buy her kids one of those toy Casio keyboards. Soon as I saw that flimsy little thing, I started fiending to play it. It called to me.

"Hey, Joann," said Willie Pearl, "look how your boy is eyeing that instrument. Think he can play it?"

"I believe he can," Mom said.

"Well, let him try."

I put my fingers all over the Casio. I wanted to be one of those guys who could sit down and play whatever was on the radio. But I couldn't. With two or three fingers, I could fool around baby chords. I heard simple melodies in my head, and those were the only ones I could manage to play on this toy keyboard.

I started into this song called "Orphanage," about a little boy who'd lost his mother and father. The story flowed out of me; I didn't try for it. It was just there. I found the right notes on the Casio and the right words to tell my little tale.

"Good God almighty," Willie Pearl exclaimed, "your boy can sing, Joann. Your boy can really sing! Where'd you learn that song, Rob?"

"Just made it up."

"No, you didn't."

"Oh yes, he did," my mother said. "Rob has a mind for making up music."

"That's beautiful," said Willie Pearl. "I believe he's blessed. Y'all keep this Casio down here. My boys don't care nothing about it. But your Rob, well, he's got a thing for it. Rob will use it."

"You mean that?" I asked Willie Pearl.

"Indeed I do, child. Now you go on and write some songs. Write one for your mama."

Next day when Willie Pearl came over, I had my new song ready.

"What's it called, son?" she asked.

"'Hard Times,'" I said.

"And it's for your mama?"

"Yes, ma'am, it's all about Mom."

"Hard Times" was a simple melody in a deep blues bag. When I started singing, I could see that I'd tapped a main vein; I could see it in Willie Pearl's eyes, which were wet with tears.

"Hard times," I sang, "she working night and day. Hard times, just to keep the landlord away. Hard times, she does it all alone. Hard times, her love keeps us strong."

"Sing it again, son," Willie Pearl requested.

I sang it again, and before I knew it, the woman was calling every last person living in Vista Gardens to come over and hear me sing 'bout these "Hard Times."

"He don't sing like no boy," said Willie Pearl. "Robert sings like a man." She was showing me off like I was her own son.

After that, many were the times Willie Pearl would come over just to hear me sing. Some of those times I could see that she was flying high in a friendly sky. Other times she was sober as a church mouse. But every time she made me feel special. In her loving way, she let me know that my songs lifted a heavy burden off her shoulders. It's a powerful feeling that I still cherish to this day, knowing that something I created can lift burdens and lighten loads.

As Willie Pearl closed her eyes and sat back with a sweet smile on her face, I let new melodies come to my fingers and new stories come to my lips.

Willie Pearl—this beautiful woman who let me use that little Casio—inspired me to create.

"You touch my soul, boy," she said. "You touch my heart."

Her words of encouragement fueled my reaching some of my highest Soulacoaster moments.

I was smiling at the same time I was frowning. I was feeling funny about the whole thing. I knew I had gotten a pass.

I knew I hadn't earned this diploma.

HOOPING AHEAD

My hoop skills got me on my elementary school basketball team. Our team did really well and the school was proud of us. As a result, I had some positive energy moving through me. Basketball was a way for me to feel good about myself.

Our coach, Mr. Wright, was a smart and honest man. When it came to ball, Coach was all business; he demanded the best from you. He was firm but fair. I wasn't the greatest player in the world, but I had a great desire to win, my hard work, and my hustle. Coach saw my desire and encouraged it. He knew how bad I wanted to win. I respected his attitude, and he respected mine. He started me as a forward.

My jump shot might have looked a little funny, but it was falling. I was reading the defense, forcing turnovers, cashing in on fast breaks. The basketball court was where I shined. The basketball court was never the problem. The problem was the classroom.

Because of my reading, I kept falling further behind. I had ways of covering it up—skipping classes, pretending I lost my book—but I knew that one day it'd all catch up with me. And it did—I was held back a few grades. But because of basketball, I was allowed to slide at school.

This reading problem hurt my heart so bad because of how I longed to know what was in those books. I had a desire for learning. I had an imagination that drew me to stories. When I looked through picture books, for instance, the pictures seemed to be waving at me. If our class took a field trip to a museum, I became part of the paintings on the walls. If there was a picture of a man on a boat in the middle of the sea, I'd make up a story in my mind: The man had dreamed of an enchanted island where a princess

85

was waiting for him. She was the love of his life, and he was sailing all the way around the world to find her.

I felt like a bird without wings. I had the desire to fly but just couldn't do it. I had the desire to read stories but just didn't know how. To me, stories were the most beautiful things in the world.

I'm in love with hearing a good story.

When our class went to see *The Black Stallion*, the story jumped off the screen into my soul. The movie was so powerful and inspiring to me. A boy and a horse, surviving a shipwreck, stranded together on a deserted island. After they were rescued, they achieved the impossible. *The Black Stallion* made me believe that I could survive my struggles, that I could overcome the obstacles in my life; things that I didn't think I could ever do, I believed now that I could.

We also saw *Star Wars*. That movie touched me, too. I could relate to Luke Skywalker overcoming Darth Vader. I understood what the Force was about. From that day on, I wanted to believe "the Force" was with me and would get me through those dark days at school.

During my last year of elementary school, nothing could stop our basketball team. We buried the rest of the league, and we wound up undefeated champs.

But I also couldn't be any sadder because there was no way I could graduate with the rest of the team. I had too many F's. My failures had caught up with me. I was going to be held back in elementary school while the rest of the guys would move on to high school.

Then came the news. A teacher called me into her office and said it plainly: "You'll be graduating with everyone else."

I couldn't believe it. I thought she had me confused with another student. I even asked her to repeat it.

"It's no mistake, Robert," she said. "You will be graduating. We all know that you have a strong desire to win. You've proven that in basketball. So we're hoping that when you get to high school, you'll show that desire in the classroom.

But you must realize that high school won't fool with you. If you don't try harder and make passing grades, high school will kick you out."

I thanked her and left, but her words hung heavy over my head; her words were echoing inside my brain when, a week later, my mother and I went to my elementary school graduation.

I was smiling at the same time I was frowning. I was feeling funny about the whole thing. I knew I had gotten a pass. I knew I hadn't earned this diploma. All the families were there, everyone happy and proud, aunts and uncles, cousins and grandmas, crowding around the graduates, taking pictures, congratulating, hugging, wishing 'em well.

As they called out the names of my classmates, I was flashing on all the games we won, the points I scored, the plays I made, the championship, the trophy, the pride that came with victory. I also remembered how the other kids learned to write and read while I couldn't, flashing on all those times when, staring at words on a page, my eyes went bleary and my mind went blank, flashing on how it felt to get all F's. In my heart, I knew that I didn't deserve the diploma. The feeling haunted me and I felt like I was living a waking nightmare.

When the principal called out out our names, each of us got up to get a handshake and a certificate.

"Terrence Smith . . ."

Terrence got up and hurried across the stage where he was handed his diploma.

"Larry Washington . . ."

Larry walked over to get his diploma.

I saw the faces of my fellow classmates and their families. Everyone was filled with pride—except me: I was filled with shame, so much shame that when they called my name, I walked across the stage, took the diploma, threw it into the audience, and ran out of the auditorium. My mother ran after me.

We were out in the parking lot when she said, "What's wrong, son?"

"I don't deserve it," I said. "I didn't earn it. I want to be able to say 'This is mine, I earned this!' Then nobody can ever take it away from me."

"The day will come when you'll feel that you did earn it, Rob. You just gotta be patient."

{ "The day will come when you'll feel that you did earn it, Rob. You just gotta be patient." }

I remember there were
40 or 50 kids in the classroom.

Everyone seemed to be old friends.

I didn't know a soul.

I took a seat in the first row and thought to
myself: *What the hell am I doing in here?*

I felt like an alien.

ROOM 126

Kenwood Academy, situated in the same Hyde Park neighborhood as the world-famous University of Chicago, where President Barack Obama and his wife Michelle once lived, was considered a great high school that attracted the smartest students, kids who wound up going to all the best colleges.

I got to go there, not because I was smart, but because I played basketball. I was happy for the chance to keep playing with my teammates and to move up to a higher league. I was totally blinded by my past, and I couldn't see into the future. In my fantasy, I had a shot at the NBA: I felt good about basketball. But I didn't feel good about high school because I knew eventually everyone would find out that I couldn't read. I was afraid that I'd lose my shot at pro basketball and my dreams of a better life. I couldn't go back to grammar school and I didn't know how I was going to get through high school. I was trapped. I'd never have teachers, like in grade school, who'd keep passing me. Besides, I didn't want that. I wanted to learn to read like everyone else.

On my first day at Kenwood I went to music class, held in room 126. I didn't know what to expect.

I remember there were 40 or 50 kids in the classroom. Everyone except me seemed to be old friends; I didn't know a soul. I took a seat in the front row and thought to myself: *What the hell am I doing in here?* I felt like an alien.

Then the teacher arrived. The minute she stepped into the room, all talking stopped. Her hair was stylishly done. I saw from how she dressed that she had class.

Her eyes were dark brown. Her eyes were looking over the room, seeing who's who and what's what. Her eyes told me that she was no substitute teacher. This lady wasn't playing.

Her name was Miss Lena McLin.

She said, "There are two students in here with gum in their mouths. I'm going to give them two seconds to put the gum in the garbage or I'll fail them." Right away 20 students got up and put their gum in the trash can. I saw that this lady was smart. If she'd said six seconds, they woulda had time to think about it and maybe only five or six kids would have gotten up. She could sure take charge of a classroom.

Next thing I knew, she was pointing right at me. I got scared and checked to see if I was chewing gum. I wasn't. I didn't know what she wanted from me.

"Do you know who you are?"

"Yes, ma'am; I'm Robert Kelly."

"No, you are God's child. The spirit of God is on you, son. You are going to be famous. You are going to write songs for Michael Jackson. You are going to travel the world. People will pay to see you. You are anointed. God has given you a gift that no one can take away."

I had never met this lady before and she had never met me. I didn't have a clue as to what she was talking about. I had heard prophecy stuff before, but never about me. Besides, I wasn't into prophecies. I didn't believe them. Even in my mother's church, I was always too shy to jump up and start hollering. I never did catch the Holy Ghost. Now here at school, this teacher was talking in tongues, and I was confused as I could be. I loved music, sure, but my main plan in life was to play basketball.

Meanwhile, Miss McLin kept on talking, even as she walked over to the upright piano and sat down. She began playing gospel chords, which seemed weird to me, I'd never seen a teacher play gospel songs.

At the time I didn't know that she was a pastor as well as a teacher. I didn't know anything. All I knew was that Miss McLin was lifting her hand with her fingers spread apart and prophesizing on me like a preacher.

While she was playing, she was praying, "Praise God. Praise His holy name. Praise Him for giving this child a talent that the world will recognize. Praise Him for putting this boy in my classroom where he can grow. Lord, let him grow. Keep him strong."

Then she looked over at me and said, "Stand up, boy. I want you to sing."

"I'm not really a singer," I said. "I'm a basketball player."

"Son, you're not a basketball player anymore. You're singing today. Just follow me."

She started singing Billy Preston's, "You are so beautiful . . . to me."

I followed her and sang the same words, the same notes. I was so shy, though, that I wouldn't face the class. I just faced her. Her face, bright and smiling, gave me confidence. Her voice inspired my voice. I started singing stuff that was amazing, even to me. Something clicked in me; I don't know exactly what. I started flying. The weirdest sensation came all over me. I was able to sing lower than I ever had; I was able to go higher; new ideas popped off in my head, and I could sing them all. The girls in the class were going crazy, and the guys were giving me the "woof-woof-woof" dog cheer. I was a new person. This woman was taking me someplace I'd never been before.

I had a new lease on life. Part of it had to do with the girls. In high school, if you were light-skinned or could sing a little, it was a wrap. I wasn't light-skinned, but having heard me sing a little, the girls were showing me serious love. That was enough to make my day . . . but not enough to make me change my mind. I still wanted to be Michael Jordan.

Next day I was at basketball practice when I saw Miss McLin coming around to talk to my new coach. No one had told him about my reading problem, so he thought I was like everyone else.

"Do you have a Robert Kelly?" she asked.

"Yes."

"Call him over here, please."

Coach called me over. I stood in front of both of them.

"I want Robert off the team," said Miss McLin.

"He's a good player," said the coach.

"Doesn't matter to me how good he is. His music comes first. Robert must be focused. Basketball is a distraction."

"But he loves it."

"I realize that. But if he plays ball and does music, he'll wind up diluting them both. He's going to have to choose."

"But shouldn't that be his choice?" the Coach asked.

"God has already made the choice," Miss McLin explained. "God has given this boy a precious gift. And I wouldn't want to defy God's will, would you?"

I had some thoughts about Miss McLin's attitude. Music was cool, but hoop was still my heart. I couldn't give up hoop.

"You aren't giving it up," she explained. "You're just giving up your place on the team. Basketball is good recreation, and I'm sure you'll be playing it for the rest of your life."

"But I need to . . ."

"You need to listen to me, young man. You need to be in this music classroom every single day. I expect you to arrive early and leave late. I expect you to work twice as hard as any of the other students."

"Why?"

"Because you're twice as talented. One day your records will be bought by millions. One day your songs will be played all over the world."

I was asking myself, *How is that possible? That's just a crazy lady talking crazy talk.*

"You think this is crazy talk," Miss McLin said, as if reading my mind, "but you can ask anyone in this school, and they'll tell you that I am not a crazy woman. I am a serious woman. I am a God-fearing woman. I am a trained musician, personally trained by my uncle, Thomas A. Dorsey. Have you ever heard of Thomas A. Dorsey, Robert?"

"No, ma'am."

"Thomas A. Dorsey was a genius. They call him the Father of Gospel Music.

He started out playing piano for the famous blues singer Ma Rainey in the twenties. You need to study these things, Robert. This is your heritage. My uncle used to go by the name Georgia Tom. In 1928, he wrote a song and recorded it with Tampa Red called 'Tight Like That' that sold millions of copies. Then in the thirties, his wife died giving birth to his son. The baby also died. My uncle was so grief stricken that he wrote a song called 'Precious Lord, Take My Hand.'"

"I know that song," I said. "My mom sings it."

"Everyone sings it. Aretha Franklin sang it at Dr. King's funeral. Before that, Mahalia Jackson sang it. I know you've heard of Mahalia Jackson."

"She sang here in Chicago."

"Mahalia got famous singing my uncle's songs, like 'Peace in the Valley.' When Uncle Thomas went from writing blues songs to gospel songs, though, some people didn't like them. I'm talking about church people. They thought his church songs sounded bluesy and jazzy. Well, they did. But Uncle Thomas knew that there's no sin in writing a gospel song with jazz chords. No sin in putting blues feeling into God's music because *all* music is God's music. You must understand, Robert, that Uncle Thomas invented modern gospel because he wasn't listening to anyone except God. He knew that God wanted His message sent out to the world. And if a jazzy feeling or a bluesy feeling made God's message more appealing, then so be it. Uncle Thomas taught me to play piano, to write music, and to recognize genius. He had genius, Robert, and I see his genius in you."

"I still have to come early and leave late every day?"

"Every single day. Not only that, but I'm going to teach you more than popular singing and gospel singing. I'm going to teach you opera."

"Opera?"

"That's right. I'm going to teach you the most difficult singing there is. The more styles you learn, the better you'll be."

I wanted to complain; I wanted to say that I still wanted to be on the basketball team; I wanted to refuse to come early and leave late every day; I wanted to reject all this hard work she was talking about. But I didn't open my mouth for one simple reason:

The lady intimidated me.

I loved Miss McLin. I loved her because I could feel that she loved God, she loved music, and she loved me. She was strong, but I was used to strong women. My mother was strong. Miss McLin couldn't sing like Mom—she didn't have Mom's powerhouse voice—but she could teach me things my mother couldn't. Miss McLin knew about breathing. She taught me to breathe deeply from my diaphragm.

"Shallow breathing leads to shallow singing," she said, "and you aren't a shallow singer, Robert. You're a singer who must sing from your soul."

When Miss McLin gave me a song where the notes were too high for me to reach, she said, "Lift your eyebrows when you sing."

I lifted my eyebrows and hit the notes.

Then when the notes got higher and I complained I couldn't hit them, she said, "Think of a jet plane soaring through the clouds. Think of the highest, tallest things that you can imagine."

I thought of the jet and the Sears tower and hit the notes.

But then, when the notes got ridiculously high and there was no way in the world I could sing them, she pressed my stomach real hard.

I hit the notes.

This is a technique that I still use to this day. That's how I hit those notes on "When A Woman Loves," by thinking about jet planes, the Sears Tower, and the sun and the stars.

Miss McLin gave me a song called "Ama del Cuore," the first love song. She said it was written in Italian 400 years ago.

"I can't sing a song that old," I said. "I can't sing a song written in Italian."

But I did. Miss McLin showed me that I could sing anything.

Miss McLin said I could write an aria. So I created an aria.

Miss McLin said I could create a gospel song, a love song, and a dance song. So I created them my way—all in the same afternoon.

She told me that she had written cantatas, masses, orchestral works for piano and violin. She'd even written electronic music.

"If I can do it, Robert," she said, "so can you."

Miss McLin was college trained. She went to Spelman in Atlanta and then earned a master's degree in music from the American Conservatory in Chicago.

"Whatever melodies I have inside me," she said, "you have even more inside you. Those melodies in you are limitless because they're coming from a limitless God. Our job is to praise Him through music. As long as you keep praising Him, He's going to keep blessing you."

I got to the point that if Miss McLin told me that I could jump off the Sears Tower and fly over Lake Michigan, I'd be jumping and flying.

When it came to music, Miss McLin did wonders for my confidence. When it came to reading, though, I was still sunk. At one point my reading was so shamefully bad I stopped going to classes altogether. I couldn't take the pressure. I ran to the music room instead. But even there I ran into trouble.

There was this guy called Charles Craig. He was a Herbie Hancock fan, a wizard of the keyboard, and another protégé of Miss McLin. Not only could Charles play great, he could also write great. Gospel, jazz, blues, pop, classical—the whole nine yards. Meanwhile, I couldn't play an instrument or read or write a single note of music; I didn't know the sharps from the flats. When I looked at a musical score, I got a headache. I did everything by ear.

Being around Charles was a little intimidating, but I saw how much Miss McLin admired him, and it made me want to learn piano. By watching him, though, I also learned something. He was a bad little guy, but when he read from the sheet music and played it flawlessly, it sounded cold. It didn't feel good. On the other hand, when he let loose and just improvised, it felt great.

I wanted to play in a way that felt great. Miss McLin always talked about following that good feeling wherever it leads. When I found this secret room at school that everyone seemed to have forgotten about, it became another place—a safe place—where I could escape from my classes and the world—and there was a piano in it.

RIBBON IN THE SKY

By the end of 9th grade, Miss McLin told me I was ready to enter the school-wide talent contest. I was still too shy and wanted to wait, but she insisted. She said I could practice it in our class before I sang it in the auditorium in front of the whole school.

But even in my music class, my shyness had me acting strange. It was Miss McLin who handed me a pair of sunglasses and told me to put them on; and it worked. I pretended to be Stevie Wonder. That was easy 'cause I was doing his "Ribbon in the Sky." My classmates encouraged me. They gave me the confidence to sing before the entire student body.

On the day of the contest I wore the shades. I even had my friend Larry Hood guide me on stage like I was blind. I was still too shy to look at the audience and sing. Charles Craig accompanied me on piano. When I got to the line that says, "There's a ribbon in the sky for our love," the screaming started. The screaming got out of hand. I was afraid that I might start a riot, but I was also overjoyed. Girls were screaming for me, everybody was screaming for me. That's the day, like Peter Parker, I got bit by the spider, a music spider. If Peter was Spider Man, I became Music Man.

I got a feeling that day that I had never gotten on the basketball court. I felt love like I had never felt from anyone except my mother. This time, it was coming from 500 people in the auditorium, but it felt like a million people to me. I wanted to experience that feeling again and again. I had taken a chance, got my courage up, and earned those screams—I'd earned the audience's love. That feeling of connection began to replace a lot of the darkness. It eased the shame I still felt inside. I went from feeling out of place to thinking that maybe, just maybe, this was the reason I graduated—maybe this school was exactly where I was supposed to be.

Miss McLin saw me as a winner and did everything in her power to make sure I saw myself the same way. But I couldn't. No matter how good it felt to make music, I couldn't get away from the fact that I was at the very bottom of my class. In a school where hundreds of kids were reading their books and finding their way, I was lost. History, geography, science, and literature—they all require reading.

I started to wear the sunglasses all the time at school, hiding behind them—hoping no one would see me, call on me, or realize I was even alive. I'd walk down the hallways, practically hugging the wall, dragging my head against it like I was crazy.

I ran from the classes and started locking myself into a little room at the back of the music room. It was really just a storage closet no one used with a lot of junk in it, some broken-down chairs and an untuned upright piano. I went in there every day, basically just to hide, but while I was hiding, I figured I might as well try to play the piano. I wanted to show Miss McLin that I could play the piano, too, like Craig. I started messing around, making these little two-finger chords. It was slow, but they sounded good to me. Two fingers became two fingers and one bass finger on the other hand, that became three fingers, then four fingers, bass became one finger, then two fingers, and so on. I kept it simple, and I started figuring out melodies on the piano. I did this for a whole year. It was really how I started writing songs on the piano. By the end of that school year, I had so many songs I had learned and written on the piano. Miss McLin tried to figure out just how I was learning so quickly. She had no idea that I was practicing and teaching myself every day in that closet.

On the negative side, I was ditching all my classes and hiding out in the storage room. When the bell rang, I'd put on my dark shades, leave the room, and walk down the hallway like I was going to class, but then turn around and go right back to the room. I never walked the hallways without my shades. I felt like they made me disappear. I kept my head down. I did this for a long time . . . and then I got caught.

The school was about to kick me out, and rather than face my mother—who'd whip my butt when she found out how much school I'd skipped—I decided to run away from home.

I was feeling a little nuts.

Somehow Miss McLin found out what was happening and called me to her office. "You've got to stay in school," she said. "You've got work to do."

"I can't do my schoolwork," I said. "I can't stay in school."

"You'll get help, Robert. I'll see to it."

"The principal says I'm beyond help. She told me that with all my failing grades and all these classes I've skipped, she's throwing me out. I don't want to be there when my mother finds out. I want to be on a bus going to Alaska."

"I'll see the principal myself."

Next thing I knew, Miss McLin took my hand and walked into the office of the principal, who was a take-no-prisoners kind of administrator. I felt like the Scarecrow brought for an audience with the Wizard of Oz.

"I'm a little busy right now," the principal said.

"So am I," said Miss McLin. "Busy training my best student to be an important musician whose influence will be felt the world over. My only problem, though, is that he says he's being expelled."

"He is."

"That's unacceptable. I cannot stand idly by. He needs an education. It's not like he's gangbanging or selling drugs. The boy's doing his best."

"That's not what my reports say."

"Your reports are wrong. I should know; I'm his teacher."

"His other teachers don't agree with you. They share my view that Robert is not an acceptable student."

"Let me be direct," said Ms. McLin.

"You always are," said the principal."Robert has failing grades," she defended, "and there's nothing more I can do."

"Well, there's something I can do," my teacher responded, standing up and pointing her finger directly at the principal. "I can go to the press and tell my story. I can tell them that we have a musical genius at Kenwood who is being kicked to the curb. I can tell them the truth. Here at Kenwood, talent has blossomed. And this young man in question is brimming with talent. Your choice is simple. You see to it that he gets help, or I see to it that your treatment is reported far and wide."

"Well, if that's how you see it, Miss McLin."

"It isn't how I see it," she said. "It's how it is."

Miss McLin saved the day. I got to stay in school.

It had taken a long time, but the turning point had arrived. Music, not basketball, became my calling. I saw that. I felt that. For the first time, I felt like I was being introduced to my true self. Meeting the real Robert was a profound healing for me.

I dedicated myself to music.

I also dedicated myself to helping Miss McLin in any way I could. I owed her everything. She took me all over the city. When they lit the big Christmas tree in downtown Chicago, she had me sing "Joy to the World"; that night I was on the news. When Oprah asked Miss McLin to put together a choir, I was in that choir.

One day my mother asked, "Why are you spending this time with that woman outside of school?"

"'Cause she's getting me on TV. She's telling the world about me. Last month she even took me to her church—the Holy Vessel—where she's the pastor. She had me sing, and during her sermon she even talked about me."

"How's a teacher gonna be a pastor, too?"

". . . sometimes God puts people in places where they life because Robert needed a certain kind of schooling.

"I don't know. But she is."

"Well you don't need to be going to her church. We got our own church. You're my boy, not hers."

The fact that my mother was jealous of Ms. McLin's being a part of my life made me love my mother even more. But Miss McLin was changing my life. She was giving me a future. I needed to keep going to her church.

When she sat down and played the piano in church, for example, she had me sitting on the bench next to her. I was there to turn the pages on her sheet music. I couldn't read the music, but when it was time to turn, Miss McLin nodded at me. I turned the page perfectly. Everything I did for Miss McLin I wanted to be perfect.

Miss McLin wanted to take me to Memphis for a gospel convention. She was going to play, and she was gonna have me sing. I was excited; never been outside of Illinois. Never been on a plane. I was going to be able to learn a lot, see a lot, and be with the choir.

"You can't go to Memphis," my mother said.

"But . . ."

"Decision is final, boy. It's too far from here, and God knows what goes on at that convention."

"It's a gospel music convention."

"You don't think gospel folk party?"

"But Miss McLin will be watching out for me."

"Miss McLin this and Miss McLin that . . . boy, all I hear you talkin' 'bout is Miss McLin. I'm tired of hearing about that woman."

I kept begging but couldn't convince my mother to let me go to Memphis. Then one night she came into my room and saw me crying.

"What's wrong, son?" she asked.

"I just gotta go to Memphis, I really do."

I could see that my mother was moved by my tears. Finally, she said, "Well, let

need to be. I know the Good Lord placed me in Robert's And for that, I'll always be grateful to God."

me just talk to this lady and see what she has to say for herself."

Right then I got a burst of joy and confidence. I felt like things were gonna work out.

A few days later, Miss McLin was in our kitchen, talking to my mother.

"I just had to meet this person who's got my son smiling more than I do," Mom admitted.

"I know I've been taking up a lot of your boy's time," Miss McLin responded.

"You sure have."

"And I know how much he means to you."

"He means the world."

"And all I can say is that no one can or will ever take your place."

"You got that right."

"You are the person who first inspired his music," Miss McLin continued, "and I know that for the rest of Robert's life, you will continue to be his main inspiration."

"Glad to hear you say that."

"Well, it's the truth. But sometimes God puts people in places where they need to be. I know the Good Lord placed me in Robert's life because Robert needed a certain kind of schooling. And for that, I'll always be grateful to God."

"Praise His holy name."

"Amen. So what I'm saying is that Robert has a destiny: You're the main ingredient in that destiny. He was born of your flesh and he contains all the music that God put in your heart. In a much smaller way, I'm also part of Robert's destiny. I was put here to show him certain things, encourage him in certain ways, and take him to certain places. I believe that Memphis is one of those places God wants me to take him."

My mom started to answer back, but didn't. At that moment I felt her jealousy melting like an ice cube in the noonday sun. Soon they were talking heart to heart, mother to mother. A week later I was on my way to Memphis.

"So what I'm saying is that Robert has a destiny: You're the main ingredient in that destiny. He was born of your flesh and he contains all the music that God put in your heart. In a much smaller way, I'm also part of Robert's destiny."

CHORUS

rk

1st row: John Thomas, Adam Rose, Tracey King, Karen Hurley, Machi Barrett, Suzanne White, Tippi Hyde 2nd row: Hermion Wyer, Ovida Brown, Ramona Jackson, Lisa Maxwell, Melanie Powell, Jonita Lattimore, Chenay McCain, Valerie Banks, Brenda Parks, Verda Wilkerson, Lena McLin, sponsor 3rd row: Maria Barjas, LaShaun Paschal, Chris Gladney, Tammy McCan, Dawn Newton, Angela Belton, Donica Lyles, Charlean Hines, DeeDee Wood, Cassandra McKay, Angela Odoms 4th row: Stephanie Miller, Angelique Swain, Kelly Russaw, Cathy Ford, Adrienne Troy, Michael Ewing, Eric France, Michele Thomas, Andrea Parker, Anita Ziegler 5th row: Karen Simpson, Matthew Swartz, Robert Kelly, Leslie Walker, Craig McLendon, Carl Taylor, Paul Daniels, Sean Dyer, Mark Cobb, Rodney Plummer, Steven Ordower

IN THE BASEMENT

In high school, I was this nappy-headed kid. Sure, it helped when I started singing, but I couldn't really compete with the guys who wore Izod shirts and the fresh Adidas sneakers. They had money, and I didn't. I came from the 'hood. I used to draw the alligator on my shirt; I'd do it carefully and hoped nobody looked too closely.

It seemed like ever since I started doing talent shows, pretty girls started paying attention to me. I met a girl in high school named Sujay who seemed to like me for who I was. I didn't have a crush on her, but she was pretty and sexy, so we ended up getting together. I appreciated how Sujay appreciated me, but I have to say, there was another girl who really got my attention.

Her name was Billie, and we're still friends today, but she'd see me only at her mom's house. She wouldn't really associate with me at school. Billie was in a clique of girls that ran with the Izod boys. All their boyfriends were basketball players. I knew I didn't come up to her standards, but she was so beautiful I didn't even care. I'd meet her on the q.t. if that's what she wanted. I'd meet her anywhere.

Then there was Charlene. She sang in the choir and was also a talented dancer. Sometimes she wore leotards to class, sometimes ballet dresses. She was gorgeous. She was the Beyoncé of Kenwood. Whenever I saw Charlene, I heard music. I got shy whenever she came into the room though. She came from a beautiful family—her mom and Miss McLin were friends—and she was talented. Man, I really wanted to get next to Charlene. But she didn't really see me that way. We were cool, but only as friends.

And the only way I could change that was in make-believe. When Miss McLin asked me and Charlene to do a musical together—she did the choreography and Charles Craig and I wrote the music—I made her my girlfriend in the play. That's how I got to kiss Charlene—on stage, in public. In private, she wasn't having it.

When I was 17, I met Chance, who was my older woman. My homie was kicking it with Chance's sister. She'd always call me "cutie pie" and shower me with affection—I had a deep crush on her. We'd take walks in the park, go to the movies, and talk all night. I fell in love with Chance, who knew more about lovemaking than me. She had experience, and I was eager to show her that I was mature for my age.

We were falling deeper in love and learning about each other's bodies. Soon I thought I knew all there was to know—except, to my surprise, I didn't. One day at my mom's house, we were making love in my room when I happened to look down and saw blood. I pulled out and saw that I was covered in blood. I panicked and started crying. What the hell was going on? I asked Chance if she was bleeding too and she said "Yeah." She tried to explain something but I ran outta the room and went straight to my sister, Theresa.

"What happened?" I demanded.

"You ain't bleeding," said Sis. "She is. She's just having her period."

Theresa explained how the monthly cycle works.

I understood, but I also didn't want to go back there. The blood was too much for me. It freaked me out. When it came to sex, I swore I was done, and I was. I didn't have sex with another girl for three or four years.

We were falling

deeper in love

and learning about

each other's bodies.

Soon I thought

I knew all there was

to know — except,

to my surprise,

I didn't.

ACT
TWO
{ Gettin' Busy }

EASY

One Saturday afternoon when I was in my late teens, I'm hangin' out with my boys and we're bored. We decide to go downtown.

"How 'bout Rush Street, Rob?"

"Rush Street is cool. Let's see what's happening on Rush Street."

Rush Street, on the north side of Chicago Avenue, had expensive restaurants, cool night spots, and lots of rich folk and tourists walking 'round, people with money and style. Rush Street was beautiful.

We got some bus transfers, rolled downtown, jumped off, and there we were, in the middle of the mix—kids from the 'hood, hanging with the rich people, checking out the scene. Rush Street was crowded with tourists, businessmen, and fine ladies. Compared to where I lived, downtown was like a whole new world, and every time I went there, I always wanted to be a part of that world.

Me and my boys were sitting on a ledge near a fancy apartment building where we had a front-row seat to what was going on.

I noticed a guy playing guitar had attracted a little crowd. His playing wasn't great, and his voice was even worse, but people were busy throwing money into his open guitar case.

That's when I got an idea. "Hey, man, watch this," I told my homies.

I put on my shades, took the Chicago Bulls baseball cap off my head, put it on the ground, and started singing "Easy Like Sunday Morning" by the Commodores, a song I knew everyone loved.

But with cars and trucks going by, it was kind of hard to be heard, so I sang really loud. I gave my solo everything that I had. Four or five people passing by stopped smiled, nodding in my direction. One guy gave me a thumbs-up and dropped some change in my cap. Another guy stopped and listened to me for a minute or two. Then he dropped in a buck. A woman did the same. Then another. And then still another. Before long, my cap was overflowing. I kept singing and folks kept dropping bills. Before I knew it, I had made close to $75; I had never seen that much money at once in my whole life.

I took me and my boys to a famous pizza place right in the middle of downtown, called Giordano's. And though it didn't look like we belonged there—four or five raggedy, young boys from the projects—I had more than enough money to feed us all, and that's just what I did. We ate good that day. I even carved my name in the wall, a Giordano's tradition.

"Great day, Rob."

"Easy day—easy like Sunday morning," I crooned. "I think I might come back here tomorrow."

No one said a word. My friends' silence gave me the idea that, even though I was treating them to pizza, they looked down on what I'd done. To them street performing was like begging, like being a bum. But I didn't care.

Street performing that day helped me discover something new and exciting: I had talent and people were willing to pay for it.

Next day I went back to Rush Street by myself and made $90. I was there for a lot longer and my throat got hoarse, but I hung in. I loved it, and so did the passing crowd. It felt really good to sing for people and make them smile. It felt even better taking money home to Mom to help out with the rent.

"You got all of this money by singing?" she asked.

"People like the way I sing, Mom," I said.

"I knew it," she said. "I always knew that your singing was good enough for you to get paid."

"Are you proud of me?" I asked.

"Son," she said, "I couldn't be prouder."

"I knew it," she said, "I always knew that your singing was good enough for you to get paid."

"Are you proud of me?" I asked.

"Son," she said. "I couldn't be prouder."

NEICE

All through my school life, kids made fun of me once they found out I couldn't read. At home, even my brothers and sister did the same—they'd call me all kinds of nasty names. I would always try to avoid getting into it with my brothers and sister 'cause every time we would get into it, the first thing that they would bring up, no matter who was around, was the fact that I couldn't read or write or spell. I remember that feeling to this day.

Donneice was a classmate who used to sit at a desk directly across from me in sixth or seventh grade. One day I noticed her watching me fumble around with my pencil while we were taking a test. She asked me if I was okay. I said right away, "Yes I'm good," and started staring intently at my test like I knew what I was doing. But her vibe let me know that she didn't believe me. I started filling in the circles fast, so that from her perspective it would look like I was acing this test. But, sadly, I was failing it in every way possible. I couldn't wait for the bell to ring because I was so embarrassed.

Recess was my only escape at the time. I would sit outside on the school steps and just watch all of the other kids, some playing around, some talking and laughing, some playing sports. I would ask myself: *Why me? Why can't I read and write like everyone else? Why do I start to yawn every time I get ready to read something? Why is it that every time I open a book, confusing music notes start to ring in my head really loud as I look at the letters?*

My mother had sat up with me many, many nights trying to help me learn to read and write. She would even give me spelling bees. She would sit me down and spell

117

out a word. Then she would make me sing the word while spelling it out, after nothing else would work. Not knowing what I was doing at the time, I would always make a sentence out of that word and sing it back to her as if it was a song. She would say: "That sounds great baby, but spell the word." And that's when everything would go blank. Blank, blank, blank. That's when I discovered that darkness did not just come from the flicking of a light switch, but it was also within me. Failing at reading hurt me a lot more than I ever let on.

So when I met Lonneice, I really appreciated her because she was the only one in school who didn't look down on me. After that first day in class, I started walking her to her next class. Then we started hanging out during recess. She would always talk about dancing, and I would always talk about being successful. Lonneice never cared about the fact that I couldn't read. She just loved to hear me talk about how I was gonna take my mom out of the 'hood and move her to some big old house up in the hills. And how the driveway would be filled with all kinds of cars, and my mom would never have a worry or care in the world when it came to having the things that she wanted. Lonneice loved the fact that my dreams of success were built around my mother's happiness. Lonneice was beautiful inside and out. She had light brown eyes, long sandy brown hair, and a dancer's body. She was a ballerina and a singer who understood my music and my talent, just like I understood hers. She could dance in any style, from classical ballet to hip-hop. She had an old soul and was wise and loyal. Lonneice always believed in me. And all of that became the ingredients in the recipe to the big pot of love that I fell in.

Neice had a grandmother named Grandma Cherrill who called everyone "darling." When I met her, it was like meeting my own grandmother because she made me feel right at home. Grandma Cherrill loved me, just like my mother loved Neice. Everyone got along like old friends. It all felt like family.

I remember the first time Lonneice took me home to meet her family. Her mom, Marcella, had some questions for me, questions like: "Where did you meet my daughter? And why did you choose her?"

"We're in the same class in school. And no disrespect, ma'am, but she kinda chose me."

She also asked me if I had a job, was I going to college, and what was I going to be in life.

I told her that at the time I didn't have a job, and I doubted very seriously that I was going to college, but that I was going to be a very successful singer. And Lonneice's mom laughed out loud and asked me: "How in the hell are you going to be successful at singing or anything else if you don't go to college?"

"I'm working on that," I told her.

Marcella just continued to size me up as she asked me, "Working on that how?" And even though I heard her, I said "Huh?"

"How are you working on that?"

That's when Grandma Cherrill interrupted, "Darling, he's not under investigation, so quit asking him all those questions. If Lonneice likes him, then I like him, too, so you all might as well get used to it."

And that's when I fell in love with Grandma Cherrill.

"He has good manners."

"Thank you, ma'am," I said. "I try."

"We better go or we'll be late for the movies," said Neice.

"What are you seeing?" asked Grandma Cherrill.

I said, "*Beverly Hills Cop.*"

"That Eddie Murphy is a good-looking boy," said Grandma.

"He sure is," Lonneice agreed.

"If y'all excuse me for just a second," I said, "I need to use your bathroom."

I had to go real bad, but, didn't want Neice's mama and grandma to know I *really* had to go. In order to make them think I was only peeing, I had to get in and out in a hurry. When I got out of the bathroom, Neice's grandmother said in a voice that couldn't have been any nicer, "Darling, you better go back in there and fix yourself."

"What's wrong?" I asked.

Neice pointed to the back of my pants. I was in such a hurry that I hadn't torn off the toilet paper that was sticking out the back of my jeans.

I ran back to the bathroom and, first thing, opened the medicine cabinet to see if there was poison. I was ready to kill myself. But there was no poison, just aspirin and bandages. I straightened myself out and got ready to face Neice's folks again. This time I made sure there was no toilet paper hanging out my backside.

"I guess I'm just a little nervous," I said to Neice's grandmother.

"We noticed," said Neice's mom.

LOCATION

LOCATION

LOCATION

THE CHITLIN BUCKET

Street performing is as old as America itself. History tells us that founding father Ben Franklin performed his poetry on public streets. A lot has changed since then. When I came of age in Chicago, if you wanted to street perform, you had to pay for a license.

When I saw the number of people that I could draw by singing, I got serious about my street act. I took it so seriously that I even got a license from the city so I could perform legally. I knew I could draw even more folks if I used my old broken-down keyboard—the old Casio that Willie Pearl had given me. Thanks to Miss McLin's hard-core and disciplined training, I could sing a cappella or sing while playing the keyboard. I also understood that it was all about location. With a better spot, I'd make better money. I found one of those spots in downtown Chicago at a busy El station at Randolph and Jackson.

I wanted my best friend, Big L, to go with me. At first he didn't want to come to watch my back because it felt a little awkward; he was one of those who thought street performing was like being a bum. But because Big L was my best friend, he didn't want to turn me down, so he did it. I had to motivate him by showing just how much money I could make.

I played at Randolph and Jackson for as long as I could, but singing over the noise of the cars, the buses, and street sounds made me very hoarse, very quick. I decided that underground, in the subway, would be a better spot because there was an echo underground and the acoustics gave my voice a better sound—reverb. The only problem was when I started to sing a lyric that I really wanted people to hear, if a train was rolling into the station, it made a lot of noise. I couldn't sing over the noise of an incoming train, so I decided to play it off and act like I was really jamming that part of the song. Then as soon as the train stopped and it got quieter, I would bring my voice up to give the illusion of continuing the song. No one could tell that I had stopped singing. The minute the train passed, I was right back into the song on cue without ever missing a beat.

I learned to read the crowd quickly. For instance, sometimes there would be a lot of white people down in the subway, and I didn't want to sing something they couldn't relate to, so I started writing songs that felt like country or pop—trying to capture the spirit of their culture. And it worked. And sometimes there'd be a lot of black people riding the train, so I would sing songs that I knew they would relate to—"Ribbon in the Sky," Stevie Wonder; "A Song for You," Donny Hathaway; and even some songs that I wrote myself.

Money was coming in steady and strong, and I began to develop something of a following, but even back then—even when I was nobody—I had some haters.

"You ain't no better than a beggar," a neighborhood singer said. "You're just a street beggar, that's all you are." I knew he was jealous because, even though he wanted to, he couldn't really sing. He had a voice like a wounded frog. Besides, even as a teenager, music was like life to me, beyond restrictions or someone else's labels.

"All singing's begging. What do you think Teddy P's doing when he sings 'Turn Off the Lights'? Or Marvin Gaye. What's Marvin doing when he's singing 'Sexual Healing.' They begging. Ain't no harm in begging, brother."

"Your begging don't get you much more than a cheeseburger."

Didn't Mom always say to turn lemons into lemonade? Well, I didn't know if McDonald's sold lemonade, but they sure sold Big Macs. People loved their Big Macs. And the underground spot where I was singing was just below McDonald's.

Right above the subway stop that I performed under was a McDonald's. People of all colors would come down to catch the train and a lot of them would have McDonald's bags in their hands. So I started singing about McDonald's, about how "when your day is through, McDonald's is the place for you." I figured if I wrote a McDonald's song and sang it as the people with McDonald's food came down, not only would they pay me, but I knew they would get a big kick out of it and go home smiling. I made up lyrics about the icy Cokes and the apple pie, the Chicken McNuggets and the tasty fries. And it worked—every time I would bust out with the McDonald's song, the people would drop more and more money into my bucket.

Things were looking up down in the subway. Before long I had enough money for a new keyboard. I'd gone from a baseball cap to a paper bag to a chitlin bucket within a month of street performing. People started hearing about me and started catching the train from that spot just so they could see me perform. I started making so much money that people started to notice; when I say "people," I mean the pickpockets down in the subway.

I used to see them trying to pick people's pockets all the time; and they never knew that I saw them because when I street performed, I would always wear black sunglasses like Stevie Wonder—it was a part of my act. So they didn't know I saw them, till one day I had made so much money that my chitlin bucket was overflowing with 10s, 20s, and one-dollar bills. Suddenly the thieves started turning their attention towards me, slickly but not wisely. I noticed it and told Big L that we had to watch these guys. He told me he was aware of it. I continued to sing.

Then out of nowhere one of the three guys that I knew was a pickpocket ran up to us real fast, snatched the bucket, and kept going. My glasses immediately flew off my face—I think it was from the speed of me getting up to chase him. Me and Big L ran so fast after this guy that we got close enough for me to catch the back of his leg and sweep-kick his ass. He fell down, and Big L started punching him. My money was flying everywhere, and I was trying to collect it all—the guy had fallen down onto the tracks. I turned around to see Big L jumped down onto the tracks after him. I remember yelling out really loud: "Don't touch the third rail!" because I had heard that the third rail is the track that could electrocute you, killing you instantly. Big L got back up on the platform, and the pickpocket ran straight down the tracks like Speedy Gonzales— out of sight.

After that I went to K-Mart and bought a big rope, and for the rest of my street-performing career, I tied one end of the rope to the chitlin bucket and the other end to my right ankle, figuring that if anybody else tried to take my money, they were going to have to take my ass right along with them. It never happened again.

I had another memorable encounter when the street was my stage—with the police. It was raining really hard that day. I had brought a chair and, of course, my keyboard, and I was ready to go. Although it was raining, it was Friday, and I felt sure the sun was going to shine on me because it was payday: that's when I made most of my money. Anyway, as I was singing and minding my own business, I had my black shades on and people were dropping bills in the bucket by the second. Business was booming . . . until all of a sudden, two cops walked up outta nowhere and said to me: "All right, Stevie, let's go."

My first thought was to act like I was blind—that's what they thought, so why not play along with it? But honesty took over. I took the glasses off and said: "What's the problem, officers?"

"You need a license to perform on the streets." So I showed them my license, but for some reason, they took me out of the subway and straight to police headquarters on 22nd Street. The police put me through all sorts of bullshit. The bottom line was that I was in my rights. I had my license. They had to let me go, but they said that if I ever tried to set up in that spot again, they'd keep chasing me away.

They released me, but they wouldn't give me a ride back to the subway. So there I was in the rain, with a keyboard and a chitlin bucket with money in it. I wasn't worried about the money getting wet, but I do remember being really mad because my keyboard was getting wet. I knew that it would soon short out and not work anymore.
I was so pissed because of the injustice that I made my way to another spot three stations away from where the cops had chased me and started singing "Superstar" by the Temptations. A line in that song—"remember how you got where you are"—seemed to give me motivation.

I sang it with so much soul, folks just had to stop and listen. It was then that I discovered the true power of my voice because that day I made more money than I had ever made as a street performer.

*I sang it with so much soul,
folks just had to stop
and listen.*

{ fall in love with the future }

DON'T LOOK BACK

When I finally got up enough nerve to tell Miss McLin that I couldn't read, write, or even spell, she told me about people who were brilliant, who had come before me, paving the way for people who were handicapped in some ways. She'd talk about Ray Charles and Stevie Wonder and how they were blind and overcame their disability and that the world loved them and their music in spite of that.

She would even go further back and talk about how Beethoven was deaf, but still he heard music and was one of the greatest composers ever. She even revealed a secret of hers, that she had had an operation on her hands and how it did not stop her from continuing to play the piano and composing music that is still sold today. Those inspiring examples gave me the hope that I needed. They were the light at the end of the tunnel that I had yearned for since the discovery of my disability.

"If they did it, Robert," she'd say, "then I know you can do it." And for the first time in my life I believed it.

My mom taught me how to fall in love with the future.

"Don't fall in love with the present or the past, Robert," she used to say. "If you do, you'll stay in the present or you'll be stuck in the past. And if you learn to love the future, then you will get to the future." That's why I still keep my eyes on the future every day.

I believed everything that my mother told me, and I trusted Miss McLin's predictions about my future—most of the time. When she told me, "One day, Robert, you're going to be one of the greatest writers of all time," I listened. I wanted to believe. But with kids still laughing at me, it was really hard.

Once I started street performing and making money, though, there was no going back. School kept getting harder. School felt like something I could never conquer. School meant shame and humiliation. School just made me feel downright bad. I was no longer on the school's basketball team, so my on-the-court skills no longer mattered. Performing made me feel that I was worth something. The streets had become my stage, and my audience was willing to pay me.

I didn't want to face my teachers, the other students, or especially Miss McLin. I didn't want to tell them I was a street performer 'cause I knew they'd look down on that. So I stopped going to class. In spite of Miss McLin's best efforts to keep me in school, I quit—just like that. Instead, I started heading for the subway station where I could sound more like James Ingram than James Ingram; more like Jeffrey Osborne than Jeffrey Osborne. I could sound like anyone, I could be anyone and feel like a million bucks. There were no tests to fail, no books to intimidate me, no judgmental looks from stuck-up students who mocked me because I couldn't do what they did.

My street following was getting so strong that if I found that another street performer—say a sax player—got to my spot before me, I could afford to give him $150 to get him to move to another location; $150 was more than he made in two days. Meanwhile, I could make $150 in two hours.

I hustled and printed business cards, then passed them around. The cards advertised that I could sing at weddings, at birthday parties, even at funerals. I was hired to entertain at all kinds of events, including stripping at women's bachelorette parties.

Even back then I felt that whatever I did, I had to do it creatively. So when I stripped, I had to tell a story, or create a fantasy, because I had learned enough about women—by listening to women most of my life—to know they needed to escape reality sometimes. So I'd come out as Darth Vader. I'd put on the black mask and the black robe. When I dropped the robe, I'd be wearing nothing but my little patent-leather drawers. Because I had a body—I was ripped real good—women went crazy. Then I'd go from Darth Vader to Luther, singing, "Don't you remember you told me you loved me, baby . . . baby, baby, baby, oh, baby, baby."

My voice gave me an advantage over all the other strippers working. Some might have had better bodies, but when I started singing, it was a wrap. Some people thought I could dance as good as I could sing, and stripping paid well. The money was

rolling in, but so were the threats. I was naïve about the strip party scene. It was controlled by big-time thugs who weren't about to put up with some freelance kid dressed up as Darth Vader cutting into their profits. After about six months, the threats became so aggressive that I recognized I'd better stick to singing in the subway stations.

Meanwhile, finan-cially, I became my mother's biggest helper—a beautiful blessing. I loved seeing the smile on her face when I gave her money. It made me happy to arrive home with three bags of White Castle burgers and the rent money. I was a bona fide breadwinner. Instead of an imaginary brick box filled with secrets, I got a real metal cashbox where I kept my money. Soon I was paying the bills and saving hundreds of dollars—and I was still a teenager.

Then something happened that broke my heart. My metal box was stolen, and everything I had worked so hard for—all my savings—disappeared. I didn't know who did it, but obviously it was someone in our house. I didn't want to start accusing anybody, so the easiest thing for me to do was just to move out.

When I moved into the YMCA downtown, close to some of the spots where I street performed, I had a single room with barely enough space for a bed. I'd sit up all night playing my keyboard and writing songs. Drug dealers, hookers, and pimps lived up and down the hallways and right across the hall from me. You had to share a bathroom and use a public phone. I didn't care. I was in survival mode. I kept a box of cereal, a carton of milk, and was good to go.

Lonneice hung in there with me. She was my girlfriend, and she believed in my dreams. While I sang in the streets, she worked as a cashier at an Amoco station. We were in this love thing together.

What could go wrong?

Neice

NEVER ENOUGH

> How do you get to be a man when you got no man to show you what it means to be a man? You look around you. You see what the other guys want. You see how the other guys do. What I saw was that all the guys with the most swag all had more than one woman.

In grammar school, the girls looked at me as someone who couldn't even read.

In high school, even when I started singing, the girls who knew me from the classroom remembered I could barely get through a sentence without stumbling all over myself. I heard them laughing. I saw their smirks. All that rejection shit hurt.

But Neice showed me love. Neice was true. Lonneice should have been enough.

But with this newfound success, my pride started blowing up, and my ego took over. Ego started filling up all those holes of youthful insecurity. Ego made me think that one girl wasn't enough. Ego made me want to taste every single flavor.

Ego had me thinking I was all that. I was slim, cut-up, and strong. I went from playing on the streets to performing in clubs, where I'd jump on top of a giant speaker and start singing and stripping at the same time. I liked showing off my voice and my body.

Ego had me following a shorty to her crib because she said her roommate didn't mind. Her roommate was real friendly, too.

Ego had me freaking.

Neice had me loving.

Ego said, "Go crazy."

Neice said, "Go easy."

Ego said, "The more the merrier."

Neice said, "It's you and me, Rob.

It's all about you and me."

Neice said, "Rob, let's go out to Baker's Square and get that delicious coconut cream pie we love so much."

Neice said, "Let's live happily ever after."

My mother said, "I love Neice."

Neice said, "I love your mother."

Neice and I started talking about moving in together.
We were moving on up, we were styling, we were happy.
It was all good.

ABDUCTED BY MY GIFT

Sometimes I feel like I've been abducted by my gift—kidnapped and taken away to a musical place never to be found again. Music possessed me in a way that sometimes scared me. It kept growing inside me. Everywhere I go, everywhere I turn, and everything I do, the lyrics and melodies are always right there—constantly reminding me that there is no escape.

Sometimes I feel like music has made love to me. And sometimes I feel like music just had sex with me. I feel I am pregnant by music; and it is the father and mother of my child. And there will be no denying that. One day I was riding in a car with one of my homies, who was a drug dealer. He had a brand-new Mercedes-Benz; matter of fact, he had several nice cars. He was older than me and I looked up to him, not because of his line of work but because he believed in me. He always told me that I would be big and have it all.

He would protect me from the gangbangers because we played basketball for money in the 'hood and we would win a lot. Believe it or not, I had a sweet jump shot on me. When we would win sometimes, the other guys did not want to pay up. They would try to lie and say that I traveled or that I was cheating. That would always happen close to us winning the game, or on the game-winning shot itself. And my partner would always make sure nothing went down and that we got paid.

I never judged or knocked his hustle because I felt like whatever he did didn't concern me. Besides that, he respected me to the point where he never involved me in any of his business. He would pick me up every Saturday morning and we would go hoop. And we would always talk about music on the way there and on the way back.

What was new and what was hot. What songs we liked and what songs we didn't. He loved music just as much as I did, except he was not musically gifted.

He would always ask me to sing for some of his family members or even sometimes some of his girlfriends. The family members I was cool with singing for, but the girlfriends I was not so cool with because, sometimes after I would sing for them, I would feel in my spirit—and I could also see it in their eyes—that they wanted me, and that would be a little uncomfortable for me. But because he was my boy, I'd sing.

Coming from playing basketball one day, my friend took me on a drive. We were on Interstate 57, way south of the city, heading to the suburbs. He had business out there. We were going down Lincoln Highway, through the village of Matteson, to a place called Olympia Fields where the houses are big, the lawns lush and green, the vibe classy and calm. I was about 16 or 17 years old.

Suddenly I noticed a huge mansion made from giant logs. It was like a log cabin that grew up to be a mansion. The house was way back behind a huge gate on a plot of land bigger than a football field.

"Stop," I said.

I got out of the car and walked up to the gate, amazed by what I saw. At my age if you had told me that this was heaven—compared to where I lived—I would have believed it. I put my hands on the gate and just stared at this house. I'd never seen anything so beautiful.

"This is the McDonald's house," said my friend. "The guy who runs a bunch of McDonald's franchises owns it." I learned much later that James Maros, one of the first 50 owner/operators of McDonald's restaurants, owned the "McDonald's House."

"This is gonna be my house one day," I said.

"Yeah, young blood, you could have a house just like this."

I looked back at him and said, "No, I'm gonna have this house."

"Say what?"

"I just know I will."

"You're crazy, Rob."

I didn't argue. I didn't have to. I knew it was going to happen.

My friend started talking, but I held on to the gate and closed my eyes and began to drown him out, telling myself that when I opened my eyes, this house would be mine. And then we left—back to the 'hood and the hustle.

{ Back to the 'hood and the hustle }

Bakersfield
Ford City
Mount
Pinos
2692
2097
Mountains
Ventura
Santa
Cruz
Island
Long Beach
Santa
Channel Islands

SHOOTING STARS

All my life I'd heard about the city of Los Angeles and all of its glory. From music stars to movie stars, it was the land of fortune and fame. Although the stories I had heard about it seemed like a book of fairy tales, I wanted—and had to have— my name written into the story.

I knew L.A. was a step in the right direction. I had been hearing about it as long as I could remember. Miss McLin always talked about L.A. and big-time producers like Quincy Jones.

There was a producer, who was making a name for himself in Chicago, who asked me if I wanted to go to L.A. He had put together a five-member group that needed a lead singer. I auditioned and got the gig. It was 1984, and five-member groups like New Edition were hot. "Cool It Now" was the #1 R&B song in the country.

"Can you write songs as good as that?" asked the producer.

"I can," I said. And I did. I wrote four killer songs for the group. Another writer named Chuck E. Booker had also written a bunch of tunes for us to sing.

We flew out to L.A. In Chicago, it was winter; in L.A. it was summer. L.A. was all sunshine and palm trees. We stayed in a little apartment where we slept on the floor, but who cared? I was in L.A., baby. I was on my way.

The producer told us he'd locked up a deal for us at A&M Records, same label where Quincy Jones himself produced all those funky hits for the Brothers Johnson.

"Right now the label is listening to everything we've written. They're deciding which songs should go on the record."

While they were deciding, we went to a photographer's studio for our first publicity shot. *Man, this was Hollywood!*

Next day the producer came in and announced the songs A&M wanted us to record. All four of mine had been chosen. When I looked at the list, though, I didn't see my name next to my songs. I didn't get any credit.

"It's not about individual credit," said the producer. "It's a group effort."

"The singing is," I said, "but I wrote those songs alone."

"Sorry, Rob, but the deal's done. The songwriting and publishing are part of the group deal. I can't give you any ownership of that. But don't worry. We'll be getting an advance. There'll be enough money for everyone."

That night I called my mother.

"It doesn't seem right to me," she said.

"That's what I think. But we're set to go in the studio in a few days. What can I do now?"

"Demand your credit."

"I did. They won't give me any."

"Then just come on home, son."

"Just get up and leave?"

"Well, look at it this way, Rob. If they screw you now, they're gonna screw you later. Cheating is cheating, Robert. I wouldn't mess with these folk."

Three days before the recording session, I told the group goodbye. They were furious. They accused me of dogging them. But as far as I'm concerned, I wasn't dogging anyone. I was doing what was right.

I did what I've always wound up doing: I came home to Chicago.

I wasn't home all that long when I felt like I had to try again. L.A. had kicked my butt once, but I wasn't about to quit.

"I know you're discouraged," said Mom, "and you've got every right to be. The music business is cold-blooded, son. It's testing you. It's saying, 'How bad you want it, boy?' If you want it bad enough, you'll stay with it. If you don't want it that bad, you'll quit. But I just can't see my baby quitting."

Her "baby" wasn't quitting. I was focusing on the future just like she taught me. I was going back to L.A, super-intent on coming home with a record deal.

"I won't be gone all that long," I told Lonneice.

"I don't want you there at all, Rob."

"I've gotta keep after it," I said. "I've gotta catch my dream."

"As long as I'm still a part of it."

"Baby," I told her, "you are the dream."

"I want to come with you," said Neice.

"Wish you could, baby," I said. "But I don't even have enough money for me. How could I support the two of us? As soon as something happens, though, I'm sending for you. I promise."

> *"The music business is cold-blooded, son. It's testing you. It's saying, 'How bad you want it, boy?'"*

"*This is Robert Kelly,*" *he said.*
"*Our next superstar.*"

STARS

I looked up at the sky from Venice Beach on the west side of Los Angeles. The midnight air was sweet, the weather mild. The ocean breeze perfect. No one was bothering me. I was out there on the sand, laid out on a blanket. That big old full moon shone down on me like a giant spotlight. The sound of the roaring waves was hypnotizing. I closed my eyes and thought, *I can do it, I can make it, I can make it in Cali.*

It didn't matter that I didn't have a place to stay, that I was living homeless on the beach. It didn't matter that I was carrying my clothes in a paper bag. Neice and her folks sent me enough money so I could eat and buy a few clothes. When it came time to enter an amateur contest in clubs like the Red Onion, I would clean up. I got on stage and killed.

But dammit to hell, I never won. Never.

I never won a single contest in L.A. I knew I was better than the other contestants. I knew I had talent, but seemed like I was the only one who knew it.

I got a better response on the streets than in the clubs. As a street performer in Venice Beach, I attracted crowds. With no keyboard or guitar, I just belted out a big ballad like "Distant Lover" and wound up with a few bucks. Of course the competition in L.A. was fiercer than Chicago. There were jugglers, comics, and painters; there was every form of artist imaginable hawking his or her wares alongside me.

I missed home. I missed my mother and Lonneice. I missed my crew and the comforts of Chicago. But I wasn't going back, not this time, not without some sign of success.

I was like a junkyard dog. Once I got my teeth into something, I wouldn't let go. I kept hustling. One thing led to another and I got the name of a big-shot music exec at Warner Records, Benny Medina. Everyone had heard of Benny Medina. At the age of 24, Benny worked for Motown and was considered Berry Gordy's protégé. He worked with artists like Ray Charles, Rick James, Madonna, Fleetwood Mac, Biz Markie, and Big Daddy Kane. The TV show, *Fresh Prince of Bel Air*, would be based on his life growing up.

Benny could definitely sign me to a deal.

Benny agreed to see me. On the phone, he said, "Come to my office. I'll see what you can do for me. And then you'll see what I can do for you."

I arrived a half-hour early. Sitting in a chair outside Medina's office was a light-skinned black guy, waiting for Benny just like me.

We started talking. He said he sang.

"How 'bout you?" he asked.

"I'm a singer, too," I said.

He went in first. Half-hour later it was my turn.

Benny Medina was cool. Said, "Go over to the piano and play whatever you like."

"I'd like to play my originals," I said.

"I want to hear them, Robert."

I played him 12 songs. Benny was knocked out.

"Man, you're something, Robert," he said. "You're great. These are brilliant songs and your voice is tremendous. Come with me right now so I can introduce you to everyone in the building."

I was on cloud nine. Benny took me to meet all the other execs and producers. "This is Robert Kelly," he said. "Our next superstar."

"Does this mean I'm in?" I asked Benny.

"Yes, sir. Just give me a week or two, and I'll get right back to you with the papers."

I called practically everyone I knew in Chicago.

My mother said, "If it's gonna take him a little while to work up your contract, come home and do the waiting here."

I had just enough for a plane ticket, so I flew home. I had moved into the basement of Lonneice's Grandma Cherrill's house. Meanwhile, I couldn't stop thinking about that pending contract from Warner Records and Mr. Benny Medina.

A week passed. Then two. Then three.

I called Medina's office. He was out. Called again. He was on the phone. Called a third time. He was gone for the day. Another week passed. I kept calling. Benny kept ducking.

By week five, I was feeling desperate. I was calling every day. His secretary was so sick of me, the second she heard my voice, she said, "Mr. Medina cannot come to the phone."

"Why can't he just tell me what's happening?"

"He is telling you," she said. "You're just not listening."

"But he's not saying anything."

"That's the point."

BIG
BREAK

BIG BREAK

I spent my late teens missing the brass ring. My early twenties were the same story.

One day soon after I got back to Chicago, we were all sitting around watching music videos on TV at my mother's house. The video for the song called "Off On Your Own" came on.

"Wait a damn second!" I shouted, jumping off the old sofa. "Who is that?"

"That's Al B. Sure," said Neice.

"That's the light-skinned guy who was sitting next to me outside Benny Medina's office!"

I'd tried, but I couldn't find love in Hollywood. Every single door—and I mean every single door—was opened and closed on me. A hundred talent shows, and I was never the winner. A hundred possible breaks, but none of them ever broke my way.

When I got back from L.A., I decided to take a different approach. I did my homework and studied the market. Solo singers like Jeffrey Osborne weren't as popular as they used to be, and since New Edition came out a few years earlier, the group look was on the rise. Now you'd hear The Boys doing "Dial My Heart." Tony! Toni! Toné! hit with "Little Walter." Johnny Gill, once a straight-up R&B singer, joined New Edition, and got hits with "If It Isn't Love" and "You're Not My Kind of Girl." Teddy Riley's group Guy was all over the radio.

I decided I was going to get the break I'd been looking for with a group.

In 1987, I found three guys who could dance and sing. I put the group together, became the lead singer, and then set to work.

"You got a name, baby?" asked Neice.

"R. Kelly and MGM, for Musically Gifted Men."

"Why R. Kelly? Why not just Robert Kelly?"

Maybe it was the stories my mother used to tell me about great soul singers of the past or maybe it was those trips to plays and operas that Miss McLin took me to. Whatever it was, I knew instinctively that I needed a hook to get noticed.

"'Robert' is too ordinary. 'R' sounds more mysterious. It's got more intrigue behind it. People will be asking . . . who is this R. Kelly? 'R' will get lots more attention than 'Robert.'"

During the mid-1980s and into the '90s, New Jack Swing—a sound that for the first time blended R&B melodies with hip-hop beats—was all the rage. Jimmy Jam and Terry Lewis and Teddy Riley were considered its pioneers. The sound of music was changing and exciting. Rap music beats were influencing R&B music and creating something new.

I wrote a bunch of songs incorporating the beats that defined the New Jack feel, as well as a couple of ballads, which my mother loved.

The group idea was working. It wasn't long before opportunity came our way. R. Kelly and MGM started making some noise. We blew up. In Chicago, we were working practically every night. The ladies were screaming, but the money wasn't coming in yet. Our manager even signed us to a small record company based in New York and Miami. They put out a single and even made a video for a song I wrote called "Why You Wanna Play Me?"

But just as things started going our way, jealousy worked its way through the group. Because I was doing all the creative work—writing and producing the songs, singing lead, choreographing, and imaging the group—I felt envy building behind my back. I heard whispers and saw unhappy glances.

I knew there were problems, but in 1990—when we were asked to go on *The Big Break*, a TV talent show in L.A. hosted by Natalie Cole where first prize was $100,000—I put those issues aside.

We went out to the West Coast. The contest had three levels, and you had to win the first two to get to the finals. We won the first round, hands down. Then we won the second. Now it was time for the third, the one that would pay us $100,000.

Our uniforms were okay, but I didn't think they were flashy enough for the finals. So, on my own, I went out and started street performing and, just like before, made good money. I took my earnings and bought killer outfits, custom made by Barbara Bates, a Chicago-based designer who was making clothes for all the stars. We were ready.

Back in the dressing room in the Hollywood studio, an hour before we were due to sing, the other guys came up and said, "Rob, we don't think it's fair that you get half the money and we got to split the other half between us. We think if we win this $100

thou, we should split it four ways."

"You decided to just spring this on me, minutes before the show?" I asked.

"We just want to get it straight. We want what's fair."

I was pissed. "I write the songs," I said. "I do the arrangements. I'm the lead singer. I create the steps. I give you your parts. Rehearse those parts. Tell you if you're flat or sharp. I do 90 percent of the work and you want me to have 25 percent of the reward? No, sir."

Words were exchanged. Fists started flying. We finally cooled it, and I said, "Tell you what, fellas. You guys go out without me. If you win, you keep everything. Or I'll go out alone. If I win, I'll keep everything. That's fair, right?"

My offer made them even madder. They didn't accept. They accused me of manipulation.

Meanwhile, Natalie Cole had heard all the noise coming from our dressing room and decided to cancel our appearance.

"Look," I told the guys, "this is crazy. We'll figure out the splits later. Let's forget this fighting and just go out there and kill."

Everyone agreed, and we sweet-talked Natalie into letting us back on.

We went out and killed.

We won! *The Big Break* was ours. We went back to Chicago conquering heroes.

Nothing left to do but wait for my share of the prize money to come.

I waited.

And I waited some more.

152

Wait

More waiting

And wait some more

AMAZING GRACE

Hate is heavy and, in my heart, I'm not a hater.

I've got a loving nature, a forgiving nature, but it was hard to drop my upset when my share from The Big Break prize money was so slow in coming. I decided to be patient, though, because my mother said patience always pays.

I was patient for a month, and then another month, and a third. Soon my patience was gone. Somehow the money disappeared. I didn't get a dime of the $100,000 in cash and prizes. For all I know, it got lost in the mail, but I blamed MGM. I decided that I couldn't deal with them anymore. Our manager decided to stick with the group. I had no choice but to forget MGM—forever.

Around this same time, I went to an audition at the original Regal Theater where a producer was putting on a gospel musical, "Don't Get God Started," starring Vanessa Bell Armstrong and Marvin Winans of the Winans—two gospel greats. I figured I sang good enough to get a part. But I missed the bus and arrived late. The security guard told me the auditions were over and to go home.

"I can't go home," I said. "I came to sing."

"They all through singing in there."

I let out a big sigh. I thought about leaving, but something inside me said no. Instead I started singing my mother's favorite song, "Amazing Grace"; sang it loud and proud. The security guard looked at me like I was crazy, but before he could say anything, this lady showed up. I recognized her as the actress from *Good Times*, who played Penny's birth mama on the show. Her name was Chip Fields and Penny was the hen-11-year-old Janet Jackson. In real life, her daughter, Kim Fields, played Tootie on the '80's show *The Facts of Life*. Turned out she had a big part in the play, too.

"Wow," said Miss Fields, "you can really sing."

"Thank you, ma'am."

"Let me give you a script. I want to hear you read for this part."

The word "read" was a dagger to my heart. I couldn't let her know I couldn't read. Couldn't let her see me stumble over words I didn't understand.

"Oh, I can't read today," I said, scrambling for an excuse, "'cause . . . 'cause I forgot my glasses."

"No problem," said Miss Fields. "You just take the script home with you and go over it tonight. Come back tomorrow when the producer arrives from Los Angeles. That's Barry Hankerson. You've heard of him, haven't you?"

"No, ma'am," I answered.

"He manages the Winans, Vanessa Bell Armstrong, and Gladys Knight. He's

"*I can't read*

going to love your voice. There's the part of a young preacher in this play that you're perfect for. So let me give you five dollars for carfare. Please show up tomorrow at noon."

I took the money and thanked Miss Fields again.

"You're forgetting the script," she reminded me.

I went back and got the script. The script, of course, was a problem.

"I can't read the script," I told Mom soon as I got home. "Every time I look at it, the words start wiggling, and it's like being back at school. This is my big chance, and I'm about to lose it."

"There's no need for you to lose it, son. You just need to tell the truth. Tell them you can sing better than anyone, but your reading's not the best."

"It's the worst."

"They'll help you with your reading, son. Just go over there tomorrow and tell the truth."

I was nervous. Couldn't even fall asleep for all the butterflies in my stomach. I opened up the script and tried making sense of the story, but that didn't work. I couldn't keep the characters straight; couldn't comprehend the meaning; didn't know what the play was saying. Tomorrow was going to be hell.

Tomorrow turned into today. I was out of the bed by 8 A.M., still trying to figure out the script. It was no use. I decided not to show up. Then I changed my mind. I had to go through with the audition. But how?

Riding the bus on the way over, I kept hearing my mother's words: "Just tell the truth."

When I arrived, Miss Fields was happy to see me.

"You study the script?" she asked.

"The truth is . . ." I hesitated. "The truth is that I don't read very well."

"Don't worry about that, baby," she said. "I know a lot of people in show

the script"

business who don't read well. We can help you with that. Don't worry about reading today. Just sing. The producer's here and he wants to hear you sing."

"Sing what?"

"Sing 'Amazing Grace' like you did yesterday."

I went out onto the stage of the Regal Theater. I looked out into the audience, but it was too dark to see who was sitting there. I took a deep breath and sang "Amazing Grace."

"That's it!" I heard a man's voice cry. "He's got the part."

I saw a man walking toward the stage. Medium built, light skin, eyebrows looked like they were stitched together. Man, was he dressed sharp.

"I'm Barry Hankerson," he said, "and I'm offering you $700 a week to do this play—plus expenses."

I was so green I didn't know what "plus expenses" meant. I thought it was his way of being slick.

Trying to prove that I was no one's fool, I said, "I can't go with that 'plus-expenses' business."

Everyone laughed at me.

"Don't worry about it, son," said Hankerson. "We'll get all the details worked out. You just come back tomorrow."

I ran home and told everyone the good news, but the next day when I showed up at the theater, I decided I needed to take another approach.

"Look here, Mr. Hankerson," I said. "I'm not really right for this part. Can't read the lines very well, and I'm not good at memorizing. I'm an artist. I got me a bag of demos, and I just want you to hear three or four of my songs. Will you do that for me, sir?"

"I will," he said. "I'll listen to them right now."

I pulled three cassettes out of a bag. The first was an early version of "Turn Back the Hands of Time." The second was "Honey Love," and the third was "Dedicated."

Hankerson's assistant took the tapes and, one after another, put them into a boom box. Hankerson stood the whole time, listening to every note. When the last song played, he said, "You're right. You're an artist. You've got a real gift, son."

That audition turned out to be the first time I met the man who would become my manager.

PUBLIC ANNOUNCEMENT

After MGM, I had to start from scratch again. I still thought a group was a good idea because groups were still the big sellers. My new life began with me singing at Chicago's Cotton Club on S. Michigan Avenue, a joint once operated by Ralph "Bottles" Capone, Al Capone's older brother.

"Hear you're interested in forming a group?" a guy called Andre Boikins said to me one night after a gig.

"That's right."

"Well, me and two friends sing and dance a little."

"Cool. I wanna hear y'all. How about tomorrow?"

"Tell me where and when."

We met in a workout room I was using to rehearse. Dre was right. His boys, Earl Robinson and Rick Webster, were okay, so I started training them.

Training was rough. I told them from jump street, "Fellas, this ain't gonna be no picnic. We're going for the gold. We're gonna train like it's the Olympics, every day in every way. I'm not interested in us just being good. We've got to be great. We're competing with the best groups in the country, whether they be in New York, Hollywood, or Atlanta. I'll be calling practice not once a day, but three times a day. We'll be hitting it not five days a week, but seven. I'm talking about the steps, the harmonies, stage presence, the whole bit. And I'm also talking about physical training. We are more than just singers and dancers. We're athletes."

Maybe they didn't believe me that night, but when we started running the rocks along Lake Michigan, they believed me then. We were doing push-ups and sit-ups like the Chicago Bulls getting ready for the playoffs.

As I was working on putting my new group together, I was approached by a well-known house music DJ named Wayne Williams, who ran a small office and recording studio for Jive Records in Chicago.

Wayne's really the guy who discovered me. He had heard me with MGM at a backyard barbecue at a residence in North Chicago, even before we signed to the other record deal. He would later tell reporters that he was blown away when he saw us performing. Somehow, he picked up on the fact that I was the leader of the group and was impressed with our energy, choreography, and showmanship.

"I could tell right away this kid had the eye of the tiger," Williams said.

Wayne had kept track of me over the months and followed what I was doing during my MGM days. In the early '80s, Jive Records had some R&B hits with Billy Ocean, but by 1991, Jive was mostly known as one of the biggest labels for rap music with Boogie Down Productions, DJ Jazzy Jeff and the Fresh Prince, and Kool Mo Dee. Because of the deal I'd been a part of with MGM, I still had some obligations to another record company. But when Jive signed me they bought me out of my previous contract.

I named the new group R. Kelly and Public Announcement—the concept was my vision, with me writing all the songs, singing all the leads, and doing all the producing. Ten months after signing with Jive, our album, *Born into the 90's*, debuted in 1992. There I was, 24 years old, on the cover, out front with my fresh fade, suited in leather, surrounded by my boys—Public Announcement.

My dream had finally become reality: We had an honest-to-goodness album.

The sound was very much both of and ahead of its time. Of course New Jack Swing was represented, but so were my R&B roots. With the release of the first single, the New Jack Swing hit, "She's Got That Vibe," folks kept comparing my voice to Aaron Hall from Guy. It wasn't a coincidence that I sounded like Aaron. Guy was hitting big, and I wanted some of those hits. After all, Aaron sounded like Charlie Wilson of the Gap Band—and I liked Charlie. I liked Aaron. I could do what they did. If I could absorb Donny Hathaway and Marvin Gaye and Stevie Wonder when I was just a little kid, as a young man I could sure as hell be a sponge that could soak up what was hot on the radio now. Also on that first album is the ballad "Dedicated," which I had written years earlier for my mother. If you listen to my voice now and listen to it on either song from back then, you'll see it's really got the same tone.

Jive was a company with an international view, and the owner, Clive Calder,

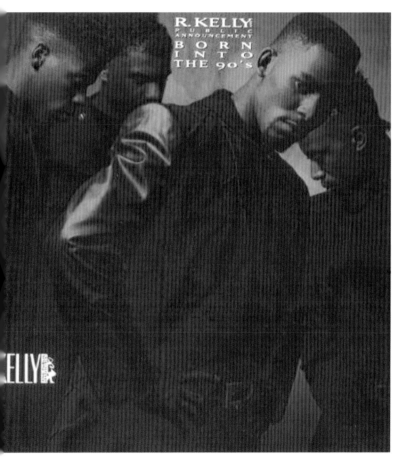

said he not only wanted to break us out in America, he wanted to promote us all over Europe and the rest of the world, too; so before I knew it, I was headed for Europe.

I could hardly wait to get to England, but I had a deep fear of flying. I still do. Up until now, I had flown a few times in the United States, but the more I flew, the deeper my fear grew. I'm a person that likes to do things that make sense, and it didn't make sense to me how a heavy plane could stay up in the air like that. It just didn't feel right. I was less fearful, though, when my mother was sitting next to me—so I made sure that my Mom came along on the tour. Her presence always had a calming effect on me. The problem was, my mother wasn't crazy about flying either, so it ended up that the first time that I took a real drink was on that flight to England. Mom and I both took a shot of Hennessy and conked out.

I'd never been out of the country before. I imagined huge crowds and pretty girls chasing us back to our hotel, but my imagination was racing way ahead of reality. To say that our first show didn't attract a huge crowd would be an understatement—there were only about five people in the audience. My group members were crushed. To this day, I've never allowed numbers to affect my performance. At intermission I told the group: "I don't care if there's only one person out there, we gotta sing like there are thousands."

Then they started playing our first single, "She's Got That Vibe," on the radio, and at the next show, maybe 20 people showed up.

My guys were still down. "Get up," I said. "It's gonna get better. I guarantee it."

By the end of our run, "Vibe'?" was all over London—becoming a top 3 record in England—and now the venues were packed.

By the time we got to Holland, "She's Got That Vibe" was one of the top-10 best-selling records in the country. Fans were screaming our name in the streets, and women were waiting for us in the lobby. As much as I wanted attention, I'd never encountered anything like it before. Sudden fame and the blitz of fans' affection tripped me out and made me a little anxious at first.

"Your dream's coming true, Rob," my mother said on the plane home. "Just like I knew it would."

Back in the U.S.A, "Vibe" was all over the radio and the video was playing on all the video shows in heavy rotation. I was eager to see the reaction of the people back home. I wanted to see if I'd be recognized. First I went to a predominantly white mall. No one recognized me.

Then I went to Evergreen Mall in a suburb of Chicago: back then we called it "Everblack" 'cause at the time it was the black mall. (It was the first indoor shopping mall in America.) At Evergreen, I went to a clothing store for high school girls. I figured someone would recognize me there. I stared a girl right in the face and even started singing my song. I wanted her to say, "Oh, are you the one who sings 'She's Got That Vibe?'" But she didn't say a thing.

Our second single, "Honey Love," had a video behind it that we shot in L.A. I've always loved movies, and I've always been very involved in the storyline and direction of all my music videos. For the "She's Got That Vibe" video, I created all the choreography; and on the way to the shoot in New York, I wanted to give us something different that no other group had, something to give us an edge. So we stopped at a store on the way to the shoot and I picked up a bunch of flashlights that we rigged onto our hats. Everybody who saw the "Vibe" video asked us where we got them. We continued to use that look at shows, and we used them again in the "Honey Love" video. Light and the use of it, or lack of it, has always played a big role in my life.

There were rumors that Miss Halle Berry plays my love interest in the "Honey Love" video. But let me put that rumor to rest; that's not Ms. Berry. It's a video actress who looks a little something like her.

When the "Honey Love" video started getting played in Chicago, I went back to Evergreen Mall. This time I went with my crew. When we got to the record store, I had one of my posse yell out, "Hey, there's R. Kelly over there." The girls came running. Man, it was a great feeling. My guys said, "He's only signing albums, no singles." The store sold a ton of albums that day. When we went on tour, we did the same routine in record stores all over the country. Meanwhile, when I went to white malls, I still got no love. Eventually I would, but it took time.

My time with Public Announcement was good. *Born into the 90's* sold a million copies; it had reached the #3 slot on the Top R&B album chart and was certified platinum.

"For every action ...
there's a REACTION!"

"YOU'RE MY GIRL"

I said those words to Lonneice time and time again. I said them because they were true. Neice inspired all my early songs.

I made enough money for me and Neice to rent an apartment together in a nice building on 75th and Lake Shore Drive. I felt like we were the Jeffersons on TV living in a high-rise up in the sky. I was rolling.

When we wanted a special night, we got a room at the Hyde Park Inn. Staying there was like being out of town. Plus, hotel rooms can heat up the loving. The loving between me and Neice was scorching hot.

Then why did I do what I did?

One night I found myself in that same room—the special room that me and Neice loved to share—with another woman. My plan was just to hit it and quit it. Just a couple of hours of pleasure I didn't want to pass up.

Somehow, though, Neice learned I was there and called the room.

"What're you doin' in our room without me, Rob?" She was crying.

I had to think quick. "I'm here to meet with Tony! Toni! Toné! They're coming over here."

"Who the fuck is Tony! Toni! Toné!?"

"You don't know who Tony! Toni! Toné! are?" Now I was getting mad that she didn't know who my alibi was!

"I don't care who the fuck they are! What does that have to do with you being in our room without me?"

"I rented the room 'cause Tony! Toni! Toné! are coming up here to audition me. They're looking for a new singer."

"Well, I want to meet Tony! Toni! Toné!" said Neice.

"They already come and gone."

"I'm coming up there anyway."

"You more than welcome, baby."

"I'm on my way."

Like lightning, I got the chick out of the room. I ran around like a crazy man, found the maid to change the sheets and the towels. I had to make it seem like I was the only one who'd been there.

By the time Neice arrived, I was cool. I thought I'd fooled her.

But I hadn't.

She knew.

As my mother used to say, "Busted, disgusted, and couldn't be trusted." Women always know when their men are cheating. And, like they say, for every action, there's a reaction.

Neice reacted by doing what I did—she found someone else.

At first I didn't want to believe it.

But then came proof. One night she and her best friend were supposed to meet me and her friend's boyfriend. They didn't show up. Something was wrong. I went to Neice's mama's house, but her folks didn't know where she was.

"Lonneice and her girlfriend said they'll be coming back here," said her grandmother.

The other guy and I turned into detectives. I found a hidden place to park our car. We sat there and waited. Finally, at 4 A.M., a big white Mercedes pulled up. A guy was driving, and Neice was sitting next to him. Her girl and another dude were in the back seat.

When the ladies got out and the guys pulled away, I popped out.

"What are you doing here?" Neice asked me.

"Wondering what the hell you're doing out till four in the morning."

"Having fun."

"I figured. Fun with who?"

"Rob, I'm not gonna stand here and get cross-examined by you of all people. You have no right."

At this moment, I knew Neice was right. I thought of the times I'd fooled around behind her back. I had nothing more to say.

We tried to work it out, but I knew she was fed up. Her mind and heart had checked out of our love.

A week later, something happened that upset her and I couldn't figure out what it was. Then I found out that the guy Lonneice had been creeping with wasn't treating her right, and that upset me.

A couple of nights later, I got an unexpected call, "Look, I got no beef with you, man, but I gotta tell you that your girl's confused. She don't know who she wants, you or me. It ain't me who's chasin' her. It's her who's chasin' me."

I confronted Neice.

"Who do you want?" I asked.

"Him."

I died inside as though I'd been shot through the heart. I felt worse than at any moment in my life.

"He's no good for you," I told her. "He's going to hurt you."

"And you haven't, Rob?"

"Not like him."

"Hurt is hurt."

"I want to make it work for us."

"It's too late," she said. "I'm gone.'"

My life with Neice was over.

"DON'T GIVE ME SOME KID OFF THE STREET ... GIVE ME THE PRESIDENT!"

I've always had a big inventory of songs. Even starting out, I had more songs than I knew what to do with. That's because songs float into my mind the way clouds float in the sky.

My work ethic was intense and insane. I thought nothing of staying up three or four nights in a row writing or recording music. At the time, I didn't know the downside of working so hard—didn't want to know it and honestly didn't care—my music was a 24/7 compulsion.

For me, it was a natural thing. Before I was even sure what "producing" meant, I was producing myself. I was figuring out the grooves; I was coming up with the parts for the keyboard, the bass, the drummer, and the guitarist. I was arranging my own background vocals and most of the time I was singing all the parts.

When I auditioned for Barry Hankerson, he asked me if I'd written the songs that I'd sung. When I told him that I had, he asked me if I could produce, too. I said "Yeah," because I had wanted him to take me on, but at the time I didn't really know what "producing" was. I went home and asked my mother.

"The way you put your music together when you're writing your songs—that means you're a producer," my mother said.

"It does?"

"Absolutely! Very few artists can produce themselves. We're talkin' about Ray Charles, Marvin Gaye, Stevie Wonder, Prince—musicians of that caliber. When you have producing talent, though, you need to work it on other artists as well as yourself."

I agreed. I realized that I wouldn't be truly great until I made another artist great. I needed to find that artist. I asked my manager to find an artist for me to produce.

One day my manager picked me up and told me I'd be producing David Peaston. I was excited to meet David, a former school teacher, who had become one of the newest hot R&B singers in the country. At that time I would have been excited to meet any celebrity. But I'd seen David on *Showtime at the Apollo* in the late 1980's. His version of Billie Holiday's "God Bless the Child" tore up the crowd. He was an amazing singer, and his fans were calling him the new Luther.

The meeting with David happened before *Born into the 90's* hit the airwaves, so David wasn't really aware of my writing or singing skills.

"Rob," said my manager, "he's gonna love your songs. You're the perfect producer to bring this guy to the next level."

We drove to the hotel where David was staying, I was in the front seat and my manager was driving. When David came out, he didn't get into the car; he came to the front and just looked in until it became clear that I needed to hop out and sit in the back seat, so that he could sit up front. David was cordial but cold. Riding over to the studio, there was hardly any talking. The vibe was nervous.

In the studio, I got to work. I played David a bunch of songs I'd written. I just knew that a couple of them were smash hits. He listened without saying a word. Then David motioned my manager to follow him into the recording booth. They didn't realize the mic was on, so I got to hear their whole conversation.

"I thought I told you to get Teddy Riley. Teddy can't do nothing but make hits. He's the king of New Jack Swing. Teddy's the President."
"Teddy's not available."

"Then make him available. Don't give me some kid off the street . . . give me the President."
"Give the kid a chance. You won't be sorry."

David finally caved, but his heart wasn't in it. He'd made up his mind that I was no hit-maker.

I tried. I said, "David, you got an unbelievable voice. Now just don't over-riff on the verse. Sing it like this . . . " And I'd show him how it went.

When it came time to record, though, Peaston changed it back to his over-riffing style and ruined the whole feel. We went back and forth like that for two hours, until I finally saw what I had to do.

I got up and left.

"Where you going?" the singer and my manager both asked me at the same time.

"I'm going to McDonald's for a double cheeseburger and fries."

"When are you coming back?"

"I'm not."

And I didn't.

I had another early encounter with a celebrity, who was a helluva lot more pleasant. In fact, it was a highlight of my life because it involved my mother.

My manager also worked with this singer who was an artist that loved my music. She was a down-to-earth lady who reminded me of my mother. And I knew my mother would love to meet her.

"Can I bring my mother over today?" I asked the singer.

"My hair's all up in curlers, my face is covered with cold cream, and I'm wearing an old housecoat."

"My mom won't care," I said.

"If she doesn't care, Rob, I don't care."

An hour or so later, my mother and I arrived. I didn't tell Mom the lady's name. I just introduced her as a friend in the music business.

"Mind if I smoke?" my "friend" asked my mother.

"Take one of my Winstons," Mom said.

They lit up, drank coffee together, and started discussing everything under the sun—their children, men in their lives, TV shows they liked, movie stars they thought were the cutest. You would have thought they'd grown up together.

After a half-hour of this, I couldn't take it anymore. I turned to my mother and said, "Mom, do you know who this lady is?"

"She's your friend. Now she's my friend, too."

I repeated. "Do you know who this lady is? Look closely at her face. Look closely in her eyes."

"I'm looking, Rob, I'm looking."

Several seconds passed by—and then my mother screamed: "Oh, my Lord! It isn't! You can't be!"

My friend started laughing. "I'm afraid it is," she said.

"You can't be!"

"I am."

"Gladys Knight?" asked my mother, still in shock.

"That's what my parents named me," said Gladys, hugging her like she was her best friend in all the world.

"Well, I broke out with some 12-play."

"One. We'll go up to my room for fun."

Then I paused and waited,
and when the people yelled out, "Two!"
I knew I had them.

12-PLAY

On the poster, my name was barely big enough to read. It was the early '90s, I was in my mid-twenties, and I was on the road with two big stars. I was the opening act.

The late Gerald Levert, of course, was royalty. His daddy, Eddie Levert, was one of the Mighty O'Jays. Gerald had been lead singer for LeVert, who had big hits with "(Pop Pop Pop) Goes My Mind" and "Casanova." He'd just released his first solo album, and the title song, "Private Line," was already a number-one hit.

Glenn Jones, who got second billing, had a hit record with "We've Only Just Begun," a song the ladies loved. He'd also been on the charts with "Show Me" and "Bring Back Your Love." Like Gerald, Glenn could sing.

I wasn't thrilled about being third on the bill because when I started singing, folks were just walking in: most of the seats were still empty. I was feeling frustrated because I had worked hard putting my show together with what I had—I didn't really have lights at all. Because I was the opener, I had what looked like a flashlight on me and I had a smoke machine to enhance my presentation. Lighting has always been extremely important to me. I want to be heard, but I also want to be seen in the right light. Lighting shapes mood. And for me, the mood's got to be right.

Meanwhile, as the tour went on, "Honey Love," my new single, started to really blow up. It got to the point where the promoters saw that I was starting to generate more heat than Glenn Jones. They decided to have him open. That meant I'd come on just before Gerald. Glenn snapped about the rearrangement, and I could understand why.

I didn't want to disrespect him, but I also wanted to reach more people. I was tired of singing to an empty house.

The first night went really well. People were in their seats and got to see me; I was feeling good about the new lineup. The second night, though, they wouldn't let me use my little light or my smoke machine. I figured if I was moving up in the show, I should get more, not less. The promoters didn't see it that way. They wanted to keep the spotlight on the bona fide star.

I respected Gerald as an artist and a man, so I went to his dressing room to discuss it.

"I feel you young fella," Gerald said, "but in this business, you got to pay your dues. My daddy did, I did, and now you're paying 'em, too. It's part of the deal."

I thanked Gerald for breaking it down for me and left. He was right. But that also didn't stop me from thinking, *What can I do that would still ignite this crowd, where I could still stand out and do me, even if I'm singing in the pitch black?* I needed a gimmick to take my show to the next level, something that would make people remember me. That's how I created "12-Play."

I thought about it for a couple of days, and I finally came up with a little skit, me just talking to the audience. At the point in the show where I would break down "Honey Love," I would start talking to the audience.

"Can I tell you all something? Can I keep it real? Can I tell you about a dream I had last night? Well, I actually had a dream where I made love to Mary J. Blige."

Everyone reacted with a big "WOOOOOOOOH!" Mary J.'s first multi-platinum album, *What's the 411?* was super-hot, and here I was talking about kicking it with her. The audience got a big kick out of picturing me with Mary.

I went on, "Hey, it was only a dream, but it was so vivid, it felt real; but in this dream, it was more than foreplay—it was 12-play. Y'all wanna hear it? Can I sing it for y'all, tell you how it went?"

Everyone yelled, "YES!"

About now, my piano player started backing me up with sexy runs on the keyboard while I sang:

"One. We'll go to my room of fun."

And the whole audience said "Two!" at the same time, as if we'd rehearsed it. That's when I knew I had them.

I sang. "I'll say give me your tongue."

The audience roared: "THREE!"

"'Cause tonight I'm gonna . . ." I grabbed my crotch and sang ". . . fulfill your fantasy!"

And the women went crazy! It was a wrap. I had never heard the crowd scream that loud during the whole tour, during anybody's show. And that was just on three!

At that moment I had an instant double dose of confidence in who I was on that stage. I knew that I could excite a crowd with more than just having and singing hit records. I now knew that I could tell a story, or give a testimony, or play a game with the audience: That was something that would set me apart from everybody else.

By the time the show got to the next city, fans had already heard about this "12-Play" and started screaming the moment I mentioned Mary J. Word spread like wildfire—and this was way before Twitter and Facebook even existed.

"Girl," a female from Detroit would tell her friend in Cleveland, "you got to get to the show and hear this R. Kelly sing about his '12-Play.' It's the bomb!"

When I went to radio stations to promote *Born into the 90's*, the DJ's just wanted to hear about "12-Play." It was the talk of every town I went to—*before* I arrived.

"Haven't recorded it yet," I'd say, "but I will. Matter of fact, it's gonna be the title of my second album."

The song was causing such a sensation that Gerald Levert's people told my manager that they didn't want me to perform it any more. The reason they gave— because I hadn't recorded it yet—was lame. Where is it written that an artist can only perform a song he's recorded? I just continued to do my show.

My management backed me up. "Long as the ladies keep yelling for it," they said, "you keep singing it."

By the end of the tour, no one could deny that the highlight of every show was when I got out there and started discussing a dream I had about loving on Mary J. Blige.

Chicago is the center of my universe—my home as a baby, a boy, a teenager, a young man, and an adult.

To me Chicago is the soul of America. It's the home of my soul.

It has its own, unique musical vibe.

THE MAKINGS OF ME

Born into the 90's had been a great buzz album, and a great way to introduce R. Kelly to the public. The guys in Public Announcement had been my background singers and dancers, but the plan had always been that on my second album, I would be a solo artist, not the leader of a group. The guys would still be in the videos and tour with me, but the second album was all about launching R. Kelly.

I wanted the next album to be something that was going to stick around for a long time, I wanted people to know that I was in it for the long ride. In order to do that, I had to take the music, my melodies, and my lyrics to the next level. So I went into the studio totally focused on achieving my goal. I wanted people to know that this was real. That I was real.

"12-Play" started out from a skit that I'd come up with to help me get through a tour, but that concept blew up and took on a life of its own. By the time I got home from the tour, the song "12-Play" was already a smash—so there was a big demand for the record. The song was so successful that I decided I would do a whole album called *12-Play*. I would spend my sound checks writing new songs for the album, so that I could record them as soon as I got home.

Chicago is the center of my universe—my home as a baby, a boy, a teenager, a young man, and an adult. To me Chicago is the soul of America. It's the home of my soul. It has its own, unique musical vibe. Chicago has launched the careers of many extraordinary artists from Sam Cooke to Kanye West. It's the home to many different kinds of amazing music and I'm determined to make sure it's properly recognized and respected.

I wrote the entire album over a month and a half. But when I started working on it, I had some concerns. I knew the song "12-Play" was strong in concert, and the ladies were loving it, but the popularity of New Jack Swing had helped get me out there. I felt I needed to develop musically if I wanted to have the longevity of a Marvin Gaye or a Stevie Wonder. The song "12-Play" had introduced me to my true self—musically—and there was no going back.

On the one hand, my management and the label were saying that because "She's Got That Vibe" and especially "Honey Love" did so well, I should be careful not to move too far away from that sound. They wanted to sell records, and the New Jack Swing thing was still the hottest seller out there.

I thought about what they said. This was to be my first album as a solo singer—no group, no one on the cover but me. I didn't want to make any foolish mistakes. I wanted to bust out with a winner.

On the other hand, I knew in my heart that it was time to take off the training wheels. It was time to introduce R. Kelly—the real R. Kelly—to the world. I felt like a fireman who'd gone through all the training and practice drills. When he finally hears that bell go off, he's ready to slide down the pole, jump on that big red fire truck, and go put out a fire.

More than just having the gift of music, I think I have the gift of having the mind of a musical scientist. I'm not afraid of research or of trying different things, stretching genres and boundaries. I wanted to bring new things to music. I wanted to be not like anybody else. That desire was as strong for me as being in the music business. I didn't want to be just some singer or some songwriter. I wanted to be great, and I wanted to be remembered for my work—having the desire, the passion, and being blessed with a gift, and being able to channel where I come from and what I've been through. Having a gift is not enough; it needs to be cultivated and shared.

When I went to record the new album, I was able to be both more patient and more innovative in the process. I started recording the songs I'd already written while I was on the road or downtown at CRC studios. But my mom's house was the hangout spot. Much as I tried, I couldn't get her to move out of the 'hood and into a nicer place. She had her friends and her life there, and that's where she wanted to stay.

"12-Play" was inspired by conversations with my Mom and the aunties and their friends hanging out on the porch. They would be listening to their favorites: Sam Cooke and Marvin Gaye and Teddy Pendergrass. One night I was chilling out on the porch with them, and we were listening Teddy Pendergrass.

"That's baby-makin' music right there!"

"That's right! Y'all was born off Teddy Pendergrass. Y'all born off Marvin Gaye!"

"What do you know about this?" one of my aunties challenged me.

And that's when the direction for the *12-Play* album became even clearer. I had to make a baby-makin' album. If Marvin Gaye did it I wanted to do it. I wanted to make an album that people want to make love to and not just make babies but want to get married, want to love somebody, want to make love to somebody. And to help expand the population. I thought I had a head start with the song "12-Play."

I was also inspired by the stories that my mom told me about going to the Regal Theater and being able to see everybody, from Marvin Gaye to Stevie Wonder. I wanted that kind of legacy for myself—I wanted people to be sitting on their porches and talking about the *12-Play* album some day, like my mom and her friends talked about their favorite artists and their songs. But I wanted to be alive and still in the game—still making hits when that day came.

As far back as my first high school performance and my days singing in the subway, my gut told me that I needed a hook—something that would make people remember my act. When I was creating *12-Play*, I wanted to create a buzz and attract attention. Sex and sensuality were going to be my hook. I saw the album as a suite in 12 parts. It was my play to win the attention and love of music fans all over the world. "Sex Me" was deliberately designed to generate a little controversy. A group called H Town had had a big hit with a song called "Knockin' Da Boots." "Sex Me" was going to take what they started to a whole new level. And because I'd been to Europe and toured America, playing in Summer Jams and major arenas, I knew how to excite a crowd. Now the challenge was to put that excitement—that was sensuous but also spiritual excitement—into a record that reflected my true heart: one that would reveal the makings of me.

"Bump N' Grind," the second single from the *12-Play* album, definitely fits in the baby-making music category. The song was originally written for the movie *Menace II Society* at the request of the directors, the Hughes Brothers. The song was supposed to play over the scene of Jada Pinkett Smith and Larenz Tate in bed together. I was excited to do it because it was the first time I'd been asked to do a song for a movie before. When they heard "Bump N' Grind," the Hughes Brothers loved the song, but the record company and my manager decided that the song should be released on my album and not the soundtrack.

There were a lot of politics about that at the time, and they ended up using "Honey Love" in the movie instead. But keeping the song for the *12-Play* album was probably the best thing for me because that song gave me my first #1 record on the *Billboard* pop chart and was the longest-running #1 record on the R&B chart at that time.

Still, I knew my second album had to better than the first. The lyrics had to be more direct; more authentic; more reflective of my experiences, emotions, and, of course, my city. I also knew it would be dedicated to my mother.

What I didn't know, though, was by the time the album came out, my world would be changed forever.

While I was making the *12-Play* album, I spent many nights in the studio. A lot of that emotion showed up on the tracks. When you hear: "Any unexpected position. Bring it on. Any secret fantasy. Baby, I will fulfill as long as you sex me" in "Sex Me, parts 1 & 2," you're hearing raw, unfiltered, youthful desires coming through in those lyrics.

I had a song that said, "It seems like you're ready," and I knew that the ladies were ready and I was ready. I wanted an album that would make love to every woman in the world. I wanted it to talk honestly to them and touch them in satisfyingly sensual ways. The spirit of seduction was heavy on me, and I saw no reason not to go for it. The album was an extended version of the concert—with all the pleading, teasing, mood-setting, foreplay, and getting nasty with "Sex Me," the gritty climactic song. I didn't see nothing wrong with a little "Bump 'N Grind." I felt "Your Body's Callin'." I liked "The Crotch On You," and I wasn't afraid to ask the ladies to "Sex Me."

While I was making the album, my mother got sick. I found out later that she'd gone to the hospital for some tests, but she downplayed them to me as well as to my brothers and my sister, telling me, "Baby, you're busy making your music. You go on and keep working. Don't worry about me. I'm gonna be fine. I'm just tired, that's all."

"But what do the doctors say?" I asked.

"The doctors say the same thing, baby. They say I'm gonna be just fine. You go do what you got to do."

"I'm supposed to head back to Europe for some concerts."

"Then go to Europe, Rob."

"You know I hate flying," I said. "Flying is always a lot easier if you're sitting next to me."

"I'll be with you next time."

"I want you with me *this* time," I said. "I don't want to get on that plane without you."

"You'll do fine without me, son. Call me every night if you want to."

"I will."

I did.

When I went to Europe this time, the crowds were four times bigger than before. That made me happy. But it wasn't the same without my mother with me.

"I got another couple of weeks out here on the road, Mom," I told her on the phone. "I really want you here with me."

"If you want me to come out there, son, I will."

"But I thought you said you gotta go back to the hospital for more tests."

"I do, baby, but the tests can wait. If I have to, I can get on a plane tomorrow."

"No, Mom, I want you to have those tests. You take care of yourself. That's more important."

"God will take care of you, son. I know He will."

In those last weeks, the European fans kept coming. The tour was a success. I couldn't wait to get home and share that success with my mother.

185

"SHE'S TEACHING ANGELS HOW TO LOVE"

When I arrived home from Europe, I was surprised to see my sister Theresa waiting at the airport.

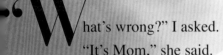

"What's wrong?" I asked.

"It's Mom," she said.

"What about Mom?"

"She's gotten worse. We need to go see her."

"How much worse?"

"Much worse."

"Why didn't anyone tell me?"

"Mama said not to. She said your tour was going good, and she didn't want anything to mess it up."

"Where is she?"

"Roseland Hospital on 111th Street."

I raced over. My brothers were sitting in the hallway.

A doctor was standing in front of the door to her room.

"Robert Kelly?" he asked.

"I'm Robert Kelly."

"Let's talk before you go in there."

"Why?"

"We need to talk. You need to prepare yourself."

I was already scared, but the word *prepared* scared me worse.

187

"Prepare for what?" I asked.

"Let's just sit and talk."

"Doctor, please, just say what you have to say."

"Your mother has incurable cancer that has reached its final stage."

"You're lying!" I shouted.

"I wish I were. I wish I could say there was hope."

"My mother says there's always hope."

"I'm sorry, Robert, but your mother is very near the end."

When I opened the door, my heart fell to the floor. My mother looked like a completely different person from the one I'd seen just a few short weeks ago. I'd never seen her look like this before. She was so much smaller. Her eyes were as yellow as a yellow crayon. Her body was all shriveled up. I went to her side and started crying.

"Oh, baby," she said, "you gotta get out of here. I told them I didn't want you to see me like this."

"I had to see you," I said.

"I don't want you to have this memory, baby. I want you to remember when I was healthy and strong."

"No one told me, Mom. No one said you'd gotten so sick."

"It happened really fast, son."

"How can you forgive me?" I asked.

"Forgive you for what, baby?"

"For not being here, for not coming home."

"I didn't want you home, Rob. I wanted you out there singing. That's what you were born to do."

I held her hand and said, "Mom, I promise you—I'm gonna be the best writer on the planet. For you, I'm gonna be the biggest singer."

"I love you, Mom."

"I love you, Rob."

"I know that, baby, and I've already seen it coming true. Now, please, get on out of here and let me be. I need to be alone."

"I don't want you to be alone, Mom. I can't live without you."

"I'll always be with you, Rob. You know that."

"I love you, Mom."

"I love you, Rob."

I left her room with tears in my eyes. I didn't know what to do or where to go—so I went to the studio. I had to be around music. I had to sing. To me, singing is like praying. It's the most powerful prayer I can send up. I was playing "A Song for You" when the call came in. Joann Kelly was gone.

I stopped playing, put my head down, and just sat there. There were people around trying to comfort me, but I didn't hear their words. At that moment I heard a new melody. I didn't have words for it, but the melody was strong. It had my mother's spirit on it. It stayed in my head. I thought of recording the melody, but something stronger was pulling at me. I knew I had to go see my mother one last time.

When I got to the hospital, I learned that they hadn't moved her from her room. I told the staff that I needed this one last time to be alone with my mother. I sat next to her bed and looked at her lifeless face. Cancer had been cruel to her, but when I looked at her, I remembered her when she was still healthy and full of life. I took her hand and said, "I swear this to you, Mom. I swear this with God as my witness. I will be the greatest artist in the world. I will do this for you because of how you always believed in me."

I got up and left. People stopped me, saying words I couldn't even hear. It may sound strange, but my mind was fixated on basketball—the only thing I could think of that might get me through the coming hours. Just being out there on the floor, running and shooting and giving it my all—the spirit of grief was so huge that only basketball could keep me going. I imagine there are people who, upon hearing horrible news, beat their fists against the wall. That's their way of coping. My way was a full-court press, bouncing that ball on the hardwood floor. I exhausted myself by playing ball for three straight hours.

Afterwards I went to the studio where that same melody kept echoing through my mind. Every time I started to sing it, though, I broke down and cried.

Mom was like God to me. She was the one who never judged me, she never abandoned me, she listened patiently to my doubts and fears, she encouraged my hopes and dreams. Without my mother, I felt there was no one to call on anymore.

I cried like a baby, cried until I felt like I had used up every tear in my body. How could I go on? How could I live without Joann Kelly by my side?

I couldn't complete the *12-Play* project without paying tribute to my mother. I thought about the melody that had invaded my mind after she had died. It was still there. But there were still no words to go with it. I'm the kind of writer who never chases a song. I wait until a song chases me. And though I knew the unwritten song was going to be one of the most important of my life, I couldn't force it into existence. I had to be patient.

But I also had to dedicate a song to Joann Kelly. I thought back on her life and remembered how, when I was just a little boy in the '70s, Mom loved the Spinners. She used to stop whatever she was doing when their lead singer, Philippe Wynne, started in on "One of a Kind (Love Affair)" or "Mighty Love" or "Love Don't Love Nobody." He also sang a song that talked about a mother named Sadie Mae: "sweeter than cotton candy" and "stronger than papa's old brandy." Every line of that song made me think of my mother. I've never been inclined to record a cover song—I've always been proud of my originals—but I knew that by singing "Sadie," I'd pay my mother the highest tribute. The song was out of her era. It was a song sung in the high style of soul that she had taught me to honor. And while it's true that *12-Play* would turn out to be a record that broke records and busted up some old taboos—an album that would be remembered for songs about sensuality and sex—the song that means the most to me is "Sadie." My mother was my Sadie, my everything.

THE DEPTHS OF MY STRUGGLES DETERMINE THE HEIGHTS OF MY SUCCESS

When my mother was still alive, I was a boy. After she died, I became a man. When my mother was still alive, my career was starting to build. After she died, my career blew up.

The most tragic event of my 26-year-old life—the death of my precious mother— coincided with the explosion of my music around the world.

Because she was gone, I was sadder than I'd ever been in my life. And not too long after my mother passed, my grandmother lost her battle with cancer and went to join her daughter, Joann. Because "Bump N' Grind" became the longest-lasting R&B hit in the history of *Billboard's* charts—not to mention a #1 pop hit as well—I was more successful than ever. Grief and joy had a hard time shaking hands. My mind was like a mixing board where the tracks—the up-tempo happy jams and the deep dark blues grooves—were leaking all over each other.

I'd reached my goal; I'd become a superstar. And while I could feel Mom's spirit still feeding me love, it hurt my heart that my eyes couldn't see her face. She was no longer there to give me a hug. And man, did I need a hug!

Looking back, I remember feeling that I couldn't go on without my mother. And, if my career hadn't taken the amazing turns that it did, maybe I would have broken down completely and spent the next year or two doing nothing but grieving. But music wouldn't let me do that. My music took over and suddenly started sweeping the country.

Suddenly I was famous. But fame almost overwhelmed me. It was like a hungry monster with an appetite that could never be satisfied. It wanted more, more, and then just when I thought it was satisfied, it asked for even more.

Things were happening so fast that I could hardly keep up with myself. These were good things—musical gifts—that were tremendous challenges and undeniable blessings. Take, for instance, the fine art of the remix.

Back in the late '80s and early '90s most hit records got a second life (and sometimes even a first life) by releasing a remixed version of the original. Usually remixes were done by hot engineers or producers to create new versions of a song, which was often for clubs. On the *12-Play* album, I decided to do the remixes of my own records instead of having someone else do them.

Because of the advances in recording technology and my growing confidence and experience in the studio, I could see how to break down the different elements of the song and put them back together in a different configuration. I could modify the groove; strip down the vocal and add new elements; throw in new sounds and accents—in short, I could re-engineer the music in a way that gave it a whole new flavor. I did two remixes of "Bump N' Grind"—the "Old School Mix" and the "How I Feel It Extended Mix," which is the version of the song we shot the video to. I also did my first remix for "Your Body's Callin'" as the B-side of the "Your Body's Callin'" single. All the remixes were huge successes. I don't know how many remixes I've done for "Your Body's Callin'," and I recently remixed "Bump N' Grind" as a choir version, for my *Love Letter* tour.

I saw the remix as a new art form to explore. I loved it as a canvas for sound. It wasn't that I no longer liked starting with a clean slate and creating a brand-new song; I'd always like doing that. But it was no longer either/or. Now I could do both. Not only could I create a new feeling out of a previously recorded song of mine, I could do it for other artists as well. Just like that, I established another major career as the remix man. Making matters sweeter, the remix of "Your Body's Callin'" sold more copies than the original.

By 1994, *12-Play* had sold more than 5 million copies, and the sexy R. Kelly brand was established. Jive's president, Barry Weiss, publicly labeled me a "pure artist" and an "old-fashioned creative genius." Jive had no problem happily allowing me to control my own creative destiny.

This kind of artistic power was a big boost to my ego. I was happy that my fans and the people I worked with accepted me as who I am. I didn't have to be phony or change my music or bow to the will and demands of others about my music.

I was riding high as a real artist and a rising star, but, according to my plans and definition of "success," I still hadn't risen high enough.

While *12-Play* was rising on the charts, Janet Jackson's *janet* album was the biggest of her career. Janet, Jimmy Jam, and Terry Lewis wrote a beautiful song called "Anytime Anyplace." It was especially appealing since, earlier in her career, Janet had a hit with "Let's Wait Awhile." Now the waiting was over and it was cool—anytime . . . anyplace. When they sent me the song to be remixed, I was ready. And when my remix went crazy on the charts, I saw that by re-imagining songs that people already loved, I could enjoy another outlet for my musical energy.

One thing was building atop another. And just when I thought it couldn't get any bigger or better, it did.

Enter Michael Jackson.

You
are
not
alone

MJ

As a kid, I watched a lot of TV and loved much of what I saw. TV was my window into worlds outside our little home. Cartoons were wonderful. They were crazy funny. Sometimes I'd picture myself jumping into the cartoons and running after the characters. But I never thought the characters were real.

Take Mickey Mouse. Mickey was the superstar of cartoon characters. Donald Duck was cool, and so was Goofy. I dug the Roadrunner and Porky Pig, whose stutter reminded me of Uncle Doug. Mickey, though, was the boss. Mickey ruled the TV screen, but I knew he was just make-believe.

Well, in a funny kind of way, I thought of Michael Jackson the same way. When the Jackson Five popped into our lives, we loved them to death. We loved Michael and Jermaine and Jackie and Tito and Marlon. We knew one from the other. We couldn't wait for them to come on TV and sing their songs about school like "ABC." They were as cool as cartoon characters—beyond human. And they were black like us! We'd been told the fairy-tale myth of how Diana Ross had discovered them. (Later I learned that that wasn't true, but as a kid I believed the myth.) When The Jackson 5 were set to appear on *American Bandstand* or *The Ed Sullivan Show*, we got to the TV a half-hour early so we wouldn't miss a single minute.

I was still a little kid—four or five—when the Jackson 5 actually became a cartoon show, where the brothers were animated like Mickey Mouse! That closed the deal; they weren't real. Michael was Mickey Mouse.

When Miss McLin came along and said that one day I'd be writing for Michael

197

Jackson, I didn't believe her. And then when Mom died and I leaned on Miss McLin even more, she kept saying the same thing. "You're more than just an artist, Rob. You're a writer whose songs will be sung by the biggest artists in the world."

I'd been going through some personal struggles, and *it seemed like everywhere I turned, I was losing people*. Just before we were about to leave on the big, 10-week *12-Play* tour, the buses were gassed up, the equipment was loaded, and I was sitting there waiting for my boys—the guys from Public Announcement who still sang backup and danced in my shows and on the videos—to show up. But they never did.

Because of all my set routines with the guys, I had to change the show. I made the necessary adjustments and, to my surprise, none of the fans seemed to miss Public Announcement. They yelled and screamed louder than ever. The tour was a huge hit.

Michael was on my mind when, towards the end of the *12-Play* tour, we were in Gary, Indiana, the Jacksons' hometown. I was also thinking about my mother and our travels to Gary to see my grandfather, and how we'd sit out on the porch; he would play his guitar for us and my mother would sing. When the thoughts of Michael and my mother came together, out came a melody—the same melody that had continued to haunt me after my mother's death.

After Mom died, I'd lost a person very dear to me—whom I loved with all my heart and soul. I wanted to let this person know that I would always be with her, even though we couldn't be together. So this time, when I heard the melody, the notes were carrying words. The words were clear. They said, "You are not alone."

I got this feeling in my gut. Goose bumps sent chills up and down my arms. I ran to the first piano I could find and started playing that melody and singing those words, "You are not alone."

It was my mother talking to me.

It was me reaching out to an incomparable loved one and letting her know that although we were apart, I would always be there for her.

The further I developed the song, the more it sounded like Michael. I heard his inflections, felt his spirit. I knew this was the right song for Michael Jackson.

Once I got to Chicago, I went to the studio and put down a demo. By then the whole story was there:

Another day has gone
  I'm still all alone
    How could this be?
      You're not here with me
        You never said goodbye
          Someone tell me why
Did you have to go
  And leave my world so cold?
    Every day I sit and ask myself
      How did love slip away?
        Someone whispers in my ear and says
That you are not alone
  I am here with you
    Though you're far away
      I am here to stay
        Just the other night
          I thought I heard you cry
Asking me to come
  And hold you in my arms
    I can hear your prayers
      Your burdens I will bear
        But first I need your hand
          Then forever can begin

When I sang on the demo, I purposely captured Michael's style, even catching the tones of his voice. That was easy since I'd been listening to Michael my entire life. I loved how Quincy Jones had produced Michael's *Off the Wall*; I loved *Thriller* and *Bad*. I knew Teddy Riley had co-produced *Dangerous*, and I really wanted to be in that company of those who had worked with Michael.

I had my manager send him the song.

A day passed.

Michael Jackson was real.

He looked at least eight feet tall.

He looked like an avatar.

My manager called.

"He wants to do it," he said.

"Michael wants to do it," I repeated. "You sure?"

"His people called. They love the song."

"That's fantastic! That's amazing!" I was shouting out the good news.

"But there's one thing, Rob."

"What's that?"

"He wants half the publishing."

The publishing represents ownership of the song. Much as I loved Michael, and much as I understood that business is business, I believed that, given the success of *12-Play*, I had earned the right to keep all my publishing and retain all the ownership.

"Tell his people," I said, "that no disrespect, but I don't want to do that. It would be the dream of my life to have Michael sing that song, but it's a song that I need to own."

"You sure, Rob? You sure you want to take that chance."

"I'm sure," I said. "If Michael really loves the song as much as I think he does, he'll sing it anyway. He'll realize he was born to sing it."

My manager conveyed my position to Michael's manager.

One day passed, then another, then still another.

I was nervous. I was thinking about nothing except whether Michael Jackson was going to sing my song.

Then the phone finally rang. My manager was on the line.

"Well?"

"Well, what?" he said, teasing me.

"Is he gonna sing it?"

"Hell, yes, he's gonna sing it."

"Thank you, Jesus!" I yelled.

"Not only is he gonna sing it, he's coming to Chicago so you can show him how to sing it."

"When?"

"Next week."

"You're kidding."

"I'd never kid about something this important, Rob. Not when it comes to you producing Michael Jackson."

Me producing Michael Jackson—he was going to sing "You Are Not Alone." I kept running those words through my mind. I still couldn't believe it. *What better way to send a radio message than through the King of Pop himself?*

I immediately got nervous and started to freak a little. It was all coming true. Michael Jackson was really getting on a plane and flying to Chicago for the express purpose of being produced by me in the studio of my choice.

My choice was CRC Studios just off Michigan Avenue in downtown Chicago. I knew it like the back of my hand. My engineers were the best. The atmosphere was cool. I knew Michael would be comfortable, and we could ensure his private space.

Wherever Michael Jackson went, though, the world knew about it. It was like there were secret agents putting out the word. So, days before he landed in Chicago, the city knew he was coming. There were mentions in the newspapers and on TV. The whole town was wired for his arrival. I was wired. I couldn't wait.

The day finally came. I got to the studio two hours early. I ordered my favorite Chinese food. I was sure to include some vegetarian dishes for Michael. I was so nervous that I started practicing in front of the food just how I would introduce Michael. Would I say, "Mike, would you like some Chinese food?" Or, "Mike, want some of this, man?" Or maybe it'd be better to say, "If you're in the mood for some Chinese food, Michael, you're welcome to it."

I was in the middle of all this when the studio phone rang. The engineer answered. All I heard him say was, "Okay?"

"Whassup?" I asked.

"They said the talent has landed and is 30 minutes away."

Michael's people had specified that they wanted only me and my engineers present during the session. My manager, though, had showed up. Like everyone else, he wanted to meet Michael.

The phone rang again.

Talent was 20 minutes away.

I went back to rehearsing how to offer Mike Chinese food.

Then another call.

Ten minutes away.

I went to the bathroom to wash my hands super-clean. I knew Michael didn't like dirt. He was a clean freak. He didn't eat meat. That's why I had those vegetarian meals ready.

"The talent has arrived," my engineer announced.

Three minutes later, his security guys appeared. They made sure they knew who was who. They made sure that the route from the car to the studio was clear.

Next we heard that the talent was in the building.

And the next thing I knew, Michael Jackson was walking through the door. Michael Jackson was real.

He looked at least eight feet tall. He looked like an avatar. He was wearing a black mask over his face. Only his eyes were showing. My manager was the first to make a move. He went over to hug him. Michael stopped the hug and offered his hand instead. Then my manager introduced him to my engineers. Michael shook their hands. Finally, Mike walked over to me. He looked in my eyes, opened his arms, and gave me the hug of my life, whispering to me in his lighter-than-air, soft, high voice, "The world's gonna be singing this song."

I blurted out something silly like, "Congratulations on everything you've done, Mike. Congratulations on being Michael Jackson."

Just about then, Bubbles the chimp pranced into the room. In my mind, I called Bubbles "Trouble." The chimp made me nervous.

"He's friendly, isn't he, Mike?"

"Oh, yes, he's not going to hurt you."

"Anyway," I said, "I'm just glad you like the song."

"I don't like it, Rob. I love it. I don't want to change one thing. I want to sing it just the way you wrote it. You captured me beautifully. That's the reason I came here. We can get started as soon as I do my vocal warm-ups."

"If you excuse me for a minute," I said, "I'll be right back."

I walked to the bathroom and just fell out on the floor. I broke down and cried. It wasn't that Michael Jackson was singing my song; it was that Michael had felt how I'd caught his spirit. *Michael Jackson had come to Chicago to work with me!*

When I got back to the studio, I heard screeching. I thought it was Bubbles throwing a fit. But it was Michael doing his vocal warm-ups. He was screeching like a wounded animal. *Man*, I thought, *this is a strange way to warm up, but he's Michael Jackson—the biggest star in the world—and if that's how he wants to warm up, it's cool with me.*

"Before we start working, Rob," said Mike, "would you mind talking to my vocal coach in L.A.? He has something he wants to ask you."

"No problem, Mike."

When we reached him, the coach said, "Mr. Kelly, Michael just wanted to ask me if it'd be okay if you only did the first verse today. You can start on the chorus tomorrow. That will help Michael conserve his voice."

"Sure thing," I said, amazed at Michael's humility. He had asked his coach to ask me if it was okay to work on Mike's timetable.

"Thanks for understanding, Rob," said Michael. "I hope this won't mess up your flow."

"I flow with you, Mike. "Anything you want, man."

For the next few hours, we worked the verse, with Michael trying as hard as he could to be true to my demo.

"It's better than the demo," I kept telling him. "Way better."

Next day, of course, I was less nervous. I knew the chorus was a killer, and Michael would nail it in no time. When he started singing, though, he immediately felt the need for background vocals.

"Rob," he said in that high, sing-song voice, "would you mind coming in here and singing backgrounds with me?"

Mind? Are you kidding? Michael Jackson was asking me to sing with him!

I had to practically stop myself from running to the vocal booth. I paced myself so I could walk slowly, but in my heart I felt like a little girl.

When we started to sing, the blend was perfect. We were butter and toast. He did that same rocking motion I'd seen him do on "We Are the World." Sitting there next to me — my voice over his, his voice over mine — I tasted heaven. Heaven on earth. Brother, this is as good as it gets.

"You know, Rob," he said later that afternoon, "sometimes it can take me a month to get a song where I want it."

"Me, too, Mike," I agreed. "Sometimes it takes me more than a month."

"I'm glad you understand. You'll be patient with me, won't you?"

"I'll be whatever you want me to be, Mike. It's still like a dream for me."

"Can I ask you something else?"

"Sure."

"Is there a mall around here, Rob?"

"Just a couple of blocks away."

"Would you go there with me? I love malls."

"I love 'em, too, Mike. Let's roll."

With Bubbles and the security team in place, we went to Water Tower Place, one of the nicest malls in Chicago. Michael headed straight for the Disney store where he was fascinated by a larger-than-life statue of Donald Duck hung above the entrance.

"That's beautiful," said Michael. "Do you think they'd sell it to me? I'd love to have Donald Duck for Neverland."

"Couldn't hurt to ask," I said.

Of course Michael Jackson walking into the Disney store caused a near-riot. When the manager appeared, Michael couldn't have been sweeter: "Is there any way I could buy that Donald Duck?" he asked.

"I'm afraid not, Mr. Jackson. It's permanently built into the front of the store."

"Oh, that's a shame," Michael said politely. "But thank you anyway, sir."

I'd never met anyone with better manners.

We spent the next three weeks perfecting the song. As far as the production went, Mike let me take the lead. Of course he had ideas for instrumental touches of his own — and they were all great. We never had a single disagreement.

After the sessions, he'd hang around the studio to talk. He was interested in my remix methods. He loved the remix on "Your Body's Callin'" and wanted to know how I'd done it. When I explained that I worked by instinct, he completely understood.

The experience of working with Mike was drama-free. Every night after he left the studio and got in his van, people were hanging out the windows of office buildings and hotels, stretching their necks to get a glimpse of him. He'd always stop and wave.

When the job was done and it was time for him to leave Chicago, he gave me another hug and said, "You're my brother."

I was too choked up to say anything.

When "You Are Not Alone" dropped as the second single off Mike's *History* album, it made the *Guinness World Records* book as the first song to debut at #1 on the *Billboard* Top 100 chart. It was #1 in the U.K. as well as in France, New Zealand, Spain, Switzerland, and Japan. Mike was right. They were singing it all over the world.

When the video came out—featuring Michael and Lisa Marie Presley, his wife at the time—I loved it for being so original. It got everyone talking.

Unfortunately, the credits on the record listed Michael as a co-writer of the song. Naturally that got me a little upset. But the minute I put a call in to Mike, he got right back to me.

"I'm so sorry," he said. "My people are so used to me co-writing everything, they presumed I'd done this as well. But mark my words, Rob, this mistake will be taken care of immediately."

And it was.

It would be some years before Michael cut another song of mine: "One More Chance" for his *Number Ones* compilations album. Before that, he invited me to his L.A. studio, just as a guest. I wound up singing on that session and having a ball. We'd talk every three months or so. He'd tell me what was happening in his life, and I'd tell him about mine.

Michael Jackson died on June 25, 2009. News of his death was like a hatchet to my chest. He meant to me what breathing means to most people. He was not only my brother and friend, he was also my mentor. I am honored and blessed to have been in Michael's presence. I got to know him like most of the world never will—on a person-to-person, soul-to-soul level. I broke down and cried when I saw a YouTube video of Michael dancing to "Ignition Remix" in the back seat of his friend's car. I mean, he was jamming; you can tell he was fully into and feeling it. I was like, "Wow, he's doing my music, he's singing to my music."

I've been in the business for over 20 years; I've written songs that have sold around the world and won all kinds of awards. But, it wasn't until I saw the great Michael Jackson busting his familiar moves to *my* song that it all became official: *"Kells" is here, baby, for real.*

In late 2009, I used part of that video in a tribute to Michael as part of my tour. The YouTube video segued into a montage of his performances and personal videos. After it played, I walked out on the stage and sang words that came to me after his death:

> *Don't say goodbye to me*
> *There is no need to*
> *Don't say goodbye to me, because I'm still with you*
> *Don't say goodbye to me, don't shed a tear*
> *Because I'm still here*
> *Go light a candle and say a prayer*
> *Scream out victory, 'cause love is still there."*

The tribute was my way of keeping Mike with me, with all of us, really. I refused to let him go and was determined not to let him die.

Because he was super-human, I was sure that Mike would live forever.

TRADE IN MY LIFE

> Understand this about me. There's the studio, the basketball court, the crib, and
> the road. The studio comes first. In the studio, the lady is music and she pos-
> sesses me more deeply than any woman. I need the basketball court for release.
> The competitive fire inside me needs to burn. If I don't burn it off, it'll burn me
> up. I need a crib for privacy and protection. I love my fans, but some of them are
> aggressive to the point of craziness.

In 1994, I found a converted church in the Lakeview section on Chicago's North Side; an upscale, in-the-city 'hood near Lincoln Park, the lakefront, and Wrigley Field. I saw the place, with its 10,000 square feet of living space, as a blank canvas that I could paint any way I wanted. I'm a perfectionist in music, and I'm a perfectionist in design. I was going to design this, my first major home, according to my vision.

For example, I envisioned an indoor pool and basketball court and a spacious indoor rehearsal/dance studio. I wanted a 27-foot stairwell in the living room, polished hardwood floors in the dining room, elaborate lighting, and breath-taking art through-out the house. There simply had to be monster sound and home theatre systems and a great room with a grand white piano as the centerpiece. I had a massive, 1500-gallon, in-the-wall aquarium installed with a pair of killer sharks swimming inside. I got that idea from a James Bond movie I saw; thought it might make my place unique and give it attitude.

My house was a place where I could take off the R. Kelly uniform and let Robert do his thing and be himself.

In an interview with *Vibe* magazine in 2007, John Monopoly—at the time manager of Kanye West, Shawnna, and Rhymefest—talked about his experience at a house party I had once thrown. It wasn't the house I just described, but the so-called "'hood shit" Monopoly described hasn't changed. He watched women braiding my hair and how we hung out in the kitchen "singing, laughing, and talking shit." To Monopoly, this was a sign of my authenticity. From his perspective, it demonstrated my "strong bond with the public" and "connection to the streets."

While what Monopoly witnessed seemed to convince him that I had genuine street cred, back in 1995, as in 2005, as in today. . . if you're hanging with me, I'm not "R. Kelly," I'm "Robert:" a mama's boy, who lives life and enjoys his life, his family, his friends, and his home. In fact, being connected with real life and real people is the only way my music can stay relevant. People tend to pamper R. Kelly, but with Robert, they can let their guard down and say what's on their minds and hearts. R. Kelly moves too fast and tries to please too many people. That's not a bad thing. In fact, it's good because it keeps me connected with my fans. But, when I separate myself from the character and come down to earth, it's Robert who picks up on the real vibes in the streets.

The road was always calling me because it allows me to connect with my fans all around the world. I want to see them and they want to see me. I want to entertain them.

I also found myself in the same position as thousands of male singers who came before me: If I sing a song that says I want to seduce you and you alone, a woman takes that personally. And I *want* her to take it personally. I want the woman to feel like I want her. And I want her to want me. All that translates into lots of ladies wanting me and, in turn, me wanting lots of ladies.

Not too many years before, I was a school kid with a reading problem whom the girls laughed at. Suddenly the kid became a superstar with a lifetime pass to an all-you-can-eat buffet. And on the menu is every kind of beautiful woman you can imagine—every shade and every shape. I was excited that my songs were so strong, excited that my female fans liked the seduction, excited that women were looking to seduce me, and I said, "Hell, yes."

My love life started operating on the same level as my musical life: It was one gorgeous song after another.

But even though I have this spirit of seduction, I also have a spirit that comes from God. The preacher in me is strong. When Mom passed away, she went straight to heaven. I truly believe that the only way I'm going to see her again is to make it to heaven.

After her death and all the sudden success—not to mention this hurricane of women coming at me—I was thrown into some serious confusion. The preacher and the seducer got to arguing.

In 1995, at the start of my second solo album, *R. Kelly*, I decided to let my fans know everything going through my head. But I wanted the preacher to deliver the message. Earth is my preacher's turf and people relate to him because they feel he's talking directly to them. The preacher is my music and my music—although it's not the same as going to church, preaches.

The intro on the record was called "The Sermon." I preached like I was in church, a church organ playing between my words, with the sisters and brothers responding to my calls, yelling "Amen" and "Preach, Brother Kelly."

I said, "Before I start, I just wanna get a few things off my chest. You see, being in the business that I am in, looks like everything I do, everywhere I go, and everything I see, seems to be through some kind of magnifying glass. Can I talk about it?

While you're looking, I suggest you take a good look. And I hope you find just what it is you're looking for. Just like that song says: 'Ain't nobody's business what I do!' Now can I move on?

I remember when I was trying to be somebody, but I just didn't know nobody. Now ever since God has blessed me, it seems that things are going a little bit different.

Folks, ain't it funny how things can change sometimes? Why, even the Statue of Liberty want some bump and grind. Can I get a witness off up in them jeeps? Amen.

I don't see nothing wrong with a little truth. You see the good book says that the truth is the light. I think it's time to turn on your lights and see the truth. Can I talk on?

You don't know where I've been. You don't know where I'm going. You don't know what I do. Can I get a witness?

So before you go trying to pass judgment on me, pass judgment on yourself. Worry 'bout yourself, and what yourself is doing, and where yourself is going, and who yourself has been with. That way, you don't have to EVER worry about nobody but Jesus."

From the pulpit I had to get right to the dance floor. "You Remind Me of Something," the first single from *R. Kelly* album, got some serious criticism. But that didn't bother me. I was proud of the song because I was freer with my metaphors. I've always wanted to express myself in ways that other guys never have. I was glad to write:

You remind me of something.
I just can't think of what it is . . .
You remind me of my jeep, I wanna ride it
Something like my sound, I wanna pump it
Girl you look just like my car, I wanna wax it
And something like my bank account
I wanna spend it . . .

    So pull up to my bumper and let the system sound
    Girl, I bet ya' I can drive you crazy

The song is a compliment to women, not an insult. We fellas love our jeeps. We love our cars. We love the speaker systems in our rides. And naturally we love our bank accounts when we got money. You can compare a woman to the moonlight and stars; you can compare her to a beautiful flower or an angel from above. All that's cool. But I wanted to come down to earth and make a comparison that was real to men.

I was happy the song got talked about. And I don't think I'm wrong in saying that the fans got a kick out of the lyrics. They proved that to me when they ran out and bought the single and it wound up hitting the #1 spot.

The power of music inside me didn't pay any attention to debates about my musical direction. It simply kept feeding me more and more lyrics, words, riffs, and rhythms. It got to a point where—and I know this may sound crazy—I talked to the notes in my head. I made them prove that they're worthy of completion.

"Come on, that all you got? What else? Bring it!"

Even before I was married to a woman, I was married to my work. Music feeds me more than I can consume sometimes. Mostly, it serves me in the wee hours of night, so my engineers and staffers have to accommodate all-night creative sessions. Because I still struggle with reading and writing, I've got old-fashioned cassette recorders all around the house, in my cars, everywhere to catch those moments of pure inspiration. When a melody comes to me, or some lines of lyrics, I've got to get them down fast. I have a near perfect memory, but I've got so many songs in my head that I've got to catch them as soon as they fight their way to the surface. So I'll hum the melody or the bass line, whatever it is that comes to me, into the cassette deck. Or now, one of my iPhones or iPads. Or I'll call the studio and have the engineer record my ideas over the phone. From those bits of melody or rhythm I'll continue to build.

In the studio, I have my longtime musical director Donnie Lyle, who is also an accomplished guitarist. I have a couple of keyboard players and programmers on staff. I'll hum or imitate with my voice all the parts of the song and Donnie will recreate the sounds in my head on the track. As the words come, I'll sing them over the track, and keep refining and refining until the song is done. I've created a life that basically revolves around music. I'm like that weird scientist who's locked himself in the basement experimenting, testing, and, every once in a while, blowing up stuff just to get that perfect formula.

When the song "I Can't Sleep" came to me, I originally wanted to cut it with Toni Braxton. It has her inflection and vocal attitude all over it. Toni had wanted me to produce her. Naturally I said yes. I love her voice.

When she came into the studio, though, she wasn't happy that "I Can't Sleep" was already written. She thought we'd be writing together. Well, that's never been my style. I'm the Lone Ranger. I prefer to write alone. Because I'm as much a word man as a music man, I have both bases covered—and I'm not looking for a collaborator. It's not that I don't recognize the greatness of other writers. But what I do, I do alone.

Toni was unprepared for my way of making music.

"Just listen to the song first, Toni," I said. "It'll fit you like a custom-made dress."

If I produced a song that fit Michael Jackson, I knew I could produce a song that fit Toni.

After listening to "I Can't Sleep," she said she liked it.

But then came the tough part—producing it.

Because I had resculpted the melody with Toni in mind, I knew exactly which way it had to go. She just had to follow my roadmap. Except Toni didn't want to follow.

"Sorry, Rob," she said. "I don't hear it that way."

"But, Toni," I said, "that's the way it's written."

"Well, I'm changing it."

"Then you're ruining it."

"Just because I'm singing it differently than you want it sung doesn't mean I'm ruining it."

"It's a hit the way it's written," I insisted.

"I don't think so."

"Well," I said, "you're certainly entitled to your opinion. And I'm entitled to take back my song. So I will."

At that point Toni and I agreed to disagree. She realized that, like the Lakers and the Celtics, we just weren't going to get along.

What Toni rejected, I accepted. I recorded "I Can't Sleep" myself on my 1995 self-titled album *R. Kelly*. It went #1.

The "Down Low" story started with me riding around L.A. where I saw Ronald Isley walking down Sunset Strip. I had my driver stop the car so I could get out and holler at him.

"Ronald Isley! Man, you don't know how much I love your music. You don't know how much my mother loved your music. I bet you don't even know who I am."

"Are you kidding, brother? You're R. Kelly. You got the hits." He looked at me

like I'd accomplished what he'd accomplished. I couldn't believe it.

All I could say was, "Well, I believe I got some hits for you. I'm looking to make the kind of music my people listened to on the porch when we were growing up. You feel me?"

"I feel you, but what do I call you, brother? What does the 'R' stand for?"

"The 'R' is for Robert, and Robert is ready to roll with the Isleys if the Isleys are ready to roll with the 'R.'"

"We roll now."

That very day we went to the studio where I played some tracks for Ronald. He loved them all. The very first song we did was "Down Low," where I sang lead but used Ronald and his brother Ernie prominently in the background. You can't help but hear the Isley vibe on that record. I was careful to respectfully label the song "Down Low (Nobody Has to Know) *featuring Ronald and Ernie Isley.*"

When it came time to make a video, I already knew the whole story—it was like a movie in my head, when I wrote the song. I was the young dude kicking it with the woman of a superbad gangsta named Mr. Biggs. I cast Ronald in the role of Mr. Biggs—and suddenly both his face and his voice were back in the media. He told me that the song and the music video propelled him into a whole new career.

Hanging with Ronald was like being with a teacher. I always learned something new from him. Like any writer or director, I took great pride in giving the Mr. Biggs character life. The Isley Brothers were one of my mom's favorite groups. I was truly humbled to work with them. My only regret was that my mom couldn't see her baby boy singing with the Isleys.

Just as "Down Low" had me looking to the past, my collaboration with the Notorious B.I.G.—"You To Be (Be Happy)"—on the same album had me looking to the future. I saw that, staying in the present, I could ride on both sides of the road: new-flavored old-school R&B and rap-heavy hip-hop.

"The

'R'

is for Robert,
and Robert is ready
to roll with the Isleys
if the Isleys are ready
to roll with the

'R.'"

GOD & MUSIC

The other side of the *R. Kelly* album testified to my relationship with God. It may be hard for some to understand, but I considered what was happening onstage with my music as steps I was taking toward God. If not for Him, I couldn't have come that far. For whatever else was happening in my crazy life, God was happening. God can't help but happen. God's always there.

With all the success of *12-Play*, with all the pain that came with my mother's death, with all the willing women surrounding me, I felt the need to reach out to the Lord for help. I needed Him bad. I loved Him deeply. Even on a love song like "Baby Baby Baby Baby Baby . . ." I asked my baby to take me to church on Sunday morning where I can thank the Lord. I sang, "Let's say a prayer together: 'Heavenly Father, which art in heaven, I pray that you keep this love together.'"

Same thing was true with "Thank God It's Friday." I took the title seriously. On one level the song was about "Friday night, disco lights, feeling right," but I had to bring God into it. I addressed the Lord when I sang: 'Heavenly Father, I thank you, I thank you, and I thank you—so many looking, looking.'"

I was one of those people looking.

As I reached the end of the album, I reached out to God again in a song called "As I Look Into My Life":

As I look into my life searching for that paradise
Oh Lord, will you help me, find me, take this crazy ghetto past of mine
And put it all behind me

I concluded the *R. Kelly* album with a prayer/song I wrote called "Trade In My Life." I sang about "sittin' here wonderin' how did things go so wrong . . ." and came to the conclusion that I had to give my life to God. I said, "I love my music and I love my fans, but I've got to step back, look at this thing like it sure-enough is. What does it profit a man to gain the world and lose his soul? I'm gonna trade it to be with you . . . from the depth of my heart."

R. Kelly ended on a holy conclusion—when the love of a woman, the love of music, and the love of God all came together in a single song. "Trade In My Life" was an affirmation of my love for Jesus, the same Jesus who, through my mother, I met as a little boy; the same Jesus who lived in the mind and soul of Lena McLin; the same Jesus who had blessed me with a talent that had taken me from the dirt to my dreams.

The *R. Kelly* album and my lyrics seriously confused many music critics and fans. Mixing the spiritual with the sensual was a hard feat for many. Some speculated that my mother's death was the beginning of "a spiritual awakening" for me. My critics wrote that *R. Kelly* was wrestling "with both sexual and spiritual concerns." And some people took offense and accused me of "twisting things up." There weren't many artists who had so boldly combined the secular and the sacred. Some detractors speculated that the album confirmed that, like so many before me, I was lost and uncertain about who I wanted to serve.

Oh, I knew who I wanted to serve all right, but I wanted to be honest. My mother's death affected me greatly, but it didn't constitute a "spiritual awakening." The seeds of God, church, and religion had been permanently planted in my life by my mother and Pastor McLin. I had never walked away from God.

In my late 20s, I was going through some personal trauma; I was thinking about my future and what I was doing with my life and career. Writing and singing about these inner conflicts onstage was just my way of taking steps toward God. He created me. Surely He'd help me, if I asked.

The rumor mill really blew up in 1997 after my surprise appearance at a gospel concert in Chicago. Looking back on my comments that night, I understand why many expected me to abandon R&B and make a full-fledged conversion to gospel.

I talked about my obsession with money and material possessions and being the center of attention for women and the media. "Here stands a broken man," I shouted. "I used to be flying in sin—now I'm flying in Jesus."

I want to be clear here, I never considered my music sinful. For the most part, what people see onstage—R. Kelly bumping and grinding, dropping my pants, seducing women—that's all show business. What I do onstage doesn't mean I jump off the stage and continue my act in my real life.

If my fans and the critics could see me as I worship, filled with the spirit, praising in praying, or seeking guidance from my pastor, they'd know that God is and has always been essential to my life.

At the concert, I was expressing my faith, acknowledging God, and honestly admitting that I had some serious work to do if I ever planned to join Joann Kelly in heaven. There is no divide between sexy and spiritual music in my world. God blessed me with the ability to create both. Take away the seductive lyrics, and they can be easily replaced with gospel.

I was grateful when one of the great contemporary gospel singers came looking for me. He knocked on my door and said, "Rob, let me help you, brother." I felt his spirit and genuine love of God. I went into his prayer circle and received many blessings from his insights into the Lord.

But because God gave me a discerning nature, even in the midst of a powerful prayer circle, I was aware of what was happening around me. Example: I was seated in a room in a prayer circle—brothers and sisters who had dedicated their life to the Lord. A sister asked us all to hold hands as she led us in prayer. When I pray, I get emotional. I give my heart over completely to the sacred moment. I can start crying, shaking, and even talking in tongues. Anything might happen when I pray. This time I fell to my knees, calling out to God and thanking Him for His grace. As I fell, though, I noticed the group leader had his little video camera aimed at me. As he was catching me on tape, I heard him talking on his cell: "Yes, we have R. Kelly with us. R. Kelly is saved. R. Kelly is in our prayer circle."

I didn't like that. Prayer is a personal thing. Prayer is private. Broadcasting my religious moment in that particular manner killed the moment for me. I wasn't on my knees to create a photo op. I was on my knees because I was humbling myself before God. I didn't need to have that image go out to the world. That kind of publicity left a bad taste in my mouth.

Today, just as it was back in the late '90s, I'll keep on expressing what's in my heart, be it sexual, spiritual, or just entertaining. People shouldn't get so deep into "psychologizing" what R. Kelly does. If you like my music, buy my music. If you don't like it, don't buy it. I will love you either way.

I loved hearing those words, but I had also made a promise to myself. I had promised to trade in my life. That meant concentrating on the spiritual gifts God had given me. I knew that spirit would grow if I could concentrate on one woman and one woman alone.

When I watched Andrea Lee dance across the stage, my eyes and heart told me that she was that woman.

"*Drea was more than just a great dancer.*"

DREA

Coming up, I was taught that every Christian has a past and every sinner has a future. As both Christian and sinner, I wanted to live in the present tense with God. I felt that my heart was ready for humanity and the demons surrounding me; for example, the drama of empty love affairs needed to stop.

And I felt like I wanted to be checked. I needed to be checked. My ego, while insisting that the music I do today is better than what I did yesterday, was not a 24-hour ego. I needed it for business negotiations and for confidence, but I was learning to keep it by my side. If I got in front of my ego, it would run me over. If I ran alongside it, I could wear it out.

I also knew that love—true love—for another human being was another way to defeat my ego.

I was auditioning dancers for an upcoming tour when I felt the first spark of that love. We'd gone through 100 dancers to choose six. Of the final six, one grabbed my full attention. She did cartwheels and splits with a flexibility and grace that knocked me out. I couldn't keep my eyes off her. She was a brilliant athlete but also an artist in the way that her movements told a story. She was sensuous, she was sexy, and she was downright spectacular.

She got the job, and before long, I got a beautiful girlfriend. Her name was Andrea Lee. Her story and mine flowed together in a natural way. Her friendly sweetness and outgoing personality reminded me of my mother. She was also a firecracker. You won't meet a stronger person. She had the heart of a lioness. Drea calmed my inner storms. She was my medicine, a wonderful woman who understood my unexplainables.

I made up my mind that I would introduce "Robert" to her. She'd seen "R. Kelly" the performer, the party guy, the player, and the music mogul. In Drea's company, I didn't need to be R. Kelly. I could be Robert, the guy without the swagger, who still loves cartoons, who praises God, and struggles with his worth and his sometimes overwhelming gift. With Drea, I could relax and reveal all of my past, my secrets, and my fears. I could open my heart.

Drea was more than just a great dancer. Like me, she could choreograph, and soon we were sharing that duty.

One day on tour I saw her in the back of the bus reading the Bible.

"You take that book seriously, don't you?" I asked.

"Sure do. Do you?"

"Very seriously."

"How would you feel if I asked you to go to church?" Drea asked.

"I'd feel good, baby. Church is what I need."

Since the experience with the prayer circle, my heart had been a little hardened toward religious leaders. But I knew that God is bigger than any of His servants. Like me, all of His servants are flawed.

"Then we'll go to church?" she asked.

"I'd love that, Drea."

We started going, which was when I started to feel committed; I saw that my relationship with God was more important than anything. If I was going to give up the party life, God was the only way.

Meanwhile, my sister Theresa had gotten saved and was active in a big church with a powerful preacher. She urged us to go to her church with her, and we did. The preacher put me in the front row, next to Theresa, and his sermons had me up on my feet. I was shouting and praising and crying out the name of Jesus with no inhibitions. It felt good.

Soon the preacher saw that I was catching the Holy Ghost and wanted me to travel with him to various cities. Part of me knew that, like the leader of the prayer circle before, he was showing me off, but another part of me felt flattered and desired his company. He was teaching me the Word.

228

When Drea and I went to church, though, I noticed that Theresa was no longer sitting in the first pew with us.

"Why?" I asked her.

"The first pew is for the important folk."

"Come on," I said. "There's no velvet rope in church."

"You stay on up there in the front," she said. "I'm cool back here."

Sometimes when I fell to my knees or started talking in tongues, I saw that the little cameras, usually aimed at the pulpit, were turning in my direction. I was on display. This time, though, I wasn't going to let that keep me from God.

I even decided to tithe. And it was a great sum of money.

"You sure you want to do this, Rob?" asked Derrel McDavid, who's been my trusted business manager from the get-go. "We're talking about millions."

"Do it," I instructed.

I also wanted to write gospel songs and join the church's music ministry. There, though, the pastor drew the line. I could sing along with everyone else, but as far as getting up there or presenting original compositions, they said no. My reputation as the bump-and-grind man didn't allow me that platform. They felt okay about taking the bump-and-grind money, but they were afraid of what the Christian community would say if my music got mixed with theirs.

Fine.

I wasn't there to argue. I was there to worship.

Weeks went by—and then months. I was doing well. Drea and I had become a loving couple. I'd managed to put most of my partying in the past. But a tour was coming up, and a tour meant the chance to party even more. A tour meant meeting a lot of female fans.

Like my albums and the music I produce for others, I want my tours to be successful. It's hard for me to concentrate on anything but success when I'm in that mode. A successful tour means parties, clubs, playing the role to get people to buy albums, guys going "woof, woof, woof" before you even come on stage and women screaming your name, throwing themselves at you.

I can't lie. Sometimes, it all feels pretty unreal.

The tour was about a week old when I knew I needed help. Temptations were up in my face. Women were handing me cards with photographs and phone numbers. I was with Drea, but my mind was wandering. I called Theresa and asked whether she'd come out on the road and bring her prayer warriors with her. She said yes.

When they arrived, we went into a room and prayed for hours. Serious praying, crying, pleading that I stay on the righteous path.

After the show, though, three ladies approached me with an offer that blew my mind. They were fine and they wanted me to join them in their room—just the four of us. They were staying in the same hotel as Drea, Theresa, and me. I said, "Wow, that sounds incredible, but I gotta pass. I'm trying to stay on the straight and narrow." "Well," said one of them, "in case you change your mind, we're in room 1305. We'll be up all night. Waiting."

I told myself not to think about it, to forget the number, but of course that's all I thought about. In my mind, the number 1305 was lit brighter than an opening-night marquee. I told myself I'd go to bed early. Drea, who had danced in the show, was tired and was ready to call it a night. We got into bed and she quickly fell asleep. I couldn't sleep. I couldn't stop imagining those three ladies.

Drea was out like a light, so when I crept out of bed she didn't hear me. I got dressed. I went to the door. Then I changed my mind. I got undressed again, put my pajamas back on, and slipped back into bed. I didn't want to do wrong. I wanted to stay with Drea. I wanted to sleep. But every time I closed my eyes, the images of those women waiting for me came back. I got out of bed a second time. I got dressed a second time. I put my hand on the doorknob. I leaned against the door. I slid down to the floor and silently prayed, "God, if you don't want me to go to these fine ladies, give me a sign. Show me something."

There was no sign. I wasn't shown a thing. I got back up, turned the knob, and, careful not to make any noise, walked out of the room into the hallway. It was an atrium hotel where you could see people walking up and down the hallways below and above you.

Room 1305. They said they'd be up all night. Said they'd be waiting.

I didn't want to go.

I wanted to go.

I was going.

Walked to the all-glass, see-through elevators. Punched the button. I was on 20. I was headed to 13. Just then, I looked up and saw Theresa on the floor above. She waved. I waved back. I felt convicted, but the devil flesh was driving my motor. There was no turning back.

Elevator arrived. Doors opened. It was empty. I walked in, punched the button that said "13." Doors closed. I waited for the elevator to start going down. But it didn't move. I pressed 13 again. Sensing something was wrong, I pressed the "open door" button. Nothing. The elevator was stuck. I got my sign! Thank you, Lord! Thank you, Jesus! I had to stay on that elevator a half-hour before the mechanics arrived to force open the door and set me free. The amount of time I spent waiting for my physical freedom helped me win my spiritual freedom.

I didn't go to room 1305. I went back to Drea.

But the story isn't that simple. Stories rarely are.

After the tour was over and we went back home, one of the women who had prayed me into the church started coming on to me. She slipped me her number and said something about how she liked to do crazy things with red lipstick. We met at her place in secret. We messed around and were ready to kick it for real when I stopped and started crying.

"We can't do this," I said. "You helped bring me back to God, and here we are doing what we know damn well God don't want us to do."

She backed off. "I'm sorry, Rob," she said. "You're a hundred percent right. I'm weak and you're strong. I need your strength to stop this."

And so we stopped. Except, a week later, when she called and said something about a new shade of red lipstick, we were back at it.

I was back in prayer.

"Father God," I prayed. "I might not be righteous now, but you know that my desire is to be righteous. That's a blessing right there, Lord. For so many years I didn't even have that desire. I pray, Father God, that you let that desire grow. I pray that I become the man I want to become—for you, for Drea, and for the family I want to lead."

I wanted a family of my own. I wanted a Cosby-like family. And I wanted Drea to be the mother of my children.

I knew what I had to do.

When I reached the decision, I was on the road. Drea was back in Chicago. I called my sister Theresa and told her to bring Drea to the private airport where I'd be landing. Except I wouldn't be landing in a plane. I had hired a helicopter.

"Bring Drea out to the tarmac," I told Theresa. "Get as close to the chopper as they'll allow. I want to make sure that she can barely hear me over the noise. I want her hair to be blowing in the wind from the propellers. I want it to look like a scene out of a movie. I want us to be in that scene. I want it to be the most romantic moment of her life."

It was. The sun was shining that day. The chopper came down out of the sky. Drea was waiting on the tarmac. I jumped out and walked over to her. Her hair was blowing in the wind. I fell on my knees. I had to scream above the roar of the engine.

"Baby girl," I roared, "I love you."

I took the small box out of my pocket and handed the ring to her.

"Baby girl," I hollered even louder. "Will you marry me?"

She was crying. She said something, but the noise of the chopper didn't let me hear it.

"Say it louder," I said.

She said it again. I still couldn't hear it.

"You got to scream, baby," I said. "You got to scream so I can hear you."

"I love you!" she screamed with all her might. "And yes! Yes! Yes! I will marry you! I will marry you!"

It was as beautiful as any scene in any movie.

A marriage, a home, a family, everything I'd ever wanted. A dream coming true.

To make the dream even better, though, and to be sure it was righteous, I decided that we should have no sex until our wedding night. Drea agreed. It was going to be difficult, but it would be worth it. It would mean that for eight months between our proposal and our marriage, love, not lust, would be growing between us. Our love would remain pure.

I had a target date for the wedding—Valentine's Day. I had the perfect place for the wedding—Denver, Colorado, a mile-high city closer to heaven. I could—and did—

design the wedding so it would look like a fairy tale. I hired a half-dozen violinists who played heavenly music. God smiled down on us and directed the snow to fall. It was romantic, and the start of something that I believed in my heart would last a lifetime.

"Will you, Andrea Lee, take this man, Robert Kelly, to be your husband in sickness and health, till death do you part?"

"I do."

"Will you, Robert Kelly, take this woman, Andrea Lee, to be your wife in sickness and health, till death do you part?"

"I do."

"Then, with God as my witness, I pronounce you man and wife."

We embraced. We cried. We were Mr. and Mrs. Robert Kelly.

FLYING

There are two ways to be in the sky—flying or falling. I prefer flying.

When the musical dream I had as a young boy came true, the cartoon characters chasing me turned out to be characters in a movie called *Space Jam*. The film featured the very song I had dreamed about—"I Believe I Can Fly." The fact that the animated/live-action film was about basketball and starred Michael Jordan (who, along with Muhammad Ali, was my biggest inspiration outside of the music world) made everything even better.

If you came up when I did, if you played hoop, and if you were raised in the streets of Chicago, Michael Jordan was the man. Even before joining the Bulls in 1984, Michael was a master hoopster at the University of North Carolina at Chapel Hill.

For us, Michael redefined the game by bringing a skill set unlike anyone before him. Not only did he have the most competitive spirit we'd ever seen, he also had moves we'd never seen. As a ballplayer, he was poetry in motion. He could twist, turn, fake, and fly; he could hit from the outside; he could hit from the inside; he could move to the hoop like a bolt of lightning; he could slam with the fierceness of an angry eagle; he could shoot it soft; he could bring it hard. There wasn't anything the man couldn't do.

Earlier in the '90s, after "Honey Love" hit, I was walking around the 'hood when I heard some kids screaming: "Michael's coming! Michael's coming down the street to see his mama."

I looked and saw a crowd of people waiting in front of a house. I didn't want to seem like a groupie, but, hell, I wanted to see Michael Jordan just like everyone else.

I wanted to see the greatest basketball player in the history of the game.

A few minutes later, Michael himself came riding up on a motorcycle. Kids flocked around him, screaming for autographs. I didn't want to look uncool, so I stood back.

After signing a few autographs, he looked up and saw me. Our eyes locked. A second passed. Did he recognize me?

"Hey, R. Kelly! What you doing around here, man?"

The kids got a little excited seeing me—a lot less excited, though, than they were to see Michael Jordan. I walked over to him.

"Michael," I said. "Can't tell you what you meant to me growing up."

A bunch of other words of praise fell out of my mouth. I kept blabbering about how much I admired him.

"Hey, man," said Michael. "I can't sing, but you can."

"Well," I said, "you know I also play ball."

"What do you mean, brother? You don't got no game." In a good-natured way, he started giving me a hard time.

"My game is pretty good," I said. "I've kept up over the years. I hoop almost every night."

"Well, keep playing, baby. And more important than that, keep singing."

"Can't stop either one."

That little encounter made a huge impression on me. Michael couldn't have been any nicer.

When I was about 10, George Benson's "The Greatest Love of All" blew me away. I had a desire to write a song like that—one that reminded kids they could achieve anything and be anything if they believed and worked hard at it.

Michael Jordan gave me that chance when he asked me to write something for the 1996 part-cartoon/part live-action film *Space Jam.*

"I Believe I Can Fly" became my biggest cross-over hit, reaching #2 on the *Billboard* Hot 100, and #1 on the U. K. Pop Charts. Believe it or not, it took me all of three hours to write. Because the tune first came to me as a child, I really do believe

God actually wrote that song. He just used me to get it out there. I prayed over the project. At the time, I was going through a lot—lawsuits, back-biting, fake friends, and folk more interested in my money than in me.

The song ministered to me, made me feel good, gave me life. It was more powerful than anything I'd ever done musically. I have never gotten over my fear of flying in airplanes and don't think I ever will. You have to practically knock me out and throw me in the baggage compartment to get me on a plane. Isn't it strange that a guy who hates flying can pen an anthem about soaring through the sky?

This is only one of the reasons I'm convinced God was involved. He put that particular song out there for everybody, including me, who needed to believe that they can achieve, that they can rise above any challenge.

My mother used to always tell me "meet greatness where it is," which meant we all walk on the ground. I tried to remember her words when I was hanging with Michael Jackson or Michael Jordan. But every now and then I had to pinch myself. One of those times was when I was playing a game of one-on-one with Jordan. I was inspired by the fact that he was so approachable and down-to-earth. The score was to 32–to-1. I might have lost pretty badly but I won a chance to play against "the man!"

Years later, after the movie came out and the song started soaring, I kept thinking about that first time I met Michael Jordan outside his mother's house on a Chicago street.

"I Believe I Can Fly" traveled all over the world, won three Grammys and so many other awards I can't remember them all. It launched me into a new orbit. Until then, I'd been seen as a sexy R&B singer. I could talk about the crotch on you; I could get the ladies to sex me, to hump bounce and go down low. I could sing pretty ballads asking you to step in my room. But before "I Believe I Can Fly," if someone had asked a music critic if R. Kelly could write a purely inspirational song, the answer would be, "You kidding? Not R. Kelly. He's too busy with the bump and grind."

Maybe the only one who wasn't surprised at the success of "I Believe I Can Fly" was me. I say that because these kinds of songs had always lived inside my soul. I call them faith anthems. They're songs that affirm my faith in God, God's faith in me, and my faith in myself. They were as deep a part of me as "Homie Lover Friend" or "Seems Like You're Ready." I knew I'd be writing these kinds of songs for the rest of my life.

I knew that my next album would have to go to a whole other level. I had lifted the bar higher—which is just what I wanted to do. After all, that's what Michael Jordan and Muhammad Ali did. They all went for the gold, and they got it. Whether I liked it or not, my blessing and burden were to try to outdo myself every time I stepped into the ring of fire. That ring burned brightest in my studio.

In the mid-'90s, something else was happening in music studios across the country—something as hot as the hottest R&B, the deepest faith anthem, or the most seductive dance groove. Rap had taken its place at the center of the musical universe. Some singers started complaining about that; some said that rappers only rap because they can't sing. I didn't see it that way. I'd grown up with rap music from the earliest days, I appreciated rap just like I did all music, and, I recognized the stories. I was influenced by the Sugar Hill Gang, Grand Master Flash, and Kurtis Blow. Everybody knew those lyrics. Times change, and musical styles started to merge.

I get upset when I hear a rapper say, "I ain't no R&B singer." They want to say "that's soft." I'm not the guy that you want to say, "Oh that guy's soft, he's an R&B guy." I'm not a fight starter, but I am a great finisher.

I wouldn't say R&B and rap belong together, but sometimes they can be a great match if the collaboration is right. I understood that rap was an art form. The challenge became clear: How can rap and R&B come together?

While I was standing in front of a hotel one sunny afternoon in Beverly Hills, the idea came to me. It came in the form of a drop-top Bentley convertible.

I was able to marry my music with rappers . . .

Slick Rick	The Notorious B.I.G.
Doug E. Fresh	Puff Daddy (Diddy)
The Game	Big Tymers
TI	Lil Jon
Elephant Man	Cassidy
Lil' Kim	Young Jeezy
Missy Elliott	Rick Ross
Wyclef (Jean)	Beanie Sigel
Snoop (Dog)	Whodini
Twista	Crucial Conflict
Do or Die	N.O.R.E.
Young BloodZ	Busta Rhymes
OJ Da Juice	Remy Ma
Swizz Beatz	Ginuwine
Chamillionaire	Birdman
T-pain	Clipse
Lucacris	Joe Budden
Huey	Chingy
Kid Rock	Fabolous
Ja Rule	Jadakiss
Big Tigger	Lil Wayne
Nelly	Gucci Mane
Fat Joe	50 Cent
Jay-Z	Lloyd
Bow Wow	K'naan
Boo & Gotti	Bei Maejor
Nick Cannon	

Put them together and you get the best of both worlds

It was 1996; I had just left the lobby of the Hotel Nikko. (We called it the Hotel Negro because so many rappers and music business folk liked staying there.) I was standing out front, waiting for my ride to arrive, when I looked up and saw Tupac Shakur driving by in a bad-ass Bentley. He was alone, and I thought to myself: *"Man, this nigga got some balls to be rolling by himself like that."*

"Yo Pac!" I yelled at the top of my voice.

He made a U-turn and jumped out of the car.

"What up, baby?" he asked.

"Just wanted to holla at you," I said. "Just had to tell you that I love everything you do."

"Hey, man," said Pac, "coming from you that's a helluva compliment."

"Lots of cats say rap and R&B live in different parts of the planet, but I don't see it that way, Pac. I see us all coming together. You feel me?"

"Been feeling the same way. It's all the same thing. Beats, words, stories."

"Man, we need to do an album."

"Would love it."

"I'm talkin' about a whole album. A whole concept. A big game-changing record."

"You got it, Kells. Tell me what studio and when to be there."

"Gonna send you some tracks," I said.

"Don't need no tracks. Just need to know you wanna work with me. That's enough. We'll just let it do what it do."

"God is good."

"All the time," said Pac.

We hugged and Pac went on his way.

As the year went on, we made tentative plans to meet, but the plans got messed up when his schedule or mine suddenly changed. That didn't change our hearts, though. Every time we talked, we talked about how this marriage of rap and R&B had to happen in a big way. We figured we were the two artists to pull it off. Pac understood that we came from the same 'hood. We had mutual respect and mutual love. I'd go around saying, "No one is better at the rap game than Pac." And Pac went around saying, "Kells is the most serious R&B thug out there."

Come September, and it looked like my schedule was opening up just before the holidays. I set up a meeting with Pac for us to plot our strategy, get firm dates, and make the musical bomb that we both knew would explode all around the world.

But another bomb exploded that no one saw coming.

I woke up on Sunday, November 8, to the news that Pac had been shot in Vegas the night before. He'd been rushed to the hospital. It didn't look good.

Six days after the shooting, on Friday the 13th, Pac died.

I was numb from the news. Didn't know what to say or what to do except praise God for giving him a gift that he gave to us—brilliant true-life stories, beautiful real-life poetry, words that will keep on living as long as there are eyes to read and ears to hear.

On many different singles, I was able to marry my music with rappers who understood the natural bond between us. Even though our approaches were different, we complemented each other. Put them together and you get the best of both worlds— a term that stayed in my mind when I decided to put together the master plan that got postponed after the death of Tupac.

I can never think of Tupac without thinking of Biggie. Because the very next year we lost another rap icon for whom I have the deepest respect.

Biggie was a lyrical genius, he was a musical painter with words. As he rapped, you would see the picture come to life as you heard his story. You hear a lot of rappers rap, you hear a lot of singers sing, but you don't see the movie in your head the way you do when you hear Biggie rap. We related in that way because I'm into painting the picture and showing you the movie of what I'm singing about, so it was natural thing for us to collaborate. Something would have been wrong with the Earth if we hadn't done something together. When I got to Biggie's studio in New York, Biggie was in the backroom messing around with his lyrics on the track; then he came out and showed me the first verse on "Fuck You Tonight." While I was listening to his verse, I was already hearing the chorus in my head. I didn't say anything and kept grooving to the track. And I had the chorus immediately.

Soon as I sang it: "*You must be used to me spending and all that sweet wining and dining . . .*" He stood up, he was tripping. "That's it! That's it right there." He loved it, just as much as I loved his verse. There was such a mutual respect between us. I didn't feel like I was working with just any rapper; I felt like I was working with someone who had a heart, someone who understood the significance of his own gift and of mine, and what it meant for them to merge together and for us to get together on the song. Biggie loved R&B music. He never felt that he was too tough for R&B.

As with all the other rappers I've worked with, Biggie and I shared common ground. Even though Biggie grew up in Brooklyn and I grew up in Chicago, we came from the same 'hood. We knew the same characters. We'd been through a lot of the same shit.

One time we were on tour together and we were staying at the same hotel in Detroit. It was late and the after-party was over. The hotel-lobby party was over. The hotel-room party was over. There were still people hanging out in the lobby. And I was back in the lobby where they had this piano. I had just recalled that childhood dream with the cartoon characters chasing me. I remembered the melody from that dream and was trying to figure out the rest of the lyrics, working on what would become "I Believe I Can Believe Fly." Biggie and his crew came in the lobby about four in the morning.

"What's up, baby! Great show, baby! What you doing?"

He came over to the piano, and I started to play it for him: "I believe I can fly, I believe I can touch the sky . . ." but so far that's all I had.

"I'm gonna tell you right now, B, that's a smash. That's a big hit right there. That's a Grammy winner, Rob."

When I was playing it for him, I was thinking—he's a hardcore rapper; this is gonna be too soft for him—but when I got through and looked up, his face was wet with tears.

"My brother," he said, "they gonna be playing that when you and I have moved on to the other side of time."

I was blown completely away because here was one of the greatest in rap, recognizing a song that was about humanity, about uplifting people and feeling the power of the song that took me beyond Biggie the rapper or Biggie the writer. That connected me with Biggie the man. Biggie was the first person to hear me sing "I Believe I Can Fly." That was a great moment.

The death of Biggie in 1997 hit me just as hard as Tupac's death the year before. Another genius went down for reasons I never understood—and still don't. Just a couple of months after he was killed, his album *Life After Death* dropped that included our collaboration on "Fuck You Tonight." Biggie was among the first hardcore rappers to understand that mixing in pretty R&B with his raps made them more radio-friendly. He also understood—as I did—that a club cut was different from a radio cut. Profanity had leaked from streets into rap, and then into R&B. We all got caught up in it. I didn't mind singing a lyric like "I'm fucking you tonight" in a club jam. I thought it fit into that slot perfectly, and so did millions of fans who bought the record.

After that collaboration, rapper after rapper came knocking at my door. And I was happy to open that door and let them in. I took it as a compliment that they thought I could contribute to their art form.

When Fat Joe, for example, came to see me in a studio in Miami, he came with deep respect. Thug as he was, street as he was, the man was all heart.

"Kells," he said, "you got to write me a hit, Bro."

"I'll do my best, Joe."

Fat Joe didn't come alone. His posse must have been 20 deep, all hanging in the studio, watching and waiting for me to come up with a killer jam.

"Tell you what," I said. "I do better when I work alone. Y'all take a walk or go to the beach. The ocean out here is really beautiful. Give me an hour, and I'll come up with something."

"No problem, Rob," said Joe.

Half-hour later him and his boyz were back.

"Got something, Kells?"

"Matter of fact, Joe, I do."

Played the track, sang the chorus, and Joe was all smiles.

"It's a monster, baby," he said.

"I like it myself," I said, as I kept singing the chorus:

We thuggin', rollin' on dubs . . .

The jam, "We Thuggin'," hit big in late 2001. Soon all the big-time rappers were coming around. Got to the point that a rap with a Kells chorus gave you even more street cred. Slick Rick, Doug E. Fresh, The Game, T.I., Elephant Man, Li'l Kim, Missy Elliott, Wyclef, Snoop, Twista, Do or Die, Young BloodZ, OJ Da Juiceman, Swizz Beatz, Chamillionaire, T-Pain, Ludacris, Huey, Kid Rock, Ja Rule, Big Tigger, Nelly—we all worked together. "Supaman High" and "Reggae Bump Bump" and a slew of others became club classics. These songs became part of my identity.

Both as an artist and a businessman, I liked that identity. As an artist, I was working with other serious artists. As a businessman, I saw club tracks as a new franchise that could be profitable for years to come. It was like being McDonald's and realizing that even though cheeseburgers and fries sold big, you could also make money serving up McRibs, which are always available for a limited time only.

Beyond the fact that marrying rap and R&B made good artistic and business sense, the marriage was good for music lovers. It gave them what they were looking for.

What are music lovers looking for?

First thing is romance. Life can be boring. Romance is exciting. The thought that you might find real love is a beautiful thing. And if a song brings you that thought and helps you strengthen that hope, I say, Amen.

Music also needs to speak to your spirit, your inner core, that part of your soul that can get drowned by the drama of daily life. Don't matter if it's a romantic ballad or a hot sexy song, music—at least the kind of music I do—has got to get all over your soul.

And then there's escape. Everyone needs escape. I need escape. Come Friday and Saturday, Kells is gonna party. You can't have a party without music. I don't care where you go around the world, you will see people—in Africa or England, in Jamaica or Japan—looking for a way to let off steam. During the week, we walk around all stiff and uptight. We have to be careful what we say to our boss, or our teacher, or our co-workers. We have to watch every step we take and every word that comes out of our mouths. Come the weekend, we're tired of holding it in. We got to let it out. We need release. We need *relief*. We need the club and all the good feelings that the club brings.

Being up in the club, in the VIP with the greatest rappers who ever rocked a mic, made me proud. Made me feel like I was living right where my people were living. Like I said in my first album, my career was born in the '90s. I wanted to be part of my times. And it was—and remains—a great blessing that I could swing back and forth between two cultures. Maybe I could even contribute to a conversation between those two cultures.

When it came to music, there was no shame in my game. I'm at my best when I am wanted, and whoever reaches out to me is going to get my best.

Bring on the rappers, baby. Let me keep dreaming that big dream where R&B and rap share the biggest stage in the world. Where R&B and rap go on the biggest tour in history.

That dream was deep in my soul.

It was going to happen. It had to.

I wanted to be part of my times.

Let me keep dreaming that big dream where R&B and rap share the biggest stage in the world. Where R&B and rap go on the biggest tour in history.

I put my career on hold for a season while, in 1997, at age 30, I signed up with the Atlantic City Seagulls, a semi-pro team in the United States Basketball League. This was no public relations stunt.

SEMI-PRO

My love of basketball is serious—so serious that I can't imagine life without it. Playing professionally was something that I'd always wanted. It was my first and only dream before I met Ms. McLin. Basketball is in my blood. When I get old and decrepit, I'll be shooting outside the arc from a wheelchair.

My career was blowing up so big until I needed a break from the craziness.

I was doing too much too quick. Taking off three or four nights a week to hoop wasn't enough. There were too many gigs, too many videos, too many artists wanting me to produce them, too many songs playing inside my head. I had to stop. I wanted to play ball full-time to prove to myself that I could do more than one thing professionally.

I did it. I put my career on hold for a season while, in 1997, at age 30, I signed up with the Atlantic City Seagulls, a semi-pro team in the United States Basketball League. This was no public relations stunt. I was doing it for myself.

Two months before the tryouts, I started getting in serious shape through a demanding program designed by Coach. Man, it was torture. We got to the gym at the crack of dawn. Did those suicides, running up and down the court like my life was on the line. Did drills for hours on end. When it came to conditioning, I didn't play around. I got into the best shape of my life. If it weren't for the hard-ass direction of Coach, I would never have made it.

When tryouts rolled around, I was there. I performed at the top of my game and made the team.

Some folks said I made it only because I was famous—that the team thought it would draw bigger crowds with me on the team. That might have been part of their thinking, but I know damn well I wouldn't have been selected if I didn't have game.

When reporters got on our coach for putting me on the team, he said, "Rob showed up in great shape. He has an effective open jumper. He can dribble, he can read the defense, and overall he has a fine skills set. He's also a worker. He hasn't missed a practice. Some of the guys thought he'd act like a star, but he hasn't. Rob has become one of the guys, a teammate who everyone likes. He's come to play and to win."

In our first game, the highlight came when I went up on defense and smacked the ball away as the opposing forward, Nathan Morris—the singer from Boyz II Men—was going to the hoop. The crowd went crazy.

The crowd was usually with me when I was put into the game. In our home opener, we crushed the Connecticut Seahawks by 30 points. I only got five minutes of playing time but was able to draw a hard foul and make both my free throws.

I soon realized that my opponents were playing extra tough against me. No one wanted to have his coach say, "I can't believe R. Kelly took you to the hole" or "I can't believe you let R. Kelly shoot a jumper in your face." Guys wanted to make me look bad. I can't say that I was a league leader, but I hung in game after game, I stayed in shape, I hit a few hard shots, and, mostly, I avoided humiliation. I believe I did myself proud.

Most importantly, I knew if there ever came a time to write my story, there'd be a chapter called "Semi-Pro."

It's a title I wear proudly.

When the season was over, there were hugs all around. My teammates and coaches all said I contributed to a championship season—and that was enough for me.

Meanwhile, music was calling me back to the studio.

ANGEL

"Why?"

"The public sees you as an R&B thug," said the music exec. "Celine Dion is a white Canadian woman with a squeaky-clean image. Her people are never gonna let her sing some song with a black dude from the 'hood."

"It's a ballad that I wrote for her and me. It's a love song."

"That makes it even worse. She won't go near it."

"Do you know her?" I asked.

"I don't need to. I know how this business works. You're running in one lane and she's running in another."

"What about 'I Believe I Can Fly'?" I asked. "That crossed over to every lane there is."

"Yes, but you sang that alone. Give her an R. Kelly song she can sing alone and she probably will. Tell her you want to sing a duet with her and she'll laugh in your face."

"I don't believe that. I want you to get this song to her and tell her I want to sing with her."

"Sorry, Rob, but that's just a waste of my time."

I left that meeting feeling discouraged but not defeated.

The exec didn't know what I knew: Celine was supposed to do this song. I wrote it shortly after my first daughter, Joann, was born. My baby had asthma. One night, she was coughing and wouldn't stop coughing. After she was calm and sleeping, I looked down on her and said, "Man, she's an angel."

253

A song was about to be birthed. As I wrote it, I heard Celine's voice all over it. It had to be. I didn't hear anybody else on that song.

I had my own connects. I'd get the song to Celine on my own.

A week later I was in the studio when an assistant handed me a note that said, "Celine Dion on the phone."

"Robert?" she asked. "May I call you Robert?"

"Of course. May I call you Celine?"

"Yes—and may I tell you that I absolutely love this song. 'I'm Your Angel' is beautiful. I understand that you'd like to sing it with me."

"I'd love to, if you hear us doing it together."

"I don't hear it any other way. Will you come to Canada? I want you to meet my husband and my family. I think you'll like the recording facilities here."

A week later, I was there. Canada was beautiful, and so was Celine's family. Everyone was gracious. The session was a breeze. Celine was happy to let me produce the song the way I envisioned it. We were in total harmony.

"I'm Your Angel" soared up the charts. When Celine was booked in Vegas, she invited me to her show. She got me a killer suite and treated me VIP all the way. Her show was off the chain.

When the music exec called to congratulate me on the success of the song—the same exec who'd been convinced that she'd never sing it with me—I accepted his best wishes. I wanted to tell him that he'd been full of shit. But I didn't have to. He already knew.

"I'm Your Angel" came out on the *R* album, along with "I Believe I Can Fly." It would be my last album of the '90s. I'd written so much new material that the CD was two discs with 29 tracks. The single that popped out first was "If I Could Turn Back the Hands of Time." In contrast to the club jams, "Time" was old school. I'd like to think it's a song that Sam Cooke could have sung. I had originally written it years before for my girlfriend Lonneice. Then when Mom died, I revisited the song, and it suddenly had deeper meaning. I kept revisiting it over the years, changing a note here or a lyric there. I always felt it was one of those forever songs, but, like all stories, I knew it would have its special place in time—if I could only be patient. The spirit would tell me when it was time to release it.

It came out at a special time in my life. In 1998, Drea had given birth to our daughter, Joann, named after my mom. What a moment! For years, people would tell me, "Rob, we made babies to your music." I had achieved one of the goals I set back on that porch with my Mom and her friends. Well, I got to the point where I wanted to make babies of my own. When I learned Drea was pregnant, I was overjoyed. My dream of a family was coming true.

I got to confess, though, that the night Drea went to the hospital, I didn't go with her. I'm one of those brothers who can't handle participating in the actual birth. It's a little too intense and the stakes are a bit too high for me if anything goes wrong. Birth is God's great miracle, and I thank Him for the gift, but the Lord and I have agreed that I'm supposed to head to the hospital after the baby is born and everyone's all cleaned up.

So, I paced the floor at Rock and Roll McDonald's near the hospital in downtown Chicago. Rock and Roll McDonald's is about the nicest McDonald's there is. You can be comfortable sitting there for hours. So while Drea was dealing with labor, I was drinking coffee with three creams and six sugars and feeling very nervous until they came and told me that, at long last, I was a father.

The first thing I saw in the face of my beautiful, gorgeous daughter was the face of my mother. Joann looked like Joann. Thank you, God.

Two years later, our second daughter Jaya was born, and three years after that, our son, Robert, Junior. All three times had me waiting at Rock and Roll McDonald's. All three times had me running to the hospital when word came that the baby was born. All three times had tears flowing from my eyes as I looked into the eyes of my children. They were, are, and will always be the greatest blessings of my life.

I adore my kids. When they were crawling on the floor, I crawled around with them, making a fool out of myself to make them laugh. When they got older and started talking, I found ways to keep them laughing. I played the games they played, watched the cartoons they watched. I love being a father.

In the beginning, Drea and I found ways to keep our love alive.

One afternoon I drove her 25 miles south of Chicago on Interstate 57. When we got off the highway, I had her put on a blindfold.

"Why?" she asked.

"You'll see," I said.

I pulled up in front of the giant gates of the mansion I had seen when I was 17 years old and a nobody—the same mansion I swore that one day would be mine. It had changed hands since I'd first seen it and was no longer the McDonald's house. The guy who'd I bought it from owned a Black hair products company; he'd turned the original house into the "Olympia Fields Castle" with a casino and marble fountains and all kinds of things in it. So I tore down the house and had a new one custom built from the ground up, a surprise I'd been working on in secret for months. I'd just shot a music video, and the location was kind of a ski lodge. I loved that warm, cozy feel so I took that look and remixed it.

"You can take off the blindfold now," I told Drea.

Right there in front of her, beyond the gate, was the biggest house she had ever seen. The grounds were enormous.

"It's ours," I said. "It's for our family."

She didn't know what to say.

"Our dreams are coming true, Drea." I said. "The fairy tale is real."

I wanted the fairy tale to last forever. On Valentine's Day I gave a big party and invited our friends. We had a picnic on the lawn, and at a designated time a helicopter flew over. I gave the signal and suddenly hundreds of red roses came falling out of the sky. It was raining red roses. Boxes with earrings and purses came down for the ladies. And for Drea, there was an oversized Gucci suitcase with furs inside. That was a good day. Other days weren't so good.

The love between Drea and me was under strain. Part of that was my fault, because I never was your conventional husband.

People look at celebrities like they're not human, but I'm just like the next man. I see fine women every day. Sometimes, I'm like, "Wow, wouldn't it be nice . . ." It's the way I was raised. I'm human. I'm flawed. I'm a man.

I've always carried two cell phones. One was for family calls, the other for nonfamily calls. Coming out of the gym one day, I mistakenly thought I had hung up on Drea when I took a call on the nonfamily phone. It was a woman I was sweet-talking.

Drea heard the whole thing. I tried to play it off, but couldn't. Finally Drea just said, "Robert Kelly, do you have something to tell me?"

"I do, and I'm sorry."

I was sorry that I didn't stop partying like I should have. I should have been a one-woman man, and I wasn't.

Another part of our problem came from Drea's love of dancing. That love got stronger and stronger.

From the start of our marriage, I made it clear that I needed a woman to raise our children and be my best friend and biggest supporter. This was the idea I'd put in the song "Homie Lover Friend" off *12-Play*. I couldn't fool myself. I always knew I wanted a stay-at-home wife to make my life work. Drea understood and, being a strong person, she tried her best. But when we went to see plays like *The Lion King* or dance companies like Alvin Ailey American Dance Theatre, the choreography thrilled her and reminded her how badly she wanted to get back into show business.

After one show, I made the biggest mistake of our marriage by introducing her to Debbie Allen. Debbie is Drea's idol. Meeting her was one of the true highlights of her life. I could feel the inspiration pass through Debbie into Drea. On one hand, that was great. On the other hand, it made Drea even unhappier because she wasn't able to dance full-time.

The times she helped me choreograph my shows weren't enough for her. She wanted to fulfill her own gifts. She wanted to get back into dance by employing a full-time teacher to give her private instructions. Naturally I was leery. I saw his picture. He was a good-looking guy, all cut and buff.

"You don't have to worry," said Drea.

Her word, though, wasn't enough for me. I went to meet the dude. Nice guy, and real honest, too.

"What are you doing talking to the man?" she asked.

"Look," I said, "he's got this real touchy-feely technique of teaching, and I have a right to know who the guy is."

"You got no right to stop me from studying with him."

"I got every right."

The dance instructor became a huge issue. It caused heavy resentment. But I put my foot down. Then I came up with a way to make things right.

"I'm buying you a dance studio," I said to Drea.

"A studio?"

"A whole studio."

"What am I gonna do with a studio?"

"Whatever you like, baby. You can teach there. You can rehearse there. You can put on recitals there. It's all yours. I'm even gonna help you design it. But you'll take the lead."

It happened. For a while, the studio made Drea happy. It got her back to dancing. It channeled her energy and gave her a new canvas for her creativity. It was a healthy and helpful professional outlet for her. Our relationship, though, was continually challenged.

Maybe it was me.

Maybe it was her.

Whatever it was, no matter how we adored our kids, no matter how hard we tried, the waters got rougher. Then the boat sprung a leak that kept getting bigger. The more we tried to bail out the water to keep us afloat, the more water we took on. Neither of us wanted this marriage to go under, but what could we do to keep it from sinking?

My relationship with Drea wasn't in good shape, But I was determined to rise to the challenge. *How could I turn up the heat?*

THE ISLEY BROTHERS
FEATURING
RONALD ISLEY
AKA MR. BIGGS

CONTAGIOUS

1. **CLEAN RADIO EDIT** (4:27)
2. **RADIO EDIT** (4:27)
3. **LP VERSION** (5:46)
4. **INSTRUMENTAL** (5:47)
5. **A CAPPELLA** (5:40)
6. **CALL-OUT HOOK** (:34)
7. **CALL-OUT HOOK #2** (:03)

(Zomba Songs Inc./R. Kelly Publishing, Inc. admin. by Zomba Songs Inc. BMI)

PRODUCED, WRITTEN AND ARRANGED
BY R. KELLY FOR BASS PRODUCTIONS, LTD
EXECUTIVE PRODUCERS
LOUIL SILAS, JR. AND RONALD ISLEY

CONTAGIOUS

Miami was a hot spot. I could connect to the music vibe in the studios and the sensuous vibe on the streets. Miami had that tropical fever that pushed creativity.

I was working on my new record when Ronald and Ernie Isley came to town.

Ever since Ron debuted in the role of Mr. Biggs, in our video for "Down Low," he'd been rolling. The Isley Brothers brand was back. Now they were looking for another hit.

"Wish I had one," I said, "but right now I've been pushing hard on other stuff. I'm really tapped out."

That's when the Isleys told me they just had a death in their family, and they needed something to lift their spirits.

"I understand," I said, "but nothing's poppin' off in my mind."

"Can't you make it pop off?" asked Ernie, who was getting angry. "Aren't you the guy who can knock off the hits just like that?"

"Well, Rob's a creative artist," said Ron, taking up my part, "and creativity ain't something you can turn on like a faucet."

"He's done it before," said Ernie. "Don't see why he can't do it again."

"Rob don't need that kind of pressure," said Ron.

"Or maybe he does," said Ernie.

It wasn't any fun listening to the brothers arguing.

"It's better that I have some time alone," I said, "to figure out a song for y'all. Once I get it, I'll call you."

"We got a plane to catch in two hours," said Ernie. "You sure you can't do it before we leave?"

"I'm sure," I said.

"No worries," said Ron. "You'll hit us when you got it."

"I will."

We said goodbye, and the brothers headed out to the airport.

I started listening and feeling my way into the music.

I understood that Ernie was down because of the death in the family. He was sad and wanted something to lift him up. I got that. But his feelings toward me were harsh and angry, and I was glad he was gone because those feelings could be contagious.

Contagious—that word stuck with me. Interesting word. Interesting concept. Interesting experience. An interesting story that could link up to where "Down Low" left off. I went to the keyboard and started fooling around with a little melody. The melody captured me and then the story started to flow:

It's 2 A.M. I'm just getting in about to check my messages,
No one has called but my homies and some bill collectors
. . . I two-way her, she don't hit me back, something is funny.
So I called her mother's house and asked has she seen my baby
Roll my six around looking for that missing lady
Got back in, turned the TV on, and caught the news
Then I put my hand on my head 'cause I'm so confused
Then I turned the TV down 'cause I thought I heard a squeaky sound,
Something's going on upstairs, and I know nobody else lives here
"Bump bump bump" as I get closer to the stairways all I hear
Then I hear my baby's voice in my ear screaming out . . .
You're contagious, touch me baby, give me what you got
(and then a man said) sexy lady, drive me crazy, drive me wild

"Contagious" was the name of the song. "Contagious" was what I'd been looking for. "Contagious" was perfect for the Isleys.

"Get Ronald Isley on the phone," I told my assistant.

Couple of minutes later my assistant said, "They're at the airport. They're about to get on a plane."

"Tell them not to. Tell them to turn around and come back to the studio."

They came, listened to "Contagious," and fell immediately in love with the song.

"When we gonna do it?" asked Ernie.

"Now," I said.

"Just like that?" he asked, reminding me of what he'd said before.

"Yes, sir," I said. "Just like that."

A few weeks later the record dropped and blew up. After all, it was contagious.

Insecurity is also contagious. I encountered a lot of insecurity when I worked on songs inspired by the Martin Lawrence/Eddie Murphy movie called *Life* for Maxwell, an up-and-coming R&B singer. Wyclef Jean did the score while I wrote and produced 10 original songs for the soundtrack album. I used artists that I loved. I had the great Kelly Price sing "It's Gonna Rain." The Isleys did "Speechless." DJ Quick and I did "It's Like Everyday." Brian McKnight sang "Discovery," and Trisha Yearwood, the wonderful country singer, did "Follow the Wind."

When it came time for the title song, "Life," I heard it for K-Ci and JoJo.

When Maxwell heard "Life," though, he wanted to sing it.

"This is a hardcore song," I told him, "about a long time in jail. It's not something you gonna relate to."

"I relate to the fact that it's the title song," he said.

"Makes no difference, Bro. I wrote a song for you that's just as good. Even better."

"But it's not the title song."

"Just listen to it," I said.

I played "Fortunate." I knew the song was killer.

"Record this," I said, "and you'll have a smash. You'll be able to tour behind it for the rest of your life."

"I still like that 'Life' track."

"Forget 'Life.' Cut 'Fortunate.'"

"I don't think so," he said.

I pulled out. If he didn't want to sing it, I would. But then his manager called and said Maxwell had changed his mind. He had a little pad he wanted to add to the song. Was that okay with me?

"It's all good, baby," I said. "I'm tellin' you, the song's a smash."

Maxwell's version of "Fortunate" went #1. It was one of the biggest hits of 1999 and won him the *Billboard* Award, the Soul Train Award, and a Grammy nomination.

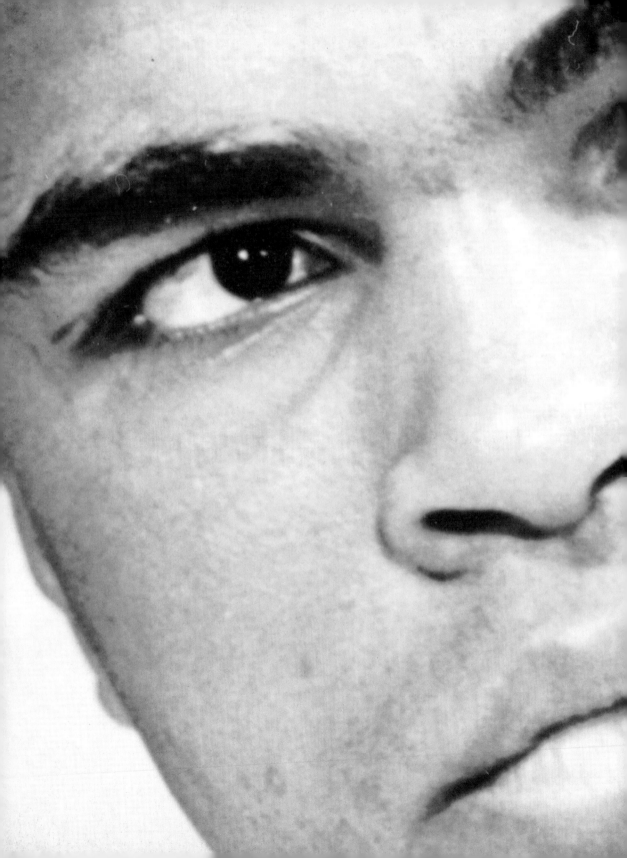

WORLD'S GREATEST

Hollywood kept calling. I did "Gotham City," a hit for *Batman and Robin*; and two songs for Samuel L. Jackson's redo of *Shaft*, "Bad Man" and "Up and Outta Here." Best of all, the producers of *Ali* asked for a song. I knew I'd have to find a groove that would float like a butterfly and sting like a bee. I knew I'd have to call it "The World's Greatest." I knew the words would have to honor this man in a way to make us both proud. I prayed for the right words, and God blessed me right away:

I am a mountain
I am a tall tree
Oh, I am a swift wind
Sweepin' the country
I am a river
Down in the valley
I am a vision
And I can see clearly
If anybody asks you who I am
Just stand up tall, look 'em in the face, and say

I'm that star up in the sky
I'm that mountain peak up high
I made it
I'm the world's greatest

267

I'm that little bit of hope

When my back's against the ropes

I can feel it

I'm the world's greatest

I am a giant

I am an eagle

I am a lion

Down in the jungle

I am a marching band

I am the people

I am a helping hand

And I am a hero

When the film premiered in Chicago, the arrangements got messed up and I found myself far from Muhammad Ali's entourage. When he found out, he sent word and had me sit right next to him during the showing. Man, you talk about a brother being proud! To have any connection with Ali was the honor of honors.

"There's a big connection, Robert," said Muhammad Ali, "because you got Sam Cooke in your soul. That connection is strong as steel."

As the movie showed, Ali and Sam had been close. Sitting next to Ali was bringing me closer to Sam.

I always had it in my mind to do something for Ali that he'd remember forever. "The World's Greatest" was a cool song, but it didn't convey everything I felt for him. A few years later, the idea hit me: like mine, his birthday is in January—I'm the 8th, he's the 17th—and I thought of the best gift I could possibly give him: an evening with Sam Cooke.

I planned a live concert at my house where I'd play the part of Sam. The living room is as large as a ballroom, and for this special night, we built a stage right in my living room. The first person I invited was Ali, but when I learned he couldn't come,

I arranged to film it and send him a copy with a card that said "Happy Birthday, to the Greatest."

I invited about a thousand people and told them to dress in period clothing. I made my band study the original arrangements for all of Sam's biggest hits. I brought in backup singers and dancers and spared no expense. I dressed in a black tux and black bow tie, and for an hour I became Sam Cooke. I sang my heart out for Ali, knowing that this was his man. But when it came time for "A Change Is Gonna Come," I had to stop and talk about me and my mother—how she'd tell me that one day my change would come and I'd entertain princes and kings. Far as I was concerned, there was no royalty more regal than Ali, no man more instrumental in instilling pride and courage in young black men.

After he watched the video at his home in Louisville, he called me to say that the show brought tears to his eyes.

"You sure Sam ain't your daddy?" he asked.

"Pretty sure," I said.

"Well, you sing like his son."

"I've never had a nicer compliment than that," I said.

Ali influenced me to do something I'd never done before. It happened in New York City, where I was booked on a popular late-night talk show. They were putting on my makeup when I looked in the monitor and saw the show host watching dogs do flips through hoops. After the flips, the trainer, a white guy, went to the couch to talk to the show host. He said some funny shit, and it was a good interview. I started wondering, *After I sing "I Believe I Can Fly"—am I going on the couch?*

"No," said my manager. "You just sing. No interview."

"Why?"

"We just want to sell records. We don't need an interview."

"But what if I want an interview? If the dog trainer can be interviewed, why can't the singer? It doesn't make sense to me."

"Don't make trouble. Just sing."

The more I thought about it, the more I didn't want to "just sing." I wanted to talk to the host.

Ali came to mind. When he was told what he couldn't do, he flat-out refused to accept it. He lived life on his terms, not the unfair terms offered to him. That's what made him a leader.

On the monitor, the announcer was saying, "Up next. R. Kelly!"

No. R. Kelly was not up next. R. Kelly was outta there. R. Kelly was leaving, getting into his car and going to McDonald's.

When the driver was about to pull away, the woman producer ran after me.

"Mr. Kelly," she said, "don't worry. We will be glad to interview you."

I went back in, went on TV, and sang my song before walking over to the couch.

In his hip style, the host cracked at me. In my own style, I cracked right back at him. We kicked it for a while. It was cool. My point had been made.

Ali

{The '90s was nothing but hits.}

R&B THUG

The '90s was nothing but hits. So I was eager to start off the new decade and fresh millennium with even more energy. I wanted to make more impact. I wanted my first record for the 2000s to be something that referred to the past but defined the future. I wanted it to be an album that showed all sides of me, and that would appeal to both my male and female fans. I called it *TP-2.com*. The *12-Play* tradition, which really started with *Born into the 90's,* was continuing, but this time I was taking it to the next level.

The first single that was released was "I Wish," a song I'd planned to do with Tupac. I originally wrote it about a friend of mine who I was supposed to go out to the club with, but I'd been so caught up recording in the studio that I told my friend to go on without me. He died that night in a car accident, and I wrote the song. I thought it would be perfect for me and Pac. You can hear Tupac's flow all over the way I sung/spoke the verses. The drama is about loss—not only the loss we felt when Pac left this Earth to go to a better place, but the loss we feel whenever a homie has moved on too soon. Violence is an ugly thing, and "I Wish" is a prayer for all violence to stop.

"Fiesta" was the next single to break out. On the album I had Boo and Gotti rapping. On the remix, Jay-Z came on board, and we had a smash hit.

Because *TP2.com* was the official follow-up to *12-Play*, I couldn't ignore the sexual theme. "Strip For You" pretty much represents the whole concept of the album. I couldn't imitate or just redo *12-Play*. I needed to figure out how to mic it differently but still be the same thing at the same time. I also had to continue the realness, so I had

273

to flip it. So on "Strip for You," instead of a girl stripping for me, I pulled a "switch-eroo," I say "Imma strip for you."

On the intro to *TP-2.com* I start out "*Hit it hard from the back. Roll around on the front. I know you heard a lot of tracks, but 12-Play's what ya want.*" When you're talking sex, it doesn't get more real than that. This time I wanted to try to go a bit more out there, but at the same time really being a little bit sarcastic, but creative at the same time. And saying, "Hey, I know what you want."

On "The Greatest Sex," I paint the scene on a bigger canvas. It's great sex—yes— but it's spiritual sex, where the lovemaking leads to the birth of a child. When I wrote it, I told people it felt like a sexual "I Believe I Can Fly" or a sexual inspirational song.

At the same time, some of my music is comical. It almost feels sexual, but if you listen to it closely, it's really funny. "Feelin' on Yo Booty" was a comedic sexual song, yet there's still a real song in there. You've got to be very silly to sing it and you've got to be a silly person to love it. I like to make people laugh and have fun. When you go to church, if the pastor at some point doesn't make you laugh, he probably ain't gonna make you join. You've gotta have a joke or two in there. You gotta do something to keep the crowd.

On *TP-2.com* I also wanted to show people who I am and let them feel the streets in me, not just the romantic Kells or the inspirational Kells. The song "R&B Thug" is about that. It's straight to the point—the streets of Kells. Where I grew up. I'm from the dirt, and a lot of people didn't know that. When they hear "Happy People" or "I Believe I Can Fly," it throws them off. I wanted the girls; at the same time, I wanted to let the guys know—no doubt about it—Kells is 'hood. I wanted to show the street side of me. I'm not a rapper, so I had to do it my way.

I wanted to conclude *TP-2.com* on a high note and leave the listener with a message of hope. I wanted to let my fans know that, no matter what they might be going through, a better day was coming. I put all that emotion in a new anthem called "The Storm Is Over Now." That song is the vegetables to go along with the meat and potatoes. Sometimes my music confuses people. I don't want people to think, *Well, Kells is just confusing me—he's gospel, he's sexual, he's trying to do too much.* But I believe in balance; no matter what, I believe in good, I believe in bad, I believe in ups and downs. I believe in partying, but then I believe in church. That's what "The Storm Is Over Now" is about.

What I didn't know, though, was that the storm had just begun—a storm like nothing I had ever seen before.

ACT THREE
{ In The Ring }

THE STORM

When you get to be a best-selling entertainer or a public figure, you're opening yourself up to attacks and lawsuits. When you're R. Kelly, everybody wants a piece. If you don't give 'em that piece, they'll find a way to get it out of you, one way or another. After you have lived long enough in the spotlight, someone will claim you did this, while another person will swear you did that. It's all part of the game. I knew that coming in.

During the '90s, I got hit with a bunch of lawsuits from several people making false claims. These suits were called "nuisance claims" and, according to my attorneys, it would cost me more money to fight the suits than to settle. The smartest thing would be to minimize the cost or I'd wind up spending 10 times the amounts fighting charges that could simply be settled out of court.

I followed my lawyers' counsel, but those suits were not about the truth—these people knew damn well that I hadn't done what they claimed; but they had hooked up with slick lawyers and were only about getting paid. I didn't like doing it, but I settled.

I've been blackmailed a million times in my career. I've been sued for ridiculous stuff that defies common sense. I can't say I'm used to it. You never get used to it. You just learn to expect it.

A superstar becomes an ATM, especially if you're the only star in your family. Everybody wants something from you, and most people feel you owe it to them.

"Buy me a car." "Buy me a house." "Furnish my house." "Buy me another house." It goes on and on. When you help your homies, they don't think you've helped them enough—so they diss you in the press. "All that mothafuckin' R. Kelly thinks about is his mothafuckin' self."

For years, I tried to balance being a responsible family member and loyal friend against the crazy demands on the part of folk trying to play me. It always seemed like if I gave someone something, it was never enough. If I gave 'em a lot, they wanted more. If I gave 'em more, they disappeared until they ran through what I gave them. Then they were back with their hands out.

Not everyone was trying to use me. Certain friends and family members showed me love without attaching a price tag. They never asked for anything. They were concerned about my welfare. They checked to make sure I was okay, not to see what they could get out of me. I loved them even more for their genuine care and affection. Devotion minus the money motive equals pure love.

Anyway, that was the '90s. Lots of annoying lawsuits, but they were all pretty much handled easily.

But then, in 2002, an H-bomb was dropped on me. After someone sent the *Chicago Sun-Times* a video that supposedly showed me having sex with a teenager, I was arrested and accused of child pornography. It didn't matter that there were real questions about the authenticity of the video; or that the girl the prosecutors claimed was on the video insisted no way it was her; or that both her parents, her grandparents, and several family members said the same thing. R. Kelly had a reputation, and R. Kelly had to pay. So what if that reputation was a fictional creation of crazy-ass music videos, sexy concert performances, and off-the-hook media hype that had nothing to do with who Robert Kelly really was. R. Kelly was going down.

I was looking at penalties involving long-term jail sentences. If I was found guilty, my career would be ruined in a single blow. Everything I ever worked for would be taken away. I'd be taken away. My kids would see their father as a criminal.

I knew the charges were bullshit; I knew I was innocent, but none of that mattered.

The press had a field day. News outlets began generating rumors and innuendo based on "anonymous" tips and interviews with supposed lovers, former employees, and associates who validated the charges against me. The media spread the lies with lightning-fast speed all over the world. I was presumed guilty long before my trial.

The flurry of uppercuts, jabs, and body blows was unstoppable. Before vowing not to participate in the media circus, I reacted like a woozy boxer throwing wild punches, hoping to slow the assault.

In 2000, my manager and I had parted ways. I thought we parted on fairly decent terms, but then I heard he'd sent a letter to reporter Jim DeRogatis at the *Sun-Times*, claiming that he had suggested I get psychiatric help for my supposed sexual addictions. I never found out if it was true, but it bothered me.

I don't have to tell you that the wheels of justice grind slowly. Man, this case grinded so slow, I thought I'd lose my mind. Nearly seven years! Seven years of having to ask the permission of the court whenever I wanted to leave Chicago. Seven years of lies, folk scandalizing my name, depicting me as a devil. Seven years of living with the sharp edge of a guillotine repeatedly hovering over my jugular. Seven years of sleepless nights and scary dreams. I was facing jail, financial ruin, the end of my career, the loss of my fans, and the loss of all respect and love.

Seven years is a long mothafuckin' time to be facing that kind of nightmare. To be honest, I felt like I was already in jail throughout those years. A lot was taken from me—my pride, my dignity, my passport, and a helluva lot of my money. It was a hell I wouldn't wish on anybody.

Throughout the ordeal, comments from many of my advisors went like this:

"Rob, you got to put a hold on recording."

"Don't tour until this legal mess is behind you, Rob."

"Robert, this is not the time to come out with sexy songs. Retreat until this thing blows over."

"The public isn't ready to accept any new material from you, Rob. Everything you write or say will be viewed under a magnifying glass. Better to say and do nothing."

I disagreed. The advice came out of concern for me, but I knew myself better than anyone. I couldn't see myself sitting around for years, twiddling my thumbs while lawyers fought with each other and court dates kept getting postponed. Truth was, if I was going to survive this ordeal, I needed my music to get through it.

I had to sing.
I had to write.
I had to produce.
I had to tour.
I had to connect with my fans.
I had to work with other artists.

Rather than retreat, I had to redouble my efforts. And I did. For those seven years, while I was under this dark legal cloud, I went out there and did more creative work than in any other period of my life. I might have done twice as much work. I turned the fear to energy. I went to work with a vengeance.

Sometimes negative situations can be more inspiring than positive ones. Struggle feeds passion; it fed my music. If I focused simply on the negatives I was going through, I would have just broken down. I didn't. My music held me together.

Not only did I need the outlet—the release from the anxiety brought on by these charges—I also needed the pure joy that comes when I'm writing a song. I needed the love that comes when I'm singing a song. I needed God, and God lives in my songs. God is strongest in me when I'm writing the melodies that He puts in my heart.

"You're wrong, Rob," said one advisor. "You're exposing too much of yourself. You're making yourself more vulnerable."

"Good," I said. "The more real that I am, the more powerful my music will be."

In the face of the charges, I was determined to sing even louder and prouder as I set out to make the most powerful music of my life.

The
more
real
that I am,
the more
powerful
my music
will
be.

WELCOME TO THE CHOCOLATE FACTORY

Welcome to the room I call the Log Cabin, the beating heart of my recording studio, the Chocolate Factory. For many years the Chocolate Factory was nestled in the basement of my home in Olympia Fields. The Chocolate Factory was my sanctuary, the place I could escape to when the weight of the world was bringing me down. And the weight often had me on my knees. The Log Cabin was where I recorded. It's made out of logs and different woods. It's small, intimate, and cozy.

There's nothing fancy about the Log Cabin. I use the same mic I've used for years. I sing my vocals right there where the engineers are sitting so that I can give them instructions, play something on the keyboard, or play one of the many instruments I keep close at hand; because while I'm singing, I'm also writing and producing. In the Log Cabin you'll also find my main engineers, Ian and Abel Garibaldi, and my musical director and guitarist, Donny Lyles—all of them have worked with me for years.

While I was hard at work in the Log Cabin, prosecutors were working overtime to build a bulletproof case. I can't tell you how many of the people making allegations were, at one time or another, the same people who had asked me for some sort of favor. A few of them were just pissed that I told them no. Sometimes people presented themselves as friends or allies and then just straight-up lied. I couldn't figure out why I was the only one who understood their motives. If someone messes up and you have to fire them, of course they're gonna be mad. The money they were getting, the fame, or whatever disappears. So anything that comes up about you, they're gonna run and say, "Yeah, he did that to me" or "Yeah, I knew that about him, too!"

I'd tell people who I thought were close to me: Listen to the facts! If you're gonna have an opinion about something, make it *your* opinion. But whatever you do, don't go by something said by somebody pissed off because they didn't get what they wanted from me."

Thank God I had the Chocolate Factory. It lifted me up. It was a safe place where I could create and reach for the sky from my basement.

As I faced the biggest challenge of my life and the brutal legal battle kicked off, I wanted to respond positively. I wanted to offer my fans—and myself—a big box of musical chocolates. I called the album *Chocolate Factory* and designed it in gold foil with a bright red ribbon on top.

Before the album came out, though, I wanted to release a single that explained where I was coming from. My life was on crutches, but I knew I'd walk again. I had many thoughts boiling up inside and I needed to get them out. Mostly, though, I needed to talk with my mother. I missed her so much. That's why "Heaven, I Need a Hug" starts with these words to her:

Dear Mama, you wouldn't believe what I'm goin' through
But still I got my head up just like I promised you
Ever since you left, your baby boy's been dealin' with
Problem after problem, tell me what am I supposed to do
See, I get lost sometimes, don't understand this place
Look in the mirror sometimes and see a troubled face
And then my tears roll down and hit the sink
Then I hold my head up high, I hope the Man upstairs can hear my cry
All these questions deep inside my mind
Like if Jesus loved me, why'd He leave my side, Mama?
I'm still trying to get the answer why
You were young, 45, and you had to die
I'm always tryin' to help people out

And it's them same people tryin' to take food out my mouth
It seems like the more money I make
The more drama y'all try to create
The more I try to move into the positive
The more y'all don't wanna let me live
Heaven, I need a hug
Is there anybody out there willin' to embrace a thug
Feelin' like a change of heart
And all I really need is a sign or a word from God
So shower down on me, wet me with our love
I need You to take me and lift me up

When I was through mixing the single, my people were telling me not to release it. Because of the court case, most radio stations had stopped playing my music. Naturally that made me mad. That meant they presumed I was guilty. I was already being punished. That's why this song, "Heaven, I Need a Hug," was so important to me.

"But that's why you can't put it out there," said one advisor.

"Why?"

"Because they'll use it against you."

"What's to use? All I'm doing is praying to my mother and God for guidance. I'm just singing what's in my heart."

"They'll twist it against you. They're just looking for material to make you look bad. You'd do better to find yourself a preacher and start meeting with him. We'll be sure the newspapers know that you've got a spiritual advisor."

"I've always had spiritual advisors—starting with my mother and continuing with Pastor Lena McLin. But I'm not gonna hook up with some well-known preacher to make me look good. I'm not gonna use a preacher to help my image. My image is in my music, not some phony public relations stunt."

"Look, Rob, 80 percent of all radio stations have banned you. Put out this song and it'll be 90 percent. Listen to me. I'm right."

I didn't listen to him because I felt he was wrong. When my fans heard my songs during that trial-by-fire period, I didn't want them to just hear a singer; I wanted them to hear a survivor. To me, it's not just writing songs, it's writing life. Whatever the story, the emotion, the calling is at that moment, I feel obligated to share it through my music.

I put out "Heaven, I Need a Hug," and the response was strong. Radio stations played it because my fans wanted to hear it. They heard my sincerity; they saw I was wearing my heart on my sleeve; and they started to send me thousands of notes and letters. Little by little, I started to get airplay again.

The hottest song on *Chocolate Factory* was "Ignition." I revisited the metaphor I had started with "You Remind Me of Something"—a woman and a car. I liked it so much I had to break off a remix and put it on the same album. In the remix, the groove got very danceable while the metaphors mixed together:

It's the remix to ignition
Hot and fresh out the kitchen
Mama rollin' that body
Got every man in here wishin'
Sippin' on Coke and rum
I'm like so what I'm drunk
It's the freakin' weekend
Baby I'm about to have me some fun

"You've lost your mind, Rob," the exec said when I told him I wanted to release "Ignition Remix" as my next single. "You can't release it with those lyrics."

"I can't change the lyrics," I said.

"Why?"

"'Cause they go with the song. They go with the mood."

"Maybe, but you've got to change the title. Given what you're facing now, you can't sing about sticking your key in the ignition."

"I don't see why not."

"They'll crucify you."

"I think the jam's so hot that they'll have to play it," I said

"I think it'll get you banned worse than before."

I didn't believe that. So I sneaked the cut to a disc jockey and asked him to test it on the air. That same night his phone lines lit up like a Christmas tree. People went crazy for it. I immediately made sure it was released all over the country, and the next thing I knew, it was sitting on top of the charts. The ban against me had been smashed by the power of music. "Ignition" turned out to be a monster hit.

It was important to me during that time to remain true to myself. To not sing about sex the way I'd always sung about it would have been an admission of guilt as far as I was concerned. Since I wasn't guilty—win, lose, or draw—I was determined to stay true to myself.

I was back. *Chocolate Factory* sold more than three million copies.

But in coming back, I wanted to show all sides of life, love, and struggle. I also wanted to give something back to my city. As the case against me lingered on, I received letters and messages of support from all over the world. But in Chicago, I received a special, familiar, soulful kind of love—the kind that just keeps stepping to you no matter the betrayal, hard times, struggle, or doubt.

I wanted to give the world the smoothest example of stepping, a Chicago dance style that I love. As I explained at the beginning of the remix of "Step in the Name of Love," stepping is more than dancing. It's a whole culture. It's a way of life. It's choreographed romance, a special mellow feeling that flows between a couple when they're out there on the dance floor. When you step, though, you step in the name of love. That's the important part. You're not just stepping to score with your lady; you're stepping and grooving in the name of love. And God is love. You're stepping but you're also feeling His spirit, His grace, His rhythms, and His holy rhymes. You got to keep on stepping, 'round and 'round, side by side, separate, and bring it back. And if anyone asks you, say, "We did it for love."

That was my strategy: beat the accusers, beat the prosecutors, beat the haters, beat them all—with love. They didn't understand: If you were hating on me, I got you beat 'cause I'm gonna keep loving on you.

People kept asking: "Rob, how is it you can keep doing what you do with all this drama surrounding you?" It may sound weird, but I just kept on stepping, kept on creating, kept on loving. Love lightened my load.

Once I knew my people were with me, I was gonna feed them the biggest R. Kelly banquet ever. I was gonna super-size my musical menu. In the same year that *Chocolate Factory* dropped—2003, when I turned 36—so did The *R in R&B Collection Volume 1*, a double-disc, hot-out-the-kitchen suite of remixes.

As the court case built, as the accusations piled on, I knew I had to keep on moving. I had to keep on keeping on. I had to stay focused and strong. I knew I had to keep playing hoop, keep releasing energy, and keep going back to the Chocolate Factory and making music.

Love lightened my load.

BEST OF BOTH WORLDS

The vision I'd wanted to bring to life with Tupac still haunted me. I wanted to marry rap and R&B in a way the world would never forget. With Biggie and Tupac gone, though, I wasn't sure who could fill the bill. There were strong rappers, but I needed the strongest.

For some time I'd been thinking about Jay-Z. He'd been moving up the food chain and building his audience. Our relationship had been cool. When he asked me to come off my *Down Low* tour to shoot the video for "Guilty 'Til Proven Innocent," I said yes.

He came to the premiere party for my video "I Wish," a song from the 2001 *TP-2.com* album. After watching it, Jay said he thought I'd captured Pac's vibe, and he asked if I wanted to work with him on something. At first Jay was thinking that we would do a single together. But when I suggested that we do an album, he was all for it.

That's how the Kells/Jay-Z collaboration began. I was excited, thinking that this could be the colossal R&B/rap merger I'd been dreaming of. We'd already done two collabos, in 2000 I'd sung the choruses on Jay-Z's "Guilty 'Til Proven Innocent" and in 2001 Jay-Z did a hot verse on "Fiesta Remix."

We cut an album together, called *The Best of Both Worlds*—the best of hip-hop meets the best of R&B—that was released in March 2002. We announced a tour that year to promote the album, but those plans were postponed after charges were issued against me. The following year, Jay dropped his *Black Album* and wanted to promote it. Just back from Europe, he needed to fill up giant venues around the country and knew I could help. *The Best of Both Worlds* did okay, but we both knew the real money could be made if we toured together.

In 2004, the idea of touring together and bringing the fans the *Best of Both Worlds* tour is what really got my creative juices flowing again. Jay and I had finished working on another album, *Unfinished Business*, with some of the unreleased tracks from our 2002 collaboration and a couple of new songs. The plan was to promote *Unfinished Business* during the tour.

I put all my energy into prepping and rehearsing for the *Best of Both Worlds* show. I had an idea for staging the opening frame: A video would run during its opening. Two tour buses—Jay in one, me in the other—would be on the run, pursued by police and media helicopters . . . One tour bus would crash through scenery on the right side of the stage; the other would crash through on the left. Then we would join up in mid-stage and do the title track, "The Best of Both Worlds," as our opening number.

Jay didn't love the idea at first, but he finally came around.

It turned out to be a spectacular opening. From there, though, things went downhill fast.

The most persistent problem was lighting. Since the start of my touring career with Levert, I've always been highly sensitive to lighting. It can make or break a performance. My lighting has to be exactly right. That's why I said, "Jay, let's settle on a mutual lighting guy—not your guy, not my guy, but a neutral guy."

"No problem," Jay agreed. "I think you're right."

At the shows my lighting was all wrong. The guy wasn't picking up my cues. The dramatic moments—when the mood needed to be dark and mysterious, or dim and sexy, or up and happy—were not lit to my satisfaction. Spotlights failed to find me on stage, and dancers were missing ques because of lighting disconnects during their routines. I tried to contain myself, but nothing means more to me than giving my fans an exceptional show. I threw a fit.

I'm a guy who choreographs his every move on stage. Now my fans couldn't see where I was on stage. I knew I wasn't imagining things because I record every tour show performance, so I can critique it the next day. Every *Best of Both Worlds'* tour tape that I played back was extremely disappointing to me and didn't measure up to my standards because of the lighting. Finally a crew member told me the truth—that the lighting guy was Jay's regular lighting guy.

I went to see Jay so we could discuss the problem without a lot of middlemen involved. I was sure that we could figure out a solution. I said, "Jay, the tour is about making us both look good."

"I realize that, Rob, and I know you're unhappy, but there's not much I can do about it."

"We can find another guy to do the lights."

"He's under contract. We're stuck with him."

We talked some more, promises were made that things would improve, and I left the meeting optimistic.

Later he came to me and asked, "Would you mind if I use that throne you built?"

"Go ahead and use it," I said, thinking that could calm the waters and get him to make his lighting man do right by me.

I had built this throne—a massive King of R&B chair—that I used during my middle segment in the show. The understanding was clear—after I used the chair, I'd leave it on stage so Jay could use it.

What happened, though, was that Jay's people got the chair for Jay to use before I came out. As a result, people were thinking that I was biting off Jay's style rather than the truth—that he was biting off mine.

Another thing: Before the show, Jay made a big deal about putting up big-screen advertisements for his *Black Album*. When I asked to have a big-screen picture of the current R. Kelly record, his people said no.

If the lighting had improved, I might have let all that bullshit go. But the lighting got worse. I did everything I could, even simplifying the lighting cues for my show so that I could at least have the bare minimum of lighting effects that I wanted, but even that didn't fix the situation. At one point, I became so frustrated that I left the stage during a show in St. Louis and went to the place that gives me comfort in times of trouble—McDonald's. But this time, I didn't go to eat. Instead I asked the guy working the drive-thru window if I could borrow his cap and uniform, and for the next three hours, I served Big Macs, fries, and Cokes to customers.

As the tour went on, Jay's crew and mine were at each other's throats; sets came to abrupt endings, shows were canceled, and all sorts of crazy shit popped off. By the time we hit Jay's hometown, New York, everyone was on edge. Considering the pending trial, the unnecessary drama was hard to handle.

Right before the Madison Square Garden concert in October 2004, I received a threatening phone call. When Jay-Z and I opened with our first act, there was a dude a few rows from the stage just glaring at me. He opened his coat in a way I considered threatening. I can't say for certain if he had a gun or not, but it was enough to put me on guard and mess up my groove. When I returned for my solo set, there was another guy in the bleachers opening his coat, gesturing like he had a pistol. When I left the stage for a costume change, I told my business manager and the promoter that I wasn't planning to risk my life finishing the show. The show's promoter convinced us that everything was cool, and we could go back out. On my way back to the stage, a member of Jay-Z's crew pepper-sprayed me dead in the face. Not only did he blast me, he got my booking agent and some of my crew as well. I had to go to St. Vincent's Hospital by ambulance where they put little tubes in both my eyes to flush chemicals out so I wouldn't lose my sight. If I hadn't been wearing my stage stunners, the doctors said that I might have gone blind.

As I was leaving the hospital, I was met by a group of reporters all asking me if I had heard what Jay-Z had said about me on the radio.

I told the reporters that I didn't know anything about it and that I had every intention of continuing on with the tour. It was only later that I found out he had said that I was jealous and insecure, and he called my actions "foolery."

When I arrived at Madison Square Garden the following day with the tour buses with my band, background singers, and dancers, we were turned away and not allowed to enter the building. In the meantime, several of Jay-Z's music friends had conveniently shown up to help Jay fill the show out and replace me. Even more conveniently, several friends had been there the night before and had finished the show while I was at the hospital. Jay-Z continued on the road without me. We found out later that the "friends" had booked their tour buses two weeks before the Garden show.

Later, I issued a press statement:

"The fans deserve better than this. I'd like the show to go on. It's really disappointing that Jay-Z and the promoter don't."

Charges, counter-charges, and lawsuits flew back and forth between me and Jay-Z, but neither one of us wanted to leave a bad taste in our fans' mouths. Our collaboration album, *Unfinished Business*, was officially released worldwide about a week before I left the tour. It debuted at #1 on the *Billboard* 200 chart in 2004 and went on to become another platinum-selling album. Although the concerts came to an abrupt end, our album delivered the full Jay-Z/R. Kelly suite to fans. The truth is, that although I'm a fan of his music, to this day, the business between me and Jay was finished.

The truth
is
the business
between me and Jay

was FINISHED.

HAPPY

It's ironic that some of the happiest music I've ever made came at the unhappiest time in my life. That's no accident. The longer the legal nightmare went on, the more I needed to make positive music. It wasn't only my natural instinct; it was my way of surviving a negative situation as well.

I was doing it for more than me. I was doing it for all people caught up in struggles. That's mostly everyone. So many of us are caught up in a financial mess, a medical mess, or a romantic mess—they're hurting for some kind of help. They need to turn their mood around and take away the pain. Music is the medicine. It's better than any drink or drug, plus there's no hangover or dangerous side effects.

Chocolate Factory had been a healing record for me and my fans. I wanted to outdo myself. I wanted to keep the love party going. I wanted to make the happiest record and, at the same time, the most spiritual record of my life. So, in 2004, I released a double-sided soul and gospel CD. One side was *U Saved Me*, and the other was *Happy People.*

I had to teach and preach my truth: Music makes me happy and saves me from misery. Name the singer who sings the saddest blues—like Billie Holiday—and I'll guarantee that while she was singing her blues, Billie's blues went away. Music cuts through the sorrow of life. It turns sad into glad. That was my purpose with "Happy People." Like Marvin Gaye's "Got to Give It Up," War's "All Day Music," or Sly and the Family Stone's "Everyday People," I wanted to give another long-lasting gift of happiness.

Throughout the record, I'm your friendly, feel-good "Weatherman," which is also the name of the first song:

1-2-3 L-O-V-E (love-love yeah)
What's up America and the rest of the world

It's the pied piper, your music weatherman
It's love-o'clock and we're broadcasting live
Right here from the Chocolate Factory
Where music ain't just music
But hit music, let's go

Steppers to the floor, steppers to the floor . . .

Around the time of *Happy People*, I was asked to sing the national anthem before the Bernard Hopkins/Jermain Taylor middleweight championship fight. I wanted to do something different, so I did a remix and created a stepper's version of the anthem. I choreographed my performance and brought real steppers into the arena while I performed. Most of the fight fans loved it. Some didn't. Someone said I had "Marvin Gayed" the "Star Spangled Banner." Time.com described my rendition as an "ill-advised smoovification" of Francis Scott Key's original song. I took all this as compliments. In the words of Sinatra, "I did it my way." And for those who said I disrespected the country, I wished them love by pointing out that singing and dancing can be beautiful forms of praise. I was praising the nation with my song, just like other songs of mine praise God.

God was the theme of the second disc, *U Saved Me*. The "3-Way Phone Call" echoed the struggle I was going through. I could be happy in *Happy People* by singing songs about sunshine and good times, but when it came to God, I had to come with all my fears. I had to come in the vulnerable state I was in. I had to call my sister and find my prayer partners. Through prayer, the rest of the songs flowed: "U Saved Me," "Prayer Changes," "I Surrender," "Spirit," "Leap of Faith," and "Prayer."

I always prayed for my wife and children. But I prayed for them more than ever during those years before my trial. For all the struggles Drea and I faced as a couple, I wished her nothing but peace of mind and happiness. Every day I thanked God for our three wonderful children—Joann, Jaya, and Robert, Jr.

The bottom line for me is always family. Nothing matters more to me than my family. No offense to God, but when my kids are around me, you wouldn't want them in heaven; you'd want them to stay at my house.

You wouldn't believe the good times we have. There's nothing I'd rather do than tell them stories about princes and princesses and castles in the air. Their minds are so open, their curiosity is addictive. My kids are my best audience, my favorite people in the entire world. I take them into the studio with me and watch them toy with the instruments with a skill way beyond their ages. They sing and write songs. And as much as little Robert loves his father's music, he might love Michael Jackson's a little more. He also has his MJ dance routine down to an art.

I love kidding and teasing my kids. Say we're watching *SpongeBob*; I'd purposely start calling Patrick—the starfish character—SpongeBob, the star of the cartoon series.

"That's not SpongeBob, Daddy," they'd scream, "that's his best friend, Patrick."

With "pretend" authority, I'd hold my ground. "Hey, kids, I know my cartoons and I know that's SpongeBob," I'd say pointing to Patrick.

When one of their friends came into the room, I'd switch over and start calling SpongeBob by his rightful name.

"That's right, Daddy," they'd say. "That's SpongeBob."

When their friend left and Patrick came on the screen again, I'd say, "Oh, here's SpongeBob about to get into more trouble."

"No!" they'd scream. "You got it all wrong!" But now they're playing along, screaming and laughing at the same time. I love making my kids laugh. But I also take pride in teaching them about success—not just the glamorous parts, but also the struggle and hard work that create success. I've always tried to be real with them about business.

At our house in Olympia Fields, Thursday was pool and pizza day. We'd spend the day together playing in the water. I remember one Wednesday night, though, I came to them and said, "Sorry, kids, but tomorrow I've got to go into the city for a meeting. I can't miss this meeting because it means a lot more money for all of us. So tomorrow I have to get all dressed up to make a good impression. I hate to miss pool and pizza day, but I have no choice."

"Daddy," said Robert, "you promised you wouldn't ever miss pool and pizza day."

"I know, son," I said, "but tomorrow is super important for my business."

The look in Little Rob's eyes made my "important" meeting seem silly.

On Thursday, I waited until the kids were in the pool before I put on a $2,000 suit, a $500 white shirt, and a $300 red silk tie. I shined my best black alligator dress shoes, grabbed a brand-new leather briefcase, and strolled out to the pool to tell the kids goodbye.

"How do I look, kids?" I asked, stepping fairly close to the pool.

"You look nice, Daddy."

"How about this suit?"

"It's a pretty suit, Daddy."

"How about this tie?" I asked, stepping a little closer.

"Pretty tie, Daddy."

"Well, your daddy's going into the city to do this big business deal," I said, stepping even closer to the edge of the pool. "And I don't want nothing to go wrong."

With that, I faked like I had slipped and, wearing all my fancy clothes and holding my briefcase, I went flying into the pool.

The kids howled with delight. I'd never seen them crack up like that. When I climbed out soaking wet, all they could say was, "Oh, Daddy, you're so crazy."

I love
making my kids laugh.

But I also take pride
in teaching them
about success

**not
just the
glamorous
parts,**

but also the struggle
and hard work.

I

never

miss

Juicy

Tuesday

JUICY TUESDAY

During my legal ordeal, not only did I keep making music at a crazy pace, I also kept playing ball like my life depended on it.

I hooped almost every single night, and tried not to miss a night; to this day, I never miss Tuesdays—they were the big night for intense hooping. It's come to be known as Juicy Tuesday. My niggas know I never missed a Juicy Tuesday: that's when the best shooters show up at the local gym. Sometimes even NBA players come down to bump elbows with me on Juicy Tuesday—it's fiercely competitive. Because I'm a night creature, we sometimes don't get started until around 1 A.M. or 2 A.M. and play for at least two hours. When my team wins, I love to ride the losers. Boasting rights are big with me. I get a kick out of pointing out how many games we've won in a row and how badly we crushed the other side.

On one particular Tuesday night in 2004, I was warming up when my security guy spotted an unfamiliar brother hanging around. He asked me what he should do about the stranger.

"Ask him his name," I replied.

After asking, the security guy came back and said, "Says his name is Charlie."

"Well, go ask his last name."

Few seconds later, my man said, "Says his name is Charlie Wilson."

"The Charlie Wilson?" I asked, "Charlie Wilson of the Gap Band?"

I went right over to him and saw that it really was *the* Charlie Wilson!

"Man," I said, "it's really good to see you—been loving your music forever. Just didn't expect to see you here. Whassup?"

"I came all the way to Chicago looking for you," Charlie answered. "The cats told me this is where you come on Tuesdays, so I figured I'd take my chances and try to catch you. I'll be honest with you, Bro. I need a hit."

"I can't believe this," I said. "Charlie Wilson is coming to me for a hit? After all those years of studying you, the least I can do is write you a hit."

"Then you're willing?"

"It'd be an honor."

"When do you think you can get started, Rob?"

"Right after I hoop. Hang around, Charlie. The minute I'm through playing, we'll head to the studio and start working."

After the game, Charlie and his woman came to my house, and I took them right to the Log Cabin. By then it was around 4 A.M. While I was fooling with ideas, they fell asleep in the easy chairs behind the engineer's board. I was happy they did. When I start writing, the early drafts are sometimes pretty crazy. The spirit of criticism in the room can sometimes dampen my groove. I need to be free to go in whatever directions, twists, or turns the song may take. If, for example, someone says, "Oh, man, that sounds terrible," it can throw me off the journey and ruin the whole operation.

Talking about operations, later when I told a business associate about how I'd met Charlie and immediately took him to the studio, the associate said, "You were going to write and produce a song for him without a contract? Didn't you want to have a signed document before you began working?"

"If a patient goes to the emergency room and asks a doctor for help," I said, "should a doctor start asking if he has insurance? The brother asked for my help, and I was the man he came to. I wasn't about to do anything except help him out and write him a song."

The song came to me quickly. The creative process followed our real-life encounter on the basketball court: I remembered when security told me someone named "Charlie" was hanging around and how I asked about his last name. That's how I came up with the song's title, "Charlie, Last Name Wilson."

When Charlie woke up, I had the song. But, before singing it for him, I felt I had to say something: "No disrespect, Charlie, but there's a whole new generation out there who don't know who you are. I want this song to be all about your name. You're introducing yourself to a whole new world of fans."

"You got that right, Rob. No argument there."

"That's why I want this song to have your name. Fact is, I want this song to be all about your name. You're not only introducing yourself to a fine honey at the club; you're introducing yourself to a whole new world of fans as well."

I played it and Charlie loved it. Right then and there he sang it. He didn't argue with any of my direction. He understood that he was putting on a custom-made suit that fit him perfectly.

"It ain't right how you turn out hits so easily," Charlie joked when we were through.

"It's easy when I'm writing for you," I said. "Real easy."

"Charlie, Last Name Wilson" did what we had hoped—it introduced Charlie to a younger R&B audience. It was the name of his first single, a major hit, and also the name of his album, which sold more than 71,000 copies in the first week of its release. The album went to the #10 spot on the *Billboard* 200 chart in 2005 and was eventually certified gold, with sales surpassing the 500,000 mark.

Charlie was back, and now everyone knew his name.

That year, my work schedule was beyond crazy. There were songs I was writing for other artists; there were the remixes of my old songs; and I was hard at work writing and recording my seventh studio album, which I'd decided to call *TP.3 Reloaded*.

The wait for the trial became even more drawn out. The pressure of the accusations served as my motivation to keep working on songs, songs, and more songs. I could go 48 hours straight without sleep. If I did manage to fall asleep, an idea would wake me and shake me until I had to run down to the studio and start recording what was in my head. Like a cannon stuffed with cannonballs, my head was stuffed with songs. Night after night, day after day, week after week, I kept firing a cannon that never emptied.

"The legal stuff is getting complicated, Robert," one of my lawyers told me, "so please, be conservative in your music."

Impossible. I couldn't rein in my music any more than a fisherman could rein in an alligator.

I was still reaching for more daring metaphors. I believed I caught a good one with "Sex In the Kitchen," where I was able to marry two human comforts—food and sex.

Girl, you're in the kitchen

Cookin' me a meal

Somethin' makes me wanna come in there and get a feel

Walk around in your t-shirt

Nothing else on

Struttin' past

Switchin' that ass

While I'm on the phone

I want sex in the kitchen

Over by the stove

Put you on the counter

By the butter rolls

Hands on the table

On your tippy toes

We'll be making love

Like the restaurant was closed

There were other sexy songs on *TP.3*. I got deep into the slow-grinding reggae jam "Slow Wind." I found another wild metaphor when I told the honey to treat me like a "Remote Control" ("Touch me, turn me on, make me sing a song, now put me on slow, push enter, now fast forward, girl, you got me programmed under your control");

"Hit It Till the Mornin'" (featuring Twista and Do or Die); and "Sex Weed" ("Girl, you got that sex weed, I just wanna hit it all the time . . . how did your sex make me feel this way, like I've been smokin' purple haze).

These songs were cool, and they kept my musical engines burning. I wanted to be heard in the club and I wanted to be played on the radio. But my mind was also expanding into a whole different form. I started seeing way past a single or even an album concept. What I saw confused me: my music started to look like an opera with a winding, connected storyline that underscores human drama and everyday complications.

You might say that the other forms—the ballad, the club jam, the sexy dance groove—were starting to make me feel a little trapped.

Trapped was a word that played nonstop inside my head.

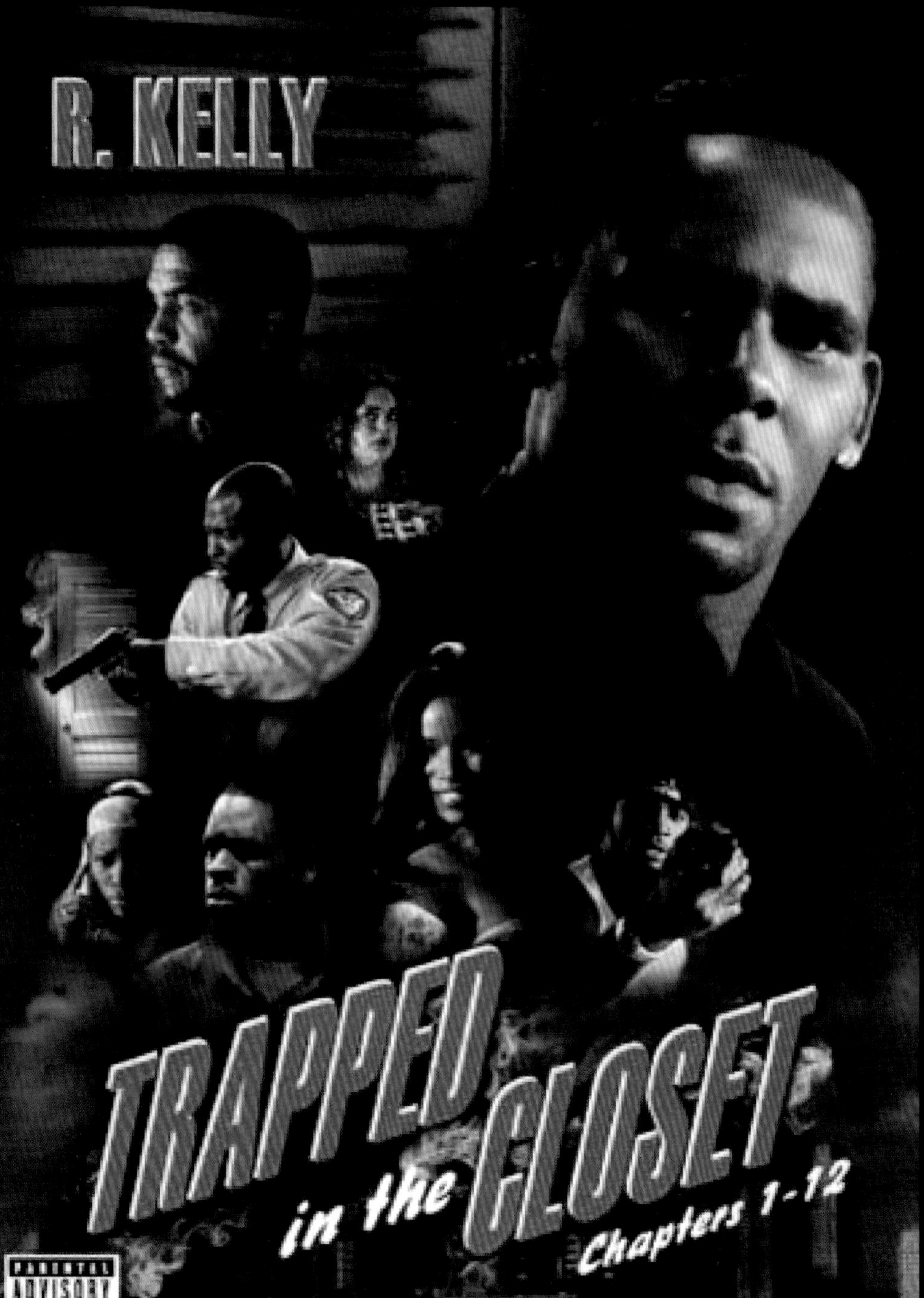
R. KELLY
TRAPPED in the CLOSET
Chapters 1-12
PARENTAL ADVISORY
EXPLICIT CONTENT
DVD

TRAPPED

You could draw a lot of conclusions as to why, during this seven-year period leading up to my trial, I suddenly felt like I needed to branch out into a longer musical form.

Maybe it was the letdown from the canceled *Best of Both Worlds* tour that made me want to retreat to my basement in the Chocolate Factory. Perhaps I was going back in time to take refuge in that period when Lena McLin exposed me to singing, theater, and opera. Maybe my legal dilemma inspired me to think about other people who were also under the gun. Maybe I was just feeling increasingly trapped and the concept was something I had to think about and deal with every day. Maybe it was all these things. Whatever it was, the idea of *Trapped in the Closet* crept up on me like an alien from another planet. I didn't go into the studio with the intent of writing a screenplay. But the lyrics:

"7 o'clock in the morning and the rays from the sun wake me,
I'm stretching and yawning in a bed that don't belong to me . . ."

Just came into my head, and as I sang them, I could picture the entire scene in my mind. Unlike my other songs, where lyrics led to video, *Trapped* came to me as a drama in need of a score.

The song scared me at first. I had no idea where the story was going; it had a life all of its own. After I was two minutes into it, still singing the verse, my crew in the studio started screaming how much they loved it. And I was just as curious as they were to find out what would happen next. Their reaction fueled my desire to move from writing verses to actually writing chapters.

311

Chapter 1 finds my character, Sylvester, the narrator, waking up in the bed of a married woman. Her husband comes home and he's forced into the closet. His cell phone rings; her husband searches for the sound. While in the closet, Sylvester sings: ". . . checks under the bed, then opens the dresser; he looks at the closet, I pull out my Beretta."

Chapter 2 opens with a confrontation at gunpoint. The woman's husband, a preacher, has a confession to make. He's been on the down-low and figures his wife's actions are good enough reasons for him to come out of the closet about his love affair with a man.

As the chapters progress, we learn that Sylvester's woman is at his house kicking it with a policeman—the same cop who gives Sylvester a ticket on his way home—and on and on until the complications can't get any more complicated.

One character led to another; one scene led to another, more intriguing scene; one betrayal seeped into other more whacked-out betrayals; and tricky situations became even trickier and each chapter ends with a cliff-hanger. Yet, everything was part of a grand scheme.

"Trapped in the Closet" started as a single, 16-minute "song" that I recorded for *TP.3*. When the executives at the label heard it, they didn't know what to make of it—a 16-minute song with no chorus and no hook? The president of the label said he wasn't sure if it was a work of genius or insanity.

To their credit, they supported that vision and let me fulfill a lifelong dream of mine. Although I'd always come up with the concepts and co-directed my music videos, but *Trapped* was so much more than a music video— this was a mini movie. I was involved in every aspect, from set design, casting, costuming, editing, teaching the actors their parts—everything. We did everything like it was a movie and a lot of the crew we hired were movie people.

In the beginning I was a little worried about whether the actors would accept me acting with them and giving them direction, because this was my first time really working outside a music video; but it was smooth, and I gained a lot of confidence doing *Trapped*. And my co-director, Jim Swaffield, had some great ideas about how we could achieve some of the things I wanted to do without having Hollywood money to do it. But I'm definitely ready for the movies now. Even before I was a singer, an artist, I wanted to be a director. I love telling stories, and *Trapped* is quite a story.

On *TP.3*, I included the first five chapters on CD, and the initial run of the album included a DVD of the mini-series. Before it was over, there were 22 chapters—and, to be honest, it's still not over. The chapters were more than songs; they were scripts. Soon they were long-form videos where I played five different roles—Sylvester, old man Randolph, Reverend Mosley, James Evans, and Pimp Lucious. Everything about *Trapped* challenged me—the writing, directing, acting, production, and the way we packaged and presented it to the public.

The plotting of *Trapped* had me in creative heaven. I could let my mind fly free at a million miles an hour. When I'm working on *Trapped*, I put the music on the speakers in the studio and the story just comes. In the beginning, I had no idea what was going to happen next; the story wrote itself and I was as curious as everybody else to find out. My biggest concern was about the rhyming. And that has had an interesting effect on the story. For example after I had introduced the character "Bridget", it was only a matter of time before I came up with the character "Little Man." It was like I was a novelist writing about how our lives are all interconnected, which was the point of the whole drama. As people living in a community and in the world, we all impact one another. What I do to you and you do to her and she does to him and he does to someone else is an endless chain of incidents with real-life consequences. No doubt I was inspired by the "stories"—the soap operas that my mother and grandmother obsessed over every day when I was growing up.

Everyone has a secret. Everyone has a closet that he or she is trapped inside of, and everyone—believe it or not—wants out of that closet.

I remembered back in Miss McLin's class at Kenwood, when she'd play an opera and tell me how I could sing and write like that. I didn't see how. "You think you can't, Robert," she said, "but I know differently. I know you have this dramatic flare and the gift to tell a long story in your own style."

Like an opera, *Trapped*, my very own "hip-hopera," is a long story where characters never stop singing. It isn't like a musical where there's talk, then a song, and then more talk. The story is told in wall-to-wall song. A single musical theme weaves it all together. And there's a conclusion to each chapter, a cliff-hanger that comes at the very end to shock and tease and make you say, "What the hell is gonna happen next?"

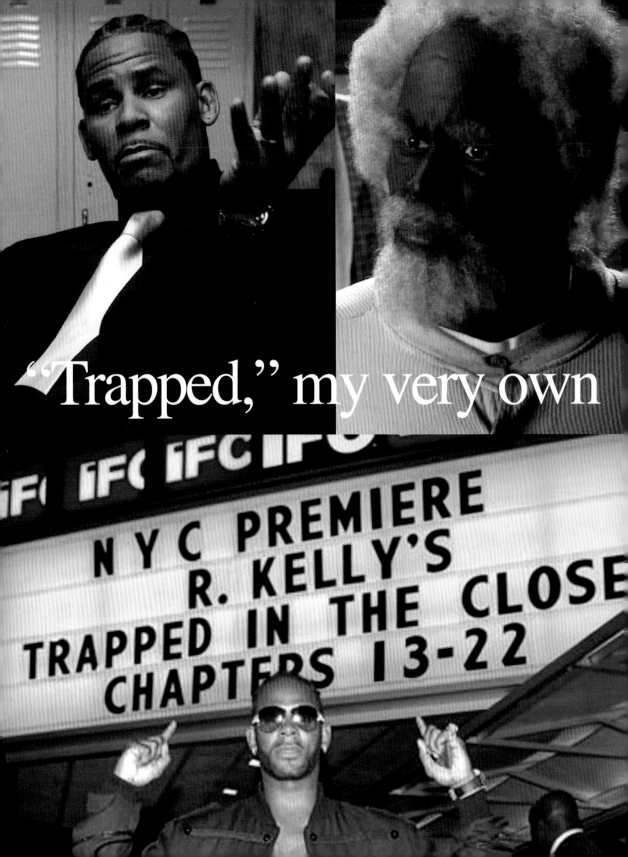

"Trapped," my very own

"hip hopera."

Stay tuned.

When I got the label to commit to filming the first five chapters of *Trapped*, some folk doubted me. They warned my producer, "Rob's a vampire. He sleeps all day and works all night, and he'll never show up at the film studio for those morning shoots. He'll never stop recording long enough to do a film project this complicated. It'll be a bust."

They were wrong. I showed up on time every day. I didn't miss a single rehearsal or early-morning call. In fact one day I even got there before the producer did! Directing and acting in *Trapped* helped me feel less trapped. While filming, something else happened that surprised and thrilled me: my producer, who also produces theatrical movies, talked about *Trapped* being a script, and she called me the "writer." I told her that I can "write songs" but I can't write; hell, I can't even spell!

If you pulled the music out of *Trapped* and just listened to the words, she answered, it's no different from any screenplay she'd ever read, except that with my work, everything rhymed.

"You're a writer, Robert. Believe that."

And for the first time, I did.

During the filming of the first five chapters of *Trapped*, I began writing the next seven chapters. We released a DVD of Chapters 1–12, and it got nominated for a Grammy for Best Long-Form Video. From 2005 to 2007, we filmed a total of 22 chapters. Chapters 13–22 debuted on IFC.com, the Website for the Independent Film Channel, over a 10-day period. The Website's traffic for that period—which normally averages around 300,000 per month—skyrocketed to 8 million in 10 days. IFC eventually played all 22 chapters strung together as a movie with no commercials. The press was crazy; everybody was loving it. Half the journalists wondered if I was a crazy genius; lots of people wondered whether I realized that it was funny. Lots of people did their own versions of *Trapped*. Weird Al Yankovich did one; Jimmy Kimmel did six chapters on his show, which featured Mike Tyson and Alanis Morrissette; and *South Park* did a *Trapped* episode that was actually banned in England.

Eventually, we compiled all 22 chapters, including a "commentary remix" and a preview of Chapter 23, into one DVD called *The Big Package*. The songs and videos earned all sorts of awards and accolades.

Chapter 22 remains the biggest cliff-hanger of all—it's the chapter where I first introduce "The Package." The package links all of the characters: One character calls another character saying, "he's got the package" about a third character. Then all of the characters are talking simultaneously about the mysterious package. The package has literally become a point of continuing intrigue. Because the package links all the characters, it shows how rumor and innuendo can spread in a community and society. I've heard a lot of theories about what the package is; some ideas are crazier than the next. Want to know what it really is? I'm saving that for the next cycle of *Trapped in the Closet*.

Stay tuned.

THE BREAKUP

The story of the end of my marriage wasn't fiction. It was a real story, a sad story. Like most stories about long love affairs gone bad, it had lots of drama.

In that way, I'm no different than millions of people struggling with their relationships. It gets good, it gets bad, it gets crazy. You want it to work because love is what brought you together. You want to regain that love, make it new, make it stronger, and hope it sees you through. You try like hell. You fail, but you get up and try again.

If you have kids, you know how much they want mommy and daddy to stay together. Divorce scares kids, confuses them, and makes them think they're the ones who've done something wrong. The last thing in the world you want is to frighten your children and mess with their security. But life can pull a man in one direction and a woman in another. No matter how much you pray to stay together, life sometimes tears you apart.

The collapse of my marriage happened during the same seven-year period when the court case against me was building while, in reaction, my creative life was boiling.

I knew that Drea wanted to be doing more with dance. Over time, it became difficult for her to accept that in our family, my career had always come before hers.

I understood her frustration, but at the same time she knew the deal going into our marriage. I never hid how important it was for me to have a stay-at-home wife. I knew myself well enough to understand that nothing else would make me happy. In the beginning, Drea seemed happy with that arrangement.

But people change. They think they want one thing and then realize they want another. That's life, I suppose. And that's why I started the dance studio where Drea choreographed two of my best tours. I thought that the studio would be enough.

It wasn't.

As time went on, Drea's resentment grew. I could understand that. It's no walk in the park being married to a man who likes to sing about sex and attracts sexy women wherever he goes. I also can't say that I was as faithful as I wanted to be or should have been. That's another reason why Drea lost patience with me.

Towards the end, our arguments got nasty. Drea doesn't give ground, and I don't either. If we were going out and I thought her hair was styled in a way that didn't bring out her beauty, she didn't want to hear about it from me.

"It's my hair," she snapped, "I don't need you to tell me how to wear it."

"Baby," I said, "you're a beautiful woman, but you don't have the right-shaped head to wear hair that high."

"That's your opinion, Robert. When I want your opinion, I'll ask for it."

"Well, excuse me, Drea, but up until now, you've always been interested in my opinion—just like I'm interested in yours."

"Right now I want to be left alone."

So I left her alone, but the more time passed, the elephant in the room got so big until there wasn't any room left for the two of us.

Once I was in the whirlpool at home. When I got out, I cut my foot on a bottle that I'd left on the floor. The cut was bad, and as I walked around the house, I left a trail of blood. It looked like a massacre. I was waiting for Drea to say something, show a little concern, but she didn't say a word. Maybe she figured I could take care of myself and get to a doctor on my own. I didn't want that. I wanted her to take care of me. She finally broke down, cried, and took me to the doctor.

There were moments when we took care of each other's feelings and were still respectful. More and more, though, there were moments when she didn't want to deal with me and I didn't want to deal with her. We were living in the same house, but we were a million miles apart.

{ *"All right," I challenged her, "if you really don't love me, I dare you to take off your wedding ring and throw it into the pond out back." Her wedding ring, by the way, cost $50,000.* }

Drea took the dare.

"plunk!"

Man, I couldn't believe it. I offered $10,000 to anyone who could fish that ring out of the pond. No one could.

Living with me was rough. Under all the pressure, I'd gotten out of shape and gained weight. I'd gone from being R. Kelly to R. Belly. I was eating wrong and not getting enough sleep. I was irritable. Drea said I was taking my frustrations out on her. She was probably right, but I gave no ground.

"The way you're acting around here," I said, "I don't think you love me anymore."

She didn't answer. She knew her silence would make me mad.

I said it again: "I don't think you love me, Drea."

Again, she said nothing.

"All right," I challenged her, "if you really don't love me, I dare you to take off your wedding ring and throw it into the pond out back." Her wedding ring, by the way, cost $50,000.

"You don't want to dare me," she said.

"The hell I don't."

"You might not like what your dare will make me do."

"I'm still daring you," I said.

Drea took the dare. She marched out to the yard and threw the ring in the pond—"plunk!" Man, I couldn't believe it. I offered $10,000 to anyone who could fish that ring out of the pond. No one could.

The drama built. Drea started talking about divorce. In a fit of anger, I told her I'd rather throw all my money into Lake Michigan than give her one cent. She said she'd take the children and, one night, she did. She was even able to get a restraining order against me. All this happened when my serious legal problems were getting more serious every day.

To Drea's everlasting credit, though, she proved loyal when it really mattered. Even as we were steamrolling toward divorce, she never bad-mouthed me to the media. As a matter of fact, she did just the opposite. In a long interview with *Essence* magazine, Drea—the woman exiting my life at the time—vouched for me. When the writer asked about the charges against me, Drea said: "C'mon, who would believe all that? That's why they call them allegations."

Being the lioness that she is, Drea said her number-one priority was keeping our kids shielded from the media madness in our lives. Although our divorce was imminent, one of Drea's comments in the *Essence* article touched my heart:

"Whatever happens to us, I will love that man to the day I die."

Her faith in my innocence took some of the bitterness out of our divorce, but it was still a tremendous blow. As a kid, I'd always dreamed of a happily-ever-after marriage. The destruction of that dream was heartbreaking for everyone—Drea, me, and especially the kids.

After I knew it was over—after I knew that all the king's horses and all the king's men couldn't put Humpty Dumpty back together again—I decided to go to the movies to get away from it all. I went by myself and saw a love story called *The Notebook*. I loved every minute of that film. It was about a man and a woman from different walks of life who made it through all kinds of obstacles. Their relationship was challenged, but their love conquered every one of their challenges. In the end, living in an old-age home, they died in each other's arms. As the film credits started to roll, I couldn't move. I burst into tears. People walking past me patted me on the back, trying to console me.

The Notebook was beautiful, and I was crying because its hero and heroine had died together. But I was also crying because I remembered a Valentine's Day—when a helicopter dropped a rainfall of roses—that had come and gone. My marriage had died. And there was nothing I could do to bring it back.

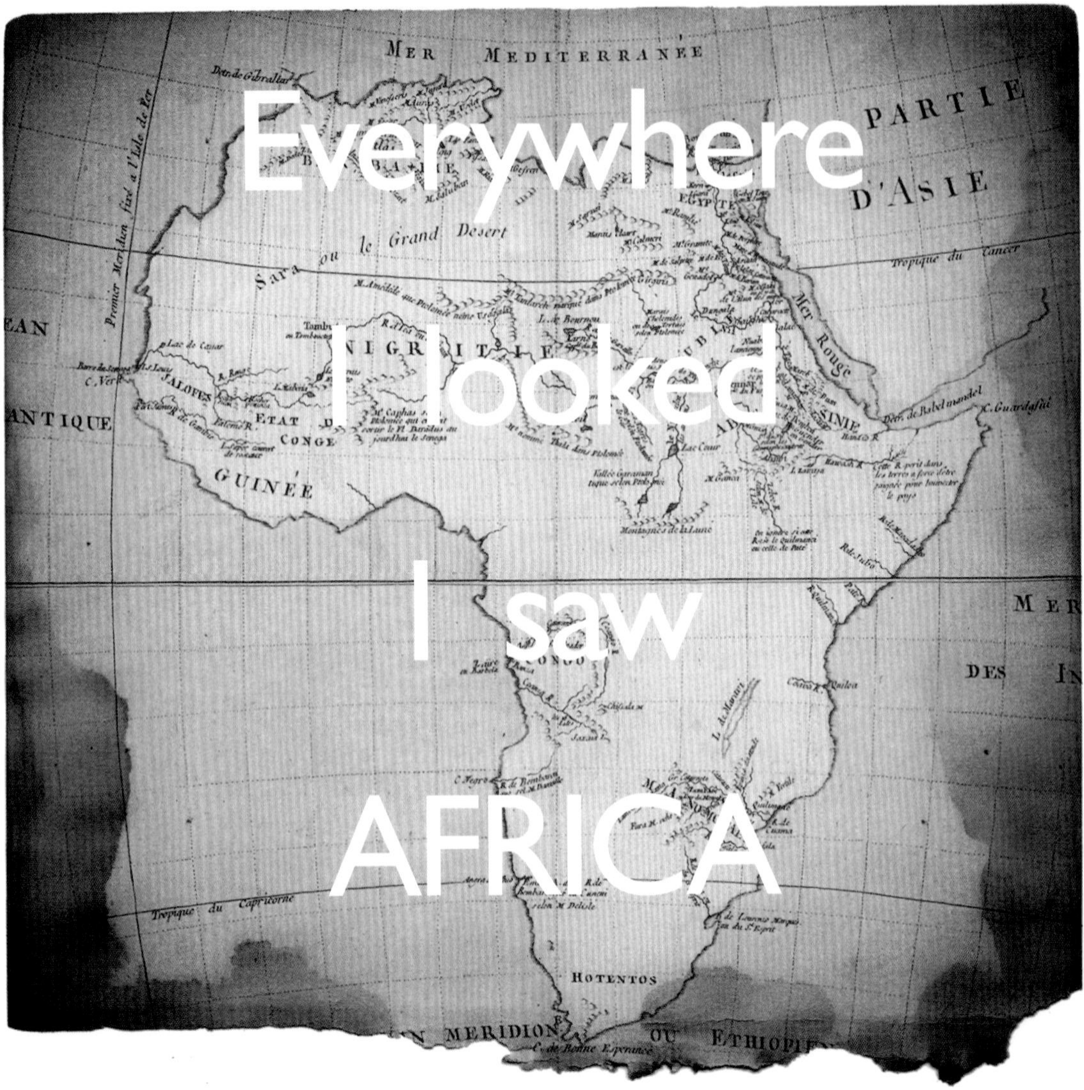

Everywhere

I looked

I saw

AFRICA

MER MEDITERRANÉE

PARTIE D'ASIE

Tropique du Cancer

Sara ou le Grand Desert

NIGRITIE

GUINÉE

ÉTAT DE CONGO

Montagnes de la Lune

MER ROUGE

SINIE

C. Guardafui

Dét. de Babelmandel

MER DES INDES

Tropique du Capricorne

HOTENTOS

MERIDION OU ETHIOPIE

C. de Bonne Espérance

Premier Meridien fixé a l'Isle de Fer

C. Vert

OCEAN ATLANTIQUE

STILL WAITING

The beginning of another new year: 2007. The hearings, the depositions, the postponements. Long years gone by, and the trial still hanging over my head. Still praying, still keeping my chin up. What to do? Make more music. Redouble my efforts. I made an album called *Double Up* that dropped in the spring of 2007, five months after my 40th birthday.

The title track had me reunited with Snoop, and on other tracks I hooked up with Swizz Beatz, Nelly, Chamillionaire, T. I., T-Pain, Usher, Huey, Ludacris, Kid Rock, Polow da Don, and Keyshia Cole.

There's a story behind the first single, "I'm a Flirt Remix." Originally I'd done the song for Bow Wow's album, and it was supposed to be his second single. But when I got a copy of the album, the song wasn't listed anywhere. Turns out they had made it a bonus track. I loved the song, and I didn't want it to go to waste, so I decided to remix it and do my own version. I called in T. I. and T-Pain to get on the track with me, and they blessed the record. From a bonus track on someone else's album, "I'm a Flirt Remix" went to #1 on the Rap Chart, #2 on the Hip-Hop and R&B charts, and #12 on the Hot 200 chart.

Double Up hit #1, and the collaborations, including "Same Girl"—my duet with Usher—were big hits. But the two songs that got lots of attention were the ones where I once again messed with the metaphors.

"The Zoo" was my very own version of the film Jurassic Park:
Girl, I got you so wet, it's like a rain forest

325

Like Jurassic Park except I'm your sex-a-saurus baby
You and me hoppin' like two kangaroos
Rattlin' and moanin' out here in these woods

The other song was "Sex Planet":

Jupiter, Pluto, Venus, and Saturn
I'm leaving Earth to explore your galaxy
Ten to zero, blast off, here we go
We'll be climaxing until we reach Mercury

For reasons I can't explain, the song became a big hit with indie rockers and made a number of their top 10 lists in 2007.

On the street though, the song that people were talking about was "Real Talk." It was raw, it was funny, it was real. I made my first viral video for "Real Talk," low budget and raw and straight to the point.

As year after year went by and the trial drew closer, my frustrations sometimes got the best of me. I prayed for calmness and acceptance, and sometimes calmness and acceptance entered my heart. Other times, though, like a caged beast, I got tired of being behind the bars of judgment. I was weary of folks assuming they knew everything about my life, assuming I just had to be guilty, and people thinking the worst of me. I was just tired of it all.

At the same time, I was listening to up-and-coming singers copying my style—from the sound of my vocals to the type of songs I write and sing. That's okay. In the beginning, I bit off the styles of Charlie Wilson and Aaron Hall, just like Ray

I'd rather be hated fc

Charles bit off Nat King Cole's style at the start of his career. Like everyone else, we need role models until we develop our own musical personalities. Everybody starts out singing what they know, what played in their houses, their neighborhoods, and on the radio. It's just the way it is.

In the beginning it was flattering. But then it became annoying when certain singers started creating press for themselves by bad-mouthing me. Suddenly they were telling me what to do. From the first day when I was starting out until this very day, I would never in a million years tell Stevie Wonder what he should do with his music. I have too much respect for the man. He came before me and paved the way for every singer that came after him. You will never hear me criticizing anything done by Stevie or Marvin Gaye or Sam Cooke or Curtis Mayfield. They taught me and inspired me.

When the press asked for my reaction, I wouldn't even discuss it; didn't want to play into the hands of media-hungry up-and-comers.

"But wait a minute, Kells," one reporter pressed. "This young singer has given his opinion of you. Shouldn't you respond?"

"No," I insisted, "because opinions should be born out of the right motive. Those opinions you're discussing come only from people looking for publicity for themselves."

"That's all you have to say?" he asked.

"One other thing," I added. "Elephants don't swat flies."

vho I am than to be loved for who I'm not.

I wasn't looking for publicity; I was still in search of new musical galaxies. The 1996 documentary, *When We Were Kings,* had a powerful impact on me.

The film captured the intensity before the heavyweight championship battle between George Foreman and Muhammad Ali in Zaire. The film showcased champions of the sports world—Ali and Foreman—and champions of the music world—James Brown, B. B. King, and Wayne Henderson. These champions drew attention back to Africa, the Motherland. I will never forget the footage of Ali traveling all over Zaire with children, adults, everyone screaming: "Ali, Boma Ye! Ali Boma Ye!" Ali's obvious love for Africans and their unshakable faith, confidence, and deep ancestral love for him were inspiring.

As a son of Africa, I wanted some of that. I wanted to feel my homeland: touch it, experience it, and sing about it. I felt a deep spiritual connection with a place I'd never been. I wanted to integrate its rhythms and harmonies, and meld its music with my music.

I had long hungered to go to Africa to see the Motherland for myself, but I had never had the opportunity. And since the court case came up, I couldn't travel outside the country because my passport had been taken away. I'd heard that I was known there, but I didn't feel the time was right for a visit. I also felt I needed to make an African album first.

I'd heard a lot about the problems in some (not all) parts of Africa—poverty, war, and the lack of things we take for granted—clean water, for example; and I also was aware of the spread of fatal diseases like AIDS and malaria. The idea of viruses and how they spread and infect people got me thinking: What if there was a positive virus, something that if people got infected with it, it would spread healing instead of sickness? In a way that's what music is—a virus that spreads hope and joy. It can bring healing by bringing people together. That's the virus that the world needs. So when I set out to write the songs for what I called the Africa album, I knew that I wanted to bring healing and love to my African brothers and sisters—a family that I had not even met yet.

I'm a "method" writer. To prepare to record what I called the Africa album, I bought every DVD and book on Africa I could find. I took them to the studio and placed them all around me. I had posters and maps of Africa hung on the walls. I had my assistant convert the Chocolate Factory into Africa; we brought in grass and sand

and trees, and everyone coming into the studio had to dress in safari gear. I wanted to bring as many props in as I could so I could get deeper into the spirit. As I sang, everywhere I looked I saw Africa. I tapped into the spirit and felt all the energy, tragedy, joy, and sadness that my ancestors had experienced. The rhythms came out. The melodies emerged. The harmonies fell from the sky. Don't ask me why or how, but I was singing songs with sounds entirely new yet incredibly old and strangely familiar.

My idea was to give the Africa album away in Africa, like a free vaccine, as a way to spread healing and inspiration. Needless to say, the record company did not support the idea of an album of all-inspirational music; it wanted me to get back to the sexual songs that are my trademark. It also didn't understand the concept of giving away music; so, for a while, the record sat on the shelves in the Chocolate Factory. But little by little I've managed to get a lot of the Africa album out over the years. The song "Let Your Light Shine" was released to raise money for victims of hurricane Katrina—a tragedy that affected me deeply. I got to perform the song on the BET telethon, but I could barely get through the song, thinking about what had happened to the people of New Orleans. "Heal It" and "Victory"—two songs on the Epic album, a collection of my inspirational songs—were also originally written for the Africa album.

It was like living in an African dream, but it was nothing like the dream that came true when I actually visited the Motherland.

TRIAL

May 9, 2008: The final legal nightmare was about to get underway. Amid all the media hoopla, the day was finally here—the day of reckoning.

Two weeks before the trial, though, a woman had popped out of nowhere with a new accusation. Our private investigators checked her out. They advised me that she was not a credible witness; nonetheless, my attorneys were nervous. This was the first time I saw them sweat. They said they thought I should cop a plea.

"But I'm not guilty," I said.

"We know that, but you'll get less time if you cop. And we're not liking the way the jury is looking."

"Well, I am liking the way the jury is looking," I countered. "I think they believe; I don't think those people want me to go to jail."

"The prosecutors are offering you a deal that means only eight months in jail."

"If the jury is looking to be against me, why is the prosecutor looking to deal?" I asked.

"Look, Rob," they said, "you do what you want, but we're extremely nervous. Eight months isn't bad."

"What's bad," I said, "is even one day. What's bad is the seven years that I've had this court case hanging over my head. One day in jail means that I've copped to these charges. How can I have a career behind that?"

"Eight months is better than 15 years."

My business manager motioned me into a separate room and said, "Rob, I think the judge is against you, and the jury will follow. I think you should take the deal."

I snapped on his ass and said, "Man, don't ever go against me. I got God with me. I got my gut instincts telling me to do what's right. I don't need you to tell me to cave in."

He kept quiet as we went back into the room with the lawyers.

"You made a decision, Robert?" they asked.

"I'm not copping to nothing," I said. "Just do the job I'm paying you to do."

"We will," they said, "but don't say we didn't warn you."

Before that moment, when people asked if I was afraid, I'd say, "No, just a little scared." My attorneys' words, though, put fear in my heart.

Yet my faith was still there. Faith got me to sleep the night before the trial. Faith got me up in the morning. Faith got me dressed and to the courtroom on time. Faith got me to stick by my decision. No deal.

My lawyers managed to show that some of the witnesses who testified against me were angry at me for personal reasons that had nothing to do with the case. Some of the witnesses contradicted themselves in their testimony, which made it hard to believe them.

Of all the witnesses who had testified against me, everyone was angry at me for personal reasons that had nothing to do with the case. One claimed I had promised him a recording deal. Another was mad that I didn't loan him money. Each was prejudiced. Each was looking for his 15 minutes of fame up there on the stand. My attorney, Ed Genson, with his expert cross-examination, caught many of them in a web of contradictions.

I knew my case was strong. But when the prosecutor stood and gave her closing argument, man, she was really strong. She almost had me believing I was guilty. She painted me as the most dangerous man on Earth. She was downright brutal. I figured, though, that was her job. Tomorrow she'd be in another courtroom calling some other dude the most dangerous man in the world.

Next was the closing argument by one of my lawyers. I prayed for him to be as persuasive as the prosecutor—and he was. He was great.

The jury was instructed to deliberate. So we waited—an hour, then two, then four, then six. Then, seven-and-a-half hours later, we were told a verdict had been reached.

Back to the courtroom, back to my seat; surrounded by my legal team.

The wait wasn't over. The judge hadn't returned to the courtroom. Meanwhile, I was sweating. Then, out of nowhere, a man handed me a card from his cigar shop. He whispered in my ear, "I know you love stogies, and we'd love to have you out to try some of the merchandise." I gave him a half-smile; I wasn't sure what his gesture meant. I told my attorney what had just happened and asked him if that was a good sign.

"Yes," he said, but he wasn't smiling.

Finally, the judge entered and called for the jury.

As they walked in, I watched their faces. Count for count, the judge asked the chief juror what they had found.

I heard the words "not guilty" spoken 12 times. Not guilty on every count.

Over and over again, I said, "Thank you, Jesus. Thank you, Jesus. Thank you, Jesus."

The policemen in the courtroom—who, up until the verdict had been read, acted like real hard asses—were now smiling and shaking my hand. I felt like the world was hugging me. Heaven was hugging me.

Someone from MTV managed to snag an interview with my attorney immediately after the trial. My lawyer broke it all down, explaining exactly why the jury found me "not guilty."

The prosecution's "star" or "surprise" witnesses never took the stand, including the woman that the prosecution believed to be the woman in the tape, in spite of her deposition to the contrary. The *Chicago Sun-Times* reporter, Jim DeRogatis, who broke the story and was the first to receive the supposed sex tape, took the Fifth and refused to testify. Instead, jurors had to rely on testimonies of "con men and hustlers," he explained. He specifically mentioned one individual, the fiancé of the state's key witness, and an attempt to solicit a payoff from me.

"He is an absolute extortionist and tried to extort me personally," my attorney told MTV. "I was angry about that. I am upset about that. I went down there, and they absolutely hit me up for $350,000 that Mr. Kelly was supposed to pay."

I heard the words

"NOT GUILTY"

spoken 12 TIMES.

Not guilty on every count.

Over and over again, I said,

"Thank you, Jesus.

Thank you, Jesus.

Thank you, Jesus."

As for me, I was too emotional to give any interviews. After the verdict was read, I went to the bathroom and broke down and cried. I had to share that moment with my mother in heaven. I could feel her crying alongside me. The moment one flood of tears ended, I'd burst into another. I just couldn't stop crying, and I couldn't stop thanking God as I left the courtroom. Tears flowed freely as people blew kisses, slapped me on the back, congratulated me, or wished me well.

I was so dazed I felt like I was being kidnapped. When I got to my car, my boys snatched me inside. Marvin Sapp, the gospel great, was blasting on the radio, singing a song I've sung at my shows, "I Never Would Have Made It," praising the one and only God who saw me through.

Within minutes, my phone was blowing up. People who had testified against me were calling to apologize, to say that they really hadn't meant it.

Did I forgive them?

Yes, I forgave everybody. I just wanted to get back to my normal life.

"Where do you want to go now?" my crew asked.

"McDonald's," I said. "I've gotta get a double cheeseburger and fries."

I
forgave
everybody

I just
wanted
to get back
to
my
normal
life

VICTORY

My dream was about to finally come true. I'd been invited to Africa, and now, after the trial, with my passport restored, the time was right.

My first trip to Africa, in July 2009, was monumental for me. I was invited to perform at two VIP concerts at the close of the ARISE Africa Fashion Awards, an annual event that spotlights up-and-coming African fashion designers. It was an experience like no other. My African fans came out in droves to the concerts in Johannesburg, Cape Town, and Nigeria.

Most fans there had grown up listening to my music but had never seen me. Because the visit was a long time coming, I was overwhelmed by raw, pure love. The last time I had that feeling was back when I was street performing. My first visit to Africa reminded me of the time when there was no pressure to live up to a megastar's image. African people just accepted me and loved me without really knowing me. It was one of the highlights of my career and the beginning of a relationship that would help me define the global significance of my music.

While there, I felt like Ali. I jogged in the streets with the kids. For two days, I ran drills and trained with the South African army. Night after night fans sang my name in their songs. I met Winnie Mandela and she took me on a tour of Soweto. I was invited to Nelson Mandela's house, which had more security than an airport. I was humbled and honored to meet the great man. Madiba, as he is called by the people of South Africa, was surrounded by many of his children and grandchildren. One of his great-granddaughters, Zenani, was a fan of mine and wouldn't let me out of her sight.

When I sat down at the piano to sing my song, "Soldier's Heart"—"You stood on the front line/You led the way/Right out of the darkness/You could have let us go astray/You were ready to die for our sake/That takes a soldier's heart"—and dedicated it to her grandfather, Zenani Mandela sat right next to me on the piano bench.

Meanwhile, back in the States, I released my ninth studio album, *Untitled*. In 2008, I had originally planned to release it as *12-Play: 4th Quarter*. But when all of the material leaked by way of the Internet, I had no choice but to scrap the idea and start from scratch. In the meantime, a management associate suggested that I release my first mixtape for the streets to tide fans over while I started recording again. That was how *The Demo Tape (Gangsta Grillz)*—remixes of popular R&B/hip-hop standards and some of my original work—came to be.

It was also around this time that I was approached by Clive Davis to work with Whitney Houston on her comeback album. I did two songs for the album and one of them, "I Look to You," was the first single released and a #1 hit for Whitney.

The *Untitled* album debuted in December 2009 at #4 on the *Billboards* 200 chart with the big club hit, "Supaman High," featuring OJ Da Juiceman. Keri Hilson and I sang "Number One," another smash. *Untitled* was a sexy record, where many of the songs like "Echo"—which had me yodeling—took me in new vocal directions. I also produced a song called "Pregnant," which blended my voice with Tyrese, Robin Thicke, and The Dream. When I wrote it, I was thinking of how Quincy Jones had done something similar with Barry White, El DeBarge, Al B. Sure, and James Ingram in "The Secret Garden." I wanted to challenge myself to see if I could do something just as lush and beautiful. For me, *Untitled* is still an undiscovered jewel. I don't think it got the kind of promotion it deserved.

Soon after the release of *Untitled*, my long-time consultant and producer of *Trapped in the Closet*, Ann Carli, told me that FIFA, the international association that governs world soccer, was seeking submissions for a special album being created for the 2010 FIFA World Cup games, which were to be held in South Africa—the first time a World Cup match would be played on the continent of Africa. They were also looking for three special songs to represent the games: the World Cup Mascots theme, the closing ceremony song, and finally the official anthem of the 2010 World Cup. Ann suggested I write and submit something. She warned me that it was a long shot—that every artist in the world was trying to get one of those slots, and that, even though I had been found innocent in the case, many corporate brands might still shy away from any association with me.

With my basketball mentality, I can get really competitive. The opportunity to have my song considered as the anthem for the World Cup games and the fact that it was a long shot got my adrenaline pumping overtime. I went to the bookstore and bought every book and DVD it had on soccer and immersed myself in my research. I watched soccer on TV and ran drills with the Chicago Fire Soccer Club, which was one of the USA teams, to get a better feel for the game. I watched *Invictus*, the Clint Eastwood film starring Morgan Freeman and Matt Damon about how Nelson Mandela used rugby to help unite the people of South Africa during the 1995 Rugby World Cup game.

I didn't want to write a song that was just about soccer or the World Cup; I wanted it to be bigger than that. I believe music can guide us into a world of peace, and I wanted a song that could speak to humanity on a global scale. I dug deep inside to find something that would inspire people like "I Believe I Can Fly" had inspired millions. In the same way that "I Believe I Can Fly" wasn't just about basketball, I wanted another song that explored the known and the unknown. We know we're missing love in this world. We know we need love to survive, but we don't know how to get there. I searched for words that spoke to the healing possibilities of love.

Keep in mind, my trial and victory were still fresh in my mind. I've always said that the depth of my struggle will determine the height of my success. If there's no fire, there's no scream. If there's no scream, no one will hear you or come to help. No continent has struggled more than Africa, especially South Africa, and "Sign of a Victory" is a testament to its struggle. It's about what Africa has been through, what it is going through, and, mainly, what Africa will overcome:

> *I can feel the spirit of the nations*
> *And I can feel my wings ridin' the winds, yeah*
> *I see the finish line just up ahead now*
> *And I can feel it risin' deep within*
> *And that's the sign of a victory*

rated, not just tolerated

The song is an uplifting
message of . . . victory. It
blends American R&B and
pop with the Soweto Spiritual
Singers' Zulu choral chants and
African musical influences.
I watched video tapes of the
Soweto Spiritual Singers,
listened to them and just fell
in love with their music
instantly. The song would not
be incomplete without a touch
of gospel.

Part of the rules for the World Cup anthem was that the song include a performance by an African artist or group. As this was a massive global event that would shine the spotlight of the world on Africa, they wanted to make sure that local African talent got some of that glow as well. I reached out to my label in South Africa and asked them if they could help me find a choir to sing on the track; they introduced me to a South African gospel choir, the Soweto Spiritual Singers. After watching some performance footage and listening to their music, I knew they would be perfect. The song would not be complete without their unique gospel touch, so I arranged to record it with the choir. The syncopated percussion beats, combined with a chorus of heavenly African voices, gave the song the stamp of authenticity.

I was humbled when Nkululeko Vilakazi, co-founder of the Soweto Spiritual Singers, described our effort:

"The song embodies the story of South Africa—hope, strength, and triumph

over adversity. It is an uplifting message of victory. It blends American R&B and pop with the Soweto Spiritual Singers' Zulu choral chants and African musical influences."

Although "Sign of a Victory" was custom-made for the event, we had to wait several weeks before we found out if the song would even be accepted for the official album. I was blown away when I learned it was selected as the official anthem for the 2010 World Cup games! It would also be the first track on *Listen Up!: The Official 2010 FIFA World Cup Album*. I felt like, instead of dominoes falling down, things were starting to go the other way: it was dominoes up—and "Sign of a Victory" was the first domino to stand.

The opening ceremonies for the World Cup were scheduled for June 11, 2010, at the newly built Soccer City Stadium in Johannesburg. Artists from the album, along with more than 1,500 other artists, dancers, singers, praise poets, drummers, and flag bearers were invited to perform at the opening ceremony. I was to have the honor of performing the official anthem and was excited about my second trip to Africa and the opportunity to get another taste of the unconditional love I had experienced a year earlier.

I wasn't sure who'd be there to greet me when my plane touched down. My hopes were high, but I just didn't know if my African fans cared enough to come greet me at the airport. Well, they showed up by the thousands—newspaper accounts put the number at 10,000. Getting off the plane and seeing the sea of beautiful black faces looked biblical to me. I was in tears. I dove into the crowd so my spirit would go out to the people. When I finally made it to the car, I jumped on the roof so my fans could see me as I pumped my fist in the air. I love going where I'm celebrated, not just tolerated, and this trip to Africa was a straight-up celebration.

The day before the World Cup opening, I attended the FIFA Fan Fest in Cape Town with the Executive Mayor, Dan Plato, to take part in a special celebration for Nelson Mandela. During the Grand Parade World Cup welcoming ceremony, I stood beside Plato when he stepped out on the balcony of Cape Town's City Hall above tens of thousands of fans. This was the same balcony from which Mr. Mandela made his first speech upon his release from prison in 1990. We were there to light the cauldron that symbolizes the everlasting light provided by Mr. Mandela's legacy. I felt very honored to be the first to light the eternal flame with the Mayor. Once the cauldron was lit, with arms outstretched and with that beautiful, lyrical African accent, Plato shouted: "CAN YOU FEEL IT?"

The crowd cheered wildly.

After the lighting of the eternal flame, we went to the stage area, where I had been asked to sing "I Believe I Can Fly." Now, I really didn't have an opening song planned for the occasion, but the mayor's words, "can you feel it," kept repeating in my head. The Soweto Spiritual Singers went on before me, and they were singing a wonderful chorus with an incredibly addictive beat. The air was filled with the sound of vuvuzelas—an African horn, almost like a supersized kazoo that gives off a piercing, majestic, some say "annoying" sound. The sound of the vuvuzelas became the soundtrack for the entire trip, as it is used for celebrations, sporting events—any kind of occasion where people are expressing joy or excitement. From backstage, I asked that the choir continue to sing out the rhythm when I took the stage. They did. I walked out on stage, singing "CAN YOU FEEL IT!" And, again, the crowd went wild.

I quickly slid into "I Believe I Can Fly," and the place erupted. It was truly humbling to see all these people, from the very young to the very old, on a continent so far from Chicago, singing my song. And they knew every single word.

While I was singing "Fly," in the back of my head the lyrics for "Can you feel it" were forming." I was onstage singing one song while mentally scribbling another. I told one of our camera crew to make sure that he got the opening of my performance, so that I could have the recording for reference. I promised myself that I'd complete the song once I got home. And I did.

More than 85,000 fans were screaming, waving, and blowing vuvuzelas when I arrived at Soccer Stadium for the opening ceremonies of the World Cup. It seemed like everyone was in accord, showing great love. There were soccer fans from all over the world, each representing their country and their favorite team. Especially excited were the South African fans, rooting for their national team, Bafana Bafana, who were competing in this first match against Mexico. Nelson Mandela himself would be in the crowd, and Joann Kelly's son would soon be performing "Sign of a Victory" with this great man in the audience. The energy of the crowd shot into me like electricity; there's just no other way to describe it. The crowds, all that love, all that energy, the very spirit of Africa electrified my senses all at once.

As I was on my way to the dressing room beneath the stadium where I was to change and wait for my cue in the ceremony, a few people from the group I had been traveling with came running towards me. Somehow, I could read their spirit. They were bringing bad news, which I did not want to hear, especially before my performance. I tried to get them to restrain themselves and hold off on whatever it was they had to tell me until later, but the news couldn't wait:

"Zenani has been killed in a car accident," they said. "Zenani is gone."

The words went through my heart like a bullet. But there was nothing I could do but go on the field. When the crowd saw me, the screaming and the vuvuzelas went crazy. The sound was like a gigantic swarm of bees.

Dressed in all black but for a gold hood and sneakers, backed by the powerful Soweto Spiritual Singers, I began the performance in a crouched position. I stood and sang the most powerful rendition of "Sign of a Victory" that I could muster. I sang for Zenani and her great-grandfather. I sang for all the grandfathers and grandmothers, all the fathers and mothers, all the brothers and sisters who have lost someone they have loved. I sang to the 85,000 people in the stadium that day and the 2 billion people watching around the world. I sang for love itself.

I
sang
for
love
itself

HANDS ACROSS THE WORLD

Music can be the calm after a deadly storm. Delivering comfort was the reason I released the single "Let Your Light Shine" in 2006 as a tribute to the victims and survivors of Hurricane Katrina, and "Rise Up" in 2007, after I heard about the massacre of innocent students at Virginia Tech.

I came back from Africa with a deeper understanding of myself and a strong desire to do even more with my music. What dwells within me is global, and my music speaks all languages. I became obsessed with the idea of world peace and accomplishing it through the brotherhood of music. Music will pave the way.

This was the motivation behind *Epic*, an album of some of my inspirational records: "The World's Greatest," "If I Could Turn Back the Hands of Time," "I'm Your Angel," and "I Believe I Can Fly." It also included five new ballads, among them "Can You Feel It?" the song I'd heard in my head while performing in Cape Town, and "Sign of a Victory." I decided to include a couple of songs from the Africa album in this collection as well. The prelude "Heal It" and the song "Victory" both fit perfectly with the album's inspirational theme. "Fireworks" was another song inspired by the World Cup; I wrote and recorded it the day that I got the news about "Sign of a Victory" being chosen as the official anthem. In my mind, I could truly see the fireworks of the ceremony. My joy is recorded in that song.

"I Believe" was inspired by the election of Barack Obama as President of the United States. The song came to me when he was still running for office. Usually, when I write inspirational songs, I see myself as a hero trying to save people with music.

As my involvement with Africa deepened, I had a strong desire to work with more African artists, to explore African talent, to strengthen my connection with Africa (the homeland). It didn't take long for that desire to become reality.

A few months after the World Cup ceremonies, I was approached by representatives from Rockstar4000/Sony Music Africa and Airtel. They asked if I'd participate in the ONE8 project; the concept was to create the first Pan African supergroup to be formed by eight of the biggest artists/groups from across Africa. I was asked to be the One in the One8; they were looking for a well-known international artist to lend his or her name to help expose African music and talent to audiences across Africa and around the world.

I was asked to write and produce a song with a group of superstars from all over the African continent: Amani from Kenya, 2face Idibia from Nigeria, Navio from Uganda, JK from Zambia, Alikiba from Tanzania, 4x4 from Ghana, Movaizhaleine from Gabon, and Fally Ipupa from Congo DRC.

My goal was to produce a song that rang out all over the world. When I sing, I sing with everything I've been through. The song needed to be something that would convince people of all colors and all nationalities that they can come out of poverty or overcome whatever problems they're dealing with—that they can fly, too.

I hadn't met any of these artists before attempting to write their song. All I had was video messages and samples of their music that they had sent me. Each artist had a unique style and characteristics. It was a true challenge. But I live for challenges, especially those that help me grow as a singer, songwriter, and music producer.

After getting a handle on their individual styles, we arranged to have all the artists flown into Chicago to record "Hands Across the World," the song I'd created for the One8 project. Usually when I work with American artists, I have some idea of their musical range—what they can or cannot do. I also know when they're being real and not-so-real.

With the ONE8 artists, everything was real. I love having fun with my music; I also love working with different people, different genres of music, and different talents and gifts. It helps stretch my talents and abilities.

Africa to America
Everywhere come on and spread some love
We got faith and a little hope
I believe that we can heal the globe
It's time to open our eyes and see
That all we need is you and me
Unity's like harmony
So let me see you stretch your hands across the world
Hands across the world . . .
I'm reaching out to the poor people,
* the sick and the alone*
I'm reaching out to the fortunate who
* can build their own homes*
I'm reaching out to the ones who seem
* to have lost their way*
And I'm calling on the ones who can
* show them a brighter day*

I will be forever humbled by the soul-to-soul connections with members of my African family.

I consider my continuing African experience among the highest highs on my Soulacoaster.

Thank you, Mom.
Thank you, Miss McLin.
Thank you, God.

"I want my song to go beyond what I wrote it for and, perhaps, touch people all around the world and inspire."

"It's extra special doing it here in South Africa, more special than anywhere else," he said, "because I believe that humanity, the spirit of people and DNA all started right here, in Africa."

LOVE LETTER

With my music, I'm always switching lanes—making U-turns, going forward to new destinations, or traveling backwards to familiar places. I don't resist the journey. I feel like I have this musical time machine that I can just get in and travel anywhere I want to.

With my time machine, I can stay rooted in the music that made me, while creating songs based on current experiences and inspirations. It feels good knowing that people depend on you to come up with songs that make them want to make love; to get on the dance floor; or to be better fathers, mothers, men, and women. But, with all the fame, fortune, and media attention, I'm also struck with the thought that this is an awesome responsibility.

This is why it's important for artists to tap into the spirit of music. Every now and then it's important to tap into the spirit of the greats so we can extend their legacies. Hopefully, you know, someday somebody will be in a studio trying to tap into the musical spirit of R. Kelly. That's what this whole thing's about—it's the power of music. Generation after generation, music is God's miracle channeled through His children who express His gifts. Our job is to just keep the miracle of music alive, express it to the best of our ability, and pass it on to those who follow.

My legacy is important to me. After I'm gone, I want to be remembered for my music and the way my music touched people around the world. I want to be remembered as a songwriter, a singer, a performer, a producer, and a good father. And honestly, I want to be remembered as one of the most versatile artists of my era.

All this was on my mind when I decided to produce my next album, *Love Letter*. It had gotten to the point where every time I switched on the radio, I'd hear my sounds and riffs. I was flattered but also concerned. This new generation, unfamiliar with my original work, might think I'm copying what they hear on the radio, when in reality I would be just doing me.

I didn't want *Love Letter* to go to the future because I didn't want to get ahead of myself. And I didn't want to stay where I was, look to the side, and see another version of my current self. Instead, I got into my musical time machine and set the dials to take me back 20, 30, and 40 years. When I landed, I found myself hanging out with Sam Cooke and Jackie Wilson—spiritually and musically. I shook hands with them, soaked in their essence. They became my teachers, fathers, uncles, big brothers. I put myself in their time zone, and when I returned to the present, I brought armfuls of new and exciting goodies. I decided that *Love Letter* was to be a concept album—an entire CD unified by the theme of "love." I love doing concept albums more than any other kind of album. They allow me to, in a way, get dressed up musically. It's not a freestyle situation; I set boundaries for myself, and the music must stay within those lanes.

Love has never failed. It has won every battle. Today and forevermore, love will go undefeated. With *Love Letter*, every song had to be about love—old-fashioned

L-O-V-E. So I programmed myself musically to come up with love-feeling tracks, songs both romantic and sexy, yet classy, like back in the day.

I had to set the proper mood in my studio. On my big-screen TV, I projected pictures of guys like Ray Charles and Marvin Gaye. I wanted to see their faces; I wanted them with me as I wrote songs, practiced lyrics, and laid down tracks. I knew these men, like all men, had their struggles. They went through trials and tribulations, but through it all, they had a heart for music and a love for people. That love shined through every song they sang. I have that same heart for music, that same love for people. But I didn't want to be R. Kelly or Kells or the Pied Piper of R&B or the Weatherman. I wanted you to feel the mama's boy inside me. I wanted you to feel Robert. I wanted the sweetest part of my soul to touch the sweetest part of yours.

I saw the album as an actual body of songs—one arm, then another arm, a head, a leg, another leg, a foot, another foot, a nose, a smile, two smiling eyes—not just a collection of individual songs. I conceived *Love Letter* as one long single—a letter filled with heart, tears, and passion on each page.

I hadn't originally planned for *Love Letter* to be my next album. As I often do, I was working on material for two albums at the same time—*Love Letter* and the project that I thought would be next up, was *Zodiac*, a continuation of the *12-Play* concept. I'd even come up with a new name for myself for that album—"January Boy," because I'm a Capricorn. But then a song so powerful came to me in the studio, that it took over and there could be no question that it was going to be my next record.

"When A Woman Loves" was the first single. Just as a righteous woman is the backbone of a man, a woman's true love can be the backbone of an album. After all, a woman's love, actually two women's—Joann Kelly and Lena McLin—made me who I am. In *Love Letter*, I'm singing about the love that comes from a mother, a grandmother, a great-grandmother. I'm singing about the love that comes from your fiancée, your wife, your daughter, your granddaughter. It's the kind of love that keeps on going and growing. I don't even consider "When A Woman Loves" a song really; it's like the heart that keeps the body alive.

Singing it was challenging because it was written in the mode of Jackie Wilson. Like so many of the great artists back then, Jackie had a powerful voice. He belted out every note; he cried out every lyric; there was no half-stepping. Sam Cooke was my spiritual soulmate as I wrote drop-down-on-your knees pleas for a woman's affection. I love that style and believe it's what's missing in songs heard on the radio today. *Love Letter* brings those powerful styles and that heart-and-soul connection back into the mainstream.

C L A S S I C

"Love Letter is a gorgeous,

15-track ode to the various stages of love,

drawing from a retro soul style

and delivered with romantic grace."

—Nekesa Mumbi Moody / Associated Press

"Radio Message" is a story set in the '50s—before using cell phones, texting, and tweeting became the norm. It's about a guy who did his girl wrong and wants to make up. He's written her but she won't write back. He gets this crazy idea. He heard about a contest the radio station is running. The next caller on the line gets two tickets and a limo ride to a concert. He knows his girl loves the radio and figures if he's the next caller, he can plead his case on the air. Maybe she'll be listening. So he makes this desperate attempt and, sure enough, his call gets through. He gets to plead his case in the form of a song, crying: *This is a radio message to my baby, and I'm begging her to come back . . .*

"Number One Hit" is a song that compares a lady to a smash hit. Having been blessed with many #1 hits, I know the tremendous adrenaline rush that comes with your very own top-of-the-chart winner. So I wanted to compare that feeling to falling in love. That's why I said, "We went past gold . . . our love blew up." I sang that she is "my Elvis and Priscilla, my Michael Jackson's *Thriller*, *Smooth Operator* by Sade, and, baby, let's not forget the *12-Play* . . . you my Titanic, my movie star, my *Coming to America*, my *Avatar*." (Avatar, by the way, is a movie I've seen about six times. It gets better each time.)

"Not Feelin' the Love" was written for Michael Jackson. We lost him before he could sing it, so on *Love Letter* I'm singing it to Michael, for Michael. In truth, he can never leave us. Michael Jackson is a permanent part of our lives. His music is so deep in us that nothing can erase it. The highlight of my career so far is working with Michael. I'm humbled by the fact that I had the opportunity to work with the greatest man to ever make music. The best way I can express my love for Michael Jackson is to make sure my music honors his legacy.

Marvin Gaye is also present on two different songs. When you talk silky, you're talking Marvin. But we're also talking about haunting, perfect harmonies. Marvin put harmonies on top of harmonies. Even when his life was filled with disharmony, when he got to the studio, everything became harmonious. In the studio, what was crazy turned sane; what was ugly turned beautiful; what was hurtful turned healing. In the studio, God took over.

I had to have that feel-good Motown vibe, so I wrote "Love Is" and sang it like Marvin singing to Tammi Terrell. My "Tammi" is K. Michelle, singer, songwriter, and my mentee. K. Michelle and I play catch with the melody and neither of us ever drops the ball.

The deeper Marvin moment comes with "Music Must Be a Lady." For years I've said that I'm married to music or that I'm pregnant with it. Music has been the one girl I would never leave, and the woman who would never leave me. Music lays out melodies for me like my mother used to lay out my clothes. Yes sir, music must be a lady.

I know that in writing *Love Letter*, God once again took over. He gave me this gift, and He demands that I not take it for granted. *Love Letter* received three Grammy nominations, including Best R&B Album and Best Traditional R&B Performance for both "When a Woman Loves" and "Radio Message." My life story, with all the challenges and rewards, has been one long love letter. God knew it was time for Robert to use His love and be real with His gift.

DOMINOES UP

> Sometimes I feel like an alien, born on a planet called Music, where there's nothing but sound. Sometimes, even in the midst of thousands, I still feel alone, because no one—including me— understands my mind, my creativity, how I'm hardwired.

I've been very honest about my inability to read words like normal people. I simply don't see words, I see music. I'm okay with that. It's part of the gift. I am so grateful that my incredible children have not been afflicted with my problem. They can all read and write better than their father, I am so very proud of them.

When asked if I consider myself a genius, I say: "No, I can't call myself a genius, but I'm on my way." I feel like I haven't been fully introduced to my gift. I always feel like there's something bigger and better out there for me. It's like I'm stuck on the runway, waiting for the best flight ever.

In countless interviews, people ask me: "If you could go back and change anything in your life, what would it be?'

My answer? "Not a damn thing!" I wouldn't change the poverty, I wouldn't change the abuse or the pain. Even though I've had some struggles and downfalls in my life, I'm still standing—strong, confident, and feeling good about life and love. I have no regrets whatsoever simply because whatever I've gone through has made me the man and artist I am today.

Chapters in my life continue to unfold, revealing mysteries I never knew about myself. Just as I was finishing this book, the strangest thing happened one late Juicy Tuesday night in Chicago. I had just finished hooping and was feeling pretty good—

my team had won about 20 games in a row. I noticed two middle-aged, neatly dressed women I'd never seen before approaching the court. I was recovering from emergency surgery to remove an abscess the size of a golf ball on my throat—a situation that, had it gone untreated for another 24 hours, could have destroyed my voice forever or even killed me. The women had read about my hospitalization in the papers and drove four hours just to check up on me.

The plot thickens: The women—whom I had never seen before in my life—claimed to be my aunts: sisters of the father I had never known and was told had abandoned me and my mother when I was born.

The women had a different version of the story. My father, they said, was present at my birth. He dearly loved my mother and me, and they said he died when I was two years old—shot to death in a bar.

Is any of this true? I have no idea, but I have to find out. It's another piece of the puzzle that is me, another *Trapped in the Closet* cliff-hanger, another twist and turn on the Soulacoaster that is my life.

As I write this, I've begun yet another chapter in my life. I've come out of my suburban cocoon, moving out of my Olympia Fields home and up into "a de-luxe apartment in the sky." Every night I gaze down on Chicago—the beautiful city that raised and fed me, and the skyscrapers that have helped me hit some of my highest notes. The Chocolate Factory is no longer in my basement—it's bigger and better than ever and still my sanctuary.

The Chocolate Factory keeps operating at full capacity. The "R. Kelly 4.5" part of me feels like I'm just starting out, like I'm still on the runway of my career, getting ready for takeoff. As always I'm working on more than one project. I was thrilled to be asked to write new songs for the remake of the movie *Sparkle*, and have my songs stand next to Curtis Mayfield's classics. *Write Me Back*, the follow-up to *Love Letter*, will be out by the time you read this. It's me stepping back into my musical time machine and having a ball. I got to imagining that I was Barry White or Teddy Pendergrass or Ray Charles. There's some Smokey and Stevie in there, too.

As the radio in my head keeps playing and sending me songs in all different genres—not just R&B, but also pop, rock, and even country. Don't be surprised if I get inspired to put out a country music album someday.

The alien that is *Trapped in the Closet* is getting ready to visit Earth again; I know everyone wants to know what "the Package" is. Get ready: you're about to find out. There are artists of all kinds knocking at my door, looking for new songs, asking me to drop a verse on their songs, or looking for remixes. I'm grateful that they've come to me and are giving me the opportunity to share their gifts.

Ideas are lined up on the runway in my head like airplanes at O'Hare. The minute one takes off, another is ready to go. There is still so much I want to achieve: Movies that I write and direct and, of course, do all the music. A one-man Broadway show. And more music. Africa is calling. So is Europe. I love London and Paris. They're telling me Tokyo took the *Love Letter* to heart and wants me to sing it to them personally. I can't wait to get over there. I feel the same about China and Russia and every other part of the world.

The world needs healing, and music is the medicine that heals. Besides the Africa album, there are Caribbean and Latin and Brazilian-inspired tracks still sitting on the shelves at the Chocolate Factory. When I created them as part of my Music Virus project, I had this idea to give the music to people in those areas for free, as a way to spread healing and inspiration. My record company wasn't exactly thrilled about that approach, but I am determined to get that music out one way or another.

I'm still amazed that healing music came my way in such quantities. I don't know why I received this gift. I can't say I deserved it. I know that I'm not immortal, but my gift is my legacy. It takes a whole lot of mess to be this blessed. I'm not here to win, but to touch.

Sometimes my gift is my enemy. My head is like an over-inflated balloon, filled with sounds that swell my brain to the extent that I fear it might explode. When it does explode, I find myself in a new and beautiful musical place.

It's taken me a lifetime to know myself, but I think I'm almost there. I'm at my best when I'm most wanted—and I know that music lovers still want great music. I know that as long as people are living on this planet, as long as they can relate to a real song about real life, I'll always be in the game.

So it is as a happy man that I come to the beginning of this book. Note I did not say "the end." As far as I'm concerned, the Soulacoaster is just getting warmed up. It's been a crazy ride up, but I know the best years are still ahead.

I give thanks to the Creator for my life every day. It could have gone either way. That bullet I took while riding a bicycle as a kid could have been the end. Shame and disconnection because I couldn't read could have become my dead-end. I have achieved what I have in this life because I was blessed with a gift and the love of two exceptional women who saw something in me I did not, could not, see within myself.

I have been knocked to my knees. I have been betrayed and maligned. I have lost love and thrown it away. My heart has been broken and I have cried an ocean of tears.

In the end, though:

I am saved by music.

I am saved by God.

I am saved by God's gift of love. And if, through my words and music, I can pass on that gift to you, I am the happiest man on earth.

A boy born in Chicago's 'hood to a loving mother has been blessed mightily. The boy became a man. The man faced a mountain of struggles, but the struggles steeled his determination. For all the storms behind him, the sun seems to always break through.

There are sunrises ahead and still thousands of songs to write and sing.

Songs that help us have fun and party all night.

Songs that let us feel the undying joy of love.

Songs that lift our earthly burdens and give us a little taste of heaven.

Songs that call for harmony, peace, and humanity.

The Soulacoaster soars to the top, the Soulacoaster roars to the bottom.

But the boy holds on.

The man holds on.

He can't and won't let go.

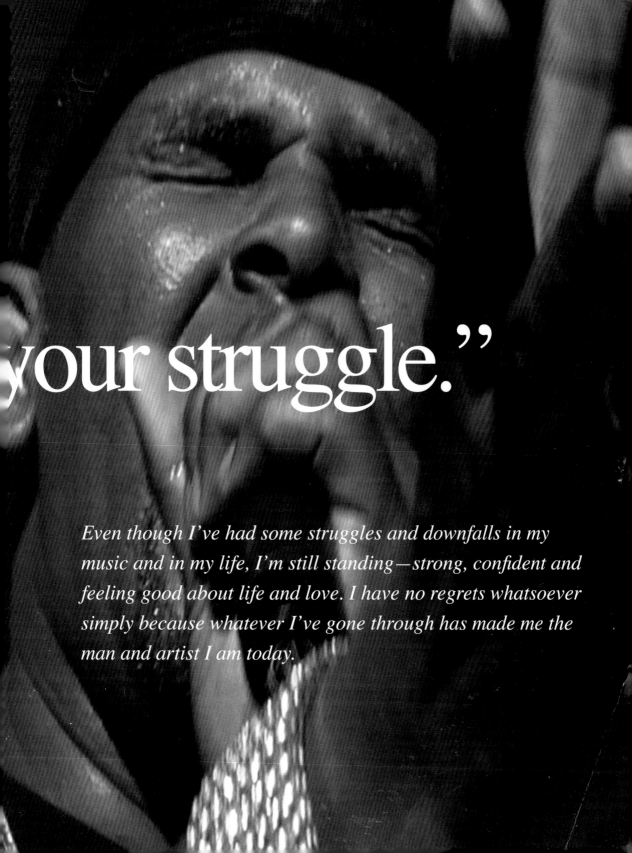

your struggle."

Even though I've had some struggles and downfalls in my music and in my life, I'm still standing—strong, confident and feeling good about life and love. I have no regrets whatsoever simply because whatever I've gone through has made me the man and artist I am today.

ACKNOWLEDGMENTS

There is no measure except infinity for the *thank yous* that I owe to the following people who have helped me turn back to the beginning—to the first page of my life.

First, I thank God for the gift of music.

Deep gratitude to:

Joann Kelly	Barry Weiss
Lena McLin	Wayne Williams
Derrel McDavid	Allan Mayer
Ann Carli	Gerry Margolis
Eric Custer	Cathy Carroll
Clive Calder	Jen Tharler

Tavis Smiley who believed in this project from the very beginning.
Cheryl Woodruff who kept it going even when it seemed impossible.

Juan Roberts / Creative Lunacy

Colby Hamilton	Paulette Robinson
Sylvester Brown, Jr.	Nicolette Salamanca
Kirsten Melvey	Lisa Reece
Thomas Louie	Steven Goff

Very special thanks to my children, Joann, Jaya and Robert Jr., whom I love so dearly. I thank God that you have been blessed with good health and you share the gift of music that I got from your grandmother, Joann Kelly, and your great-grandfather.

To all of my fans around the world—I am forever indebted. Thank you from
the bottom of my heart for supporting me during the highs and lows
of this ride throughout my career. Thank you for having my back.
I will continue to share my musical gift with you
as long as I'm breathing.

David Ritz expresses deep gratitude to Rob, whose artistry continues to dazzle and inspire
me, as well as Tavis Smiley, Cheryl Woodruff, David Vigliano, Ann Carli,
Derrel McDavid, Eric Custer, and Roberta, the love of my life for 47 years.
Thank you, Jesus.

Discography

STUDIO ALBUMS

12-Play (1993)

R. Kelly (1995)

R. (1998)

TP-2.com (2000)

Chocolate Factory (2003)

Happy People/U Saved Me (2004)

TP.3 Reloaded (2005)

Double Up (2007)

Untitled (2009)

Love Letter (2010)

Write Me Back (2012)

COLLABORATION ALBUMS

Born into the 90's (1992) (with Public Announcement)

The Best of Both Worlds (2002) (with Jay-Z)

Unfinished Business (2004) (with Jay-Z)

COMPILATION ALBUMS

Feelin' On Yo Booty—The Remixes (2000)

The R. In R&B Collection, Vol. 1 (2003)

Remix City, Volume 1 (2005)

My Diary (2005)

Playlist: The Very Best of R. Kelly (2010)

Epic (2010)

FILMOGRAPHY

Trapped in the Closet (13–22) (2007)

Trapped in the Closet (1–22) The Big Package (2007)

R. Kelly Live the Light It Up Tour (2007)

Music Credits

"12-PLAY": Words and Music by R. Kelly © 1993 • UNIVERSAL MUSIC Z SONGS

"YOU ARE NOT ALONE": Words and Music by R. Kelly © 1995 • UNIVERSAL MUSIC Z SONGS

"I'M STILL HERE": Words and Music by R. Kelly © 2009 • UNIVERSAL MUSIC Z SONGS and R KELLY PUBLISHING, INC.

"THE SERMON": Words and Music by R. Kelly and Erick S. Sermon © 1995 • UNIVERSAL MUSIC Z SONGS and ERICK SERMON ENTERPRISES, INC. c/o UNIVERSAL MUSIC-Z TUNES, LLC.

"YOU REMIND ME OF SOMETHING": Words and Music by R. Kelly © 1995 • UNIVERSAL MUSIC Z SONGS

"AS I LOOK INTO MY LIFE": Words and Music by R. Kelly © 1995 • UNIVERSAL MUSIC Z SONGS

"DOWN LOW (Nobody Has To Know)": Words and Music by R. Kelly © 1995 • UNIVERSAL MUSIC Z SONGS

"THE WORLD'S GREATEST": Words and Music by R. Kelly © 2002 • UNIVERSAL MUSIC Z SONGS

"HEAVEN I NEED A HUG": Words and Music by R. Kelly © 2002 • UNIVERSAL MUSIC Z SONGS

"IGNITION (Remix)": Words and Music by R. Kelly © 2002 • R KELLY PUBLISHING, INC. and UNIVERSAL MUSIC Z SONGS

"WEATHERMAN": Words and Music by R. Kelly © 2004 • UNIVERSAL MUSIC Z SONGS

"SEX IN THE KITCHEN": Words and Music by R. Kelly © 2005 • UNIVERSAL MUSIC Z SONGS

"TRAPPED IN THE CLOSET (Chapter 1 of 5)": Words and Music by R. Kelly © 2005 • UNIVERSAL MUSIC Z SONGS

"THE ZOO": Words and Music by R. Kelly © 2007 • R KELLY PUBLISHING, INC. and UNIVERSAL MUSIC Z SONGS

"SIGN OF A VICTORY": Words and Music by R. Kelly © 2010 • R KELLY PUBLISHING, INC. and UNIVERSAL MUSIC Z SONGS

"HANDS ACROSS THE WORLD": Words and Music by R. Kelly © 2010 • R KELLY PUBLISHING, INC. and UNIVERSAL MUSIC Z SONGS

"RADIO MESSAGE": Words and Music by R. Kelly © 2010 • R KELLY PUBLISHING, INC. and UNIVERSAL MUSIC Z SONGS

"THE DIARY OF ME": Words and Music by R. KELLY © 2011 • UNIVERSAL MUSIC Z SONGS

☗ Photo Credits

Image courtesy of Larry Busacca, Getty Images appears on the back cover.

Images courtesy of Ann Carli appear on page 70 and 368.

Image courtesy of Fortress Entertainment appears in the Foreword.

Image courtesy of Brian Franklin appears on page 352.

Image courtesy of Joe Grant appears on page 160.

Images courtesy of the Robert Sylvester Kelly Collection appear on pages 4, 29, 40, 48, 50, 84, 105, 190-191, and 314.

Images courtesy of Michael Lavine appear on pages 180, 192, 234, and 248.

Images courtesy of Parrish Lewis appear on the cover and pages 354 and 359.

Image courtesy of Anthony Mandler/ARTMIX Creative appears on page 318.

Image courtesy of Gary Mankus appears on page 64.

Image courtesy of Frank Micelotta, Getty Images appears on page 292.

Image courtesy of the National Oceanic and Atmospheric Administration/Department of Commerce, NOAA Photo Library, NOAA Central Library; OAR/ERL/National Severe Storms Laboratory (NSSL) appears on page 278-279.

Images courtesy of Randee St. Nicholas appear on pages 356 and 360.

Image courtesy of Gilles Petard, Getty Images appears on page 52.

Images courtesy of Jordan Porter appear in Act 1 and pages 21, 24, 26, 110-111, 112-113, 120-121, 125 and 276.

Images and Original Illustrations courtesy of Juan Roberts appear on pages 10, 14, 44, 60, 68, 74, 80-81, 90-91, 98, 116-117, 144-145, 154, 170-171, 186-187, 252-253, and 354-355.

Image courtesy of the Library of Congress and Ira Rosenberg appears on page 266-267.

Image courtesy of Robert Abbott Sengstacke, Getty Images appears on page 34-35.

Image courtesy of Charles A. Sengstock Jr., Used with Permission, appears on page 7.

Images courtesy of Juan Soliz, PacificCoastNews.com appears on page 342.

Images courtesy of Sony Music Entertainment appear on pages 163, 217, 272, 284, 291, 298, 310, and 314-315. Album and Video Stills courtesy of RCA Records, a division of Sony Music Entertainment.

Images courtesy of Jim Swaffield appear on the endpapers and on pages 136-137, 200-201, 220-221, 327, 338, 342-343, 344, 348, 350, 353, and 367.

Images courtesy of Reisig and Taylor Photography appear in Act 1 and pages 56, 126-127, 129, 166, 176, 210-211, 278 and 330.

Thanks to Becca from fuckyeahrkelly.tumblr.com for special photo research.

♛ About the Authors

R. Kelly, the king of R&B, makes music of epic proportions. After 18 years of stardom, the visionary songwriter, producer, and vocalist continues to forge an artistic path that caters to fantasy and captures the hearts of adoring fans. This is in essence how an artist sells over 35 million records, and wears the crown of a king. As a prolific artist, it is this uncanny ability to compose classics and deliver electrifying live performances that defines everything that is essential R. Kelly.

Kelly has been named the #1 R&B/Hip-Hop artist of the past 25 years by *Billboard* magazine and is the recipient of multiple Grammy, *Billboard*, BMI, and American Music Awards. R. Kelly lives and produces music out of his
Chocolate Factory in the heart of Chicago.

David Ritz is the only four-time winner of the Gleason Music Book Award. He has collaborated with Janet Jackson, Ray Charles, Marvin Gaye, B.B. King, Aretha Franklin, Etta James, Smokey Robinson, and Don Rickles. He also cowrote, with Gaye, the song "Sexual Healing."

SmileyBooks Titles of Related Interest

BOOKS

AMERICA I AM LEGENDS:
Rare Moments and Inspiring Words
Edited by SmileyBooks
Introduction by Tavis Smiley

HOPE ON A TIGHTROPE:
Words & Wisdom
by Cornel West

BROTHER WEST:
Living and Loving Out Loud
by Cornel West with David Ritz

BRAINWASHED:
Challenging the Myth of Black Inferiority
by Tom Burrell

PEACE FROM BROKEN PIECES:
How To Get Through What You're Going Through
by Iyanla Vanzant

BLACK BUSINESS SECRETS:
500 Tips, Strategies and Resources for
African American Entrepreneurs
by Dante Lee

FAIL UP:
Twenty Lessons on Building Success from Failure
by Tavis Smiley

FAITH IN THE FIRE:
Wisdom For Life
by Gardner Taylor, edited by Edward Taylor

HEALTH FIRST:
The Black Woman's Wellness Guide
by Eleanor Hinton Hoytt and Hilary Beard

DVD
STAND: a film by Tavis Smiley

All of the above are available at your local bookstore, or may be ordered through online retailers.

We hoped you enjoyed this SmileyBooks publication.

If you would like to receive additional information, please contact:

SMILEYBOOKS

250 Park Ave South
Suite 201
New York, NY, 10003
(646) 484-4962
(646) 484-4956 (fax)
www.smileybooks.com